THE GLEAM OF LIGHT

THE GLEAM OF LIGHT

*Moral Perfectionism and Education
in Dewey and Emerson*

NAOKO SAITO

FORDHAM UNIVERSITY PRESS   NEW YORK   2005

Copyright © 2005 Fordham University Press

All rights reserved. No part of this publication may be reproduced, stored in a retrieval system, or transmitted in any form or by any means—electronic, mechanical, photocopy, recording, or any other—except for brief quotations in printed reviews, without the prior permission of the publisher.

American Philosophy Series, No. 16
ISSN 1073-2764

Library of Congress Cataloging-in-Publication Data

Saito, Naoko.
   The gleam of light : moral perfectionism and education in Dewey and Emerson / Naoko Saito. — 1st ed.
      p. cm. — (American philosophy series ; no. 16)
   Includes bibliographical references and index.
   ISBN 0-8232-2462-7 (hardcover) ; ISBN 0-8232-2463-5 (pbk)
   1. Dewey, John, 1859–1952. 2. Emerson, Ralph Waldo, 1803–1882. 3. Perfection. 4. Education—Philosophy. I. Title. II. Series.
   B945.D44S23 2005
   191—dc22
                                                       2005003333

Printed in the United States of America
First paperback edition 2006

*For Kako Saito
and Teruko Saito*

Contents

Acknowledgments ix
Foreword by Stanley Cavell xiii

1. In Search of Light in Democracy and Education: Deweyan Growth in an Age of Nihilism — 1
2. Dewey between Hegel and Darwin — 17
3. Emerson's Voice: Dewey beyond Hegel and Darwin — 36
4. Emersonian Moral Perfectionism: Gaining from the Closeness between Dewey and Emerson — 50
5. Dewey's Emersonian View of Ends — 69
6. Growth and the Social Reconstruction of Criteria: Gaining from the Distance between Dewey and Emerson — 81
7. The Gleam of Light: Reconstruction toward Holistic Growth — 99
8. The Gleam of Light Lost: Transcending the Tragic with Dewey after Emerson — 120
9. The Rekindling of the Gleam of Light: Toward Perfectionist Education — 139

Notes 163
Bibliography 195
Index 205

Acknowledgments

The development of this book is traced through a series of personal encounters over many years. As a Japanese person drawn to American philosophy, I am accustomed to being positioned as "a foreigner"—hence, to maintaining a distance from the familiar, to being a stranger. In the course of my research, a number of people have acknowledged and responded to my experience of strangeness, and this has had a profound impact on the formation of my thought. The book is, in a sense, my attempt to acknowledge this in return.

The idea for the book, which attempts to play out a triangular conversation among John Dewey, Ralph Waldo Emerson, and Stanley Cavell, originated and developed through my sequential encounter with three philosophers at Harvard: Israel Scheffler, Hilary Putnam, and Cavell himself. I was introduced to pragmatism and the philosophy of education by Israel Scheffler in 1990, and since then he has continued to encourage and inspire my research. It was especially the example of Scheffler as a teacher that led me to understand what it means to be original in philosophy—that, in his words, we become original after going through "an imitation phase." If I had not been impressed by the power of his account of education's need for philosophy, and of philosophy's need for education, this book would not have come into being. In 1995 and 1996 I had the good fortune to take Hilary Putnam's course on pragmatism, during which I was especially struck by his lectures on Dewey and William James. In powerful words that conveyed the spirit of pragmatism, the meaning of "reconstruction in philosophy," and the idea of democracy as a way of living, his teaching motivated me to write a doctoral thesis on Dewey. I was particularly grateful to him for reading my thesis when it was nearing completion. His first visit to Japan, in the winter of 2003, when I accompanied him and Ruth Anna Putnam during their visit to Tokyo and Kyoto, was an occasion for me to recall and renew the extent of the influence that I had originally gained from him at Harvard; it gave a final boost toward the completion of the book manuscript.

My encounter with Cavell in the winter of 1996 was fateful: it determined the general path that I was to pursue thereafter, one that has led to the publication of this book. I spoke to Cavell of the way that I was struggling at the time, so it seemed, with the different voices of Emerson and Dewey within me, a relationship that, in the course of my research, emerged as pivotal for pursuing the idea—as *The Claim of Reason* puts this—of philosophy as the education of grown-ups. It was Cavell who responded to this thought and encouraged me to explore it in my work. In my continuing dialogue with him over the following years, I have pondered Emerson's idea of the "gleam of light," an idea that, I believe, is critical for any assessment of the relationship between Dewey and Emerson as philosophers of democracy.

The path of this inquiry led me to continue my doctoral work at Teachers College at Columbia University from 1997 until 2000. It was in New York that I met two teachers who were of immense importance in helping me complete this work. René Arcilla, who was my adviser, shared my passion for Emerson and Cavell, and sympathetically guided my research throughout. Nel Noddings had just arrived at Teachers College when I moved there, and her courses on the ethic of care, as well as on Dewey, were of great benefit to me as I worked on my thesis.

There are also other teachers and friends whom I would like especially to thank. Jim Garrison, who is an expert on Dewey and whom I met at the conference of the Philosophy of Education Society in Texas in 1996, has since then continued to support my research and advise on my inquiries into Dewey and Emerson. A mutual passion for Cavell's philosophy and the question of its relation to pragmatism has made me feel that I have known Vincent Colapietro for more than the three years of our acquaintance. I also met Andrew Feenberg in Japan in 2002. He brought his expertise in critical theory and philosophy of technology to a reading of some of my early drafts of chapters and raised challenging questions, especially concerning the feasibility of connecting Dewey's pragmatism and Emerson's transcendentalism. I have benefited from a number of conversations on pragmatism with Larry Hickman, both in the United States and during his visits to Japan, and I am grateful to him for introducing me to the Society for the Advancement of American Philosophy. At a late stage, in 2004, I met Steve Odin in Japan, and his careful comments on the manuscript gave me some crucial suggestions regarding the idea of the gleam of light. Tatsuhito Izuka and Richard Spear, who have been my Emersonian friends for many years, have helped me clarify my ideas in dialogue.

I thank Helen Tartar, general editor at Fordham, whom I met by chance at the annual meeting of the Society for the Advancement of American Philosophy in Birmingham, Alabama, in 2004. Her own enthusiasm for Cavell has caused me to feel a sense of gratitude that extends beyond my appreciation of her efficiency in seeing this book through to publication. I have benefited enormously from the sympathetic attention that my manuscript has received from Douglas Anderson, editor for the American Philosophy Series at Fordham University Press. The thoughtful and incisive questions raised by Fordham's anonymous reviewer have led me to enhance the text in ways I could not have conceived by myself. The writing of this book was assisted by the generosity of the National Academy of Education/Spencer Foundation by whom I was awarded a Postdoctoral Fellowship in 2002. I am very grateful for the academic and practical support that this provided.

Finally, but most important, I thank Paul Standish, whom I met in 2001 when I presented a paper on Emerson's gleam of light at the Philosophy of Education Society annual meeting in Chicago. It is not too much to say that our intense and continuing dialogue on Emerson and Cavell has brought me to this juncture in the path that I have been pursuing. Without his patient help and critical comments at various stages in the production of this manuscript, this book would not have been completed.

The gleam of light, the theme of this book, has been intensified for me in the trajectory of these relationships.

Foreword

In the past several decades in the United States there has been a remarkable revival of interest in two (perhaps *the* two) of the most famous, or influential, American claimants to the title of philosopher: John Dewey and Ralph Waldo Emerson. From the point of view of a philosopher and teacher such as myself, this revival of interest is a valuable, heartening turn of events. But I find that it has come at a high price, namely one in which Emerson's so-called transcendentalism is largely subordinated to Dewey's pragmatism. I mean that the tendency on the part of most participants in these matters has been to think of Emerson as essentially a forerunner of pragmatism, whose writings, so far as philosophically useful, are taken up, and taken forward, in Dewey's massive corpus of works. The resulting inattention to the details of Emerson's texts contributes, to my mind, to a thinning of American intellectual and cultural life, which is not unequivocally expressed by pragmatism but rather, it seems to me, by an irreducible tension between pragmatic and transcendentalist instincts and expressions. This is not something that manifests itself with particular clarity within the field of professional philosophy, where both of these instincts are themselves heavily, not of course wholly, subordinated to styles of analytical philosophy that go back to inheritances from England and from Vienna during the first half of the twentieth century. The tension is manifest most clearly, perhaps, in the history of American literature and in America's contribution to the development of the worldwide art of cinema. But these are not matters to which professional philosophy on this continent has for the most part felt that it must be responsive.

Whether and how the issue between pragmatism and transcendentalism will come to matter to philosophy generally (as I hope it will) will depend upon whether the tension proves to be an expression not merely of a parochial conflict confined within the arena of a few American professors of philosophy, but finds resonance within the experience of thinkers formed also by intellectual and cultural ferment beyond these borders. Naoko Saito is well placed to contribute to the determination of this question, in two respects. First, she takes up the interaction of Dewey and Emerson at perhaps its most sensitive and revelatory point, namely in their respective views of education. Dewey wrote in virtually all the fields into which philosophy is broken, but in none is his influence, intellectual and practical, more deeply and currently active than in the philosophy of education. Emerson, strikingly, does not divide philosophy into fields, but all of his writing can be seen as directed to what he calls the youth or the student, so that the totality of it embodies a pedagogical ambition, implicitly declaring that his culture as a whole stands in need of education. Second, the knowledge Naoko Saito deploys of the educational environments, intellectual and institutional, of both Japan and of the United States, gives her that double perspective which must enter into the philosophical assessment I find called for.

Her response to the strains shared in Dewey and Emerson brings to attention the details of their texts in a way that has so often been missing from these late debates arranged between them. Something I am particularly grateful for in her work is that, while she brings out the intimacy between the writings of these thinkers, she never loses sight of the differences between them. It is, it seems to me, precisely because of this awareness of differences that she is able, somewhat paradoxically, to reach back to the details of Emerson's decisive intervention in American culture in order to find the philosophical strength and sympathy with which to defend and enrich the reception of Dewey's work in the face of the periodic waves of criticism it has attracted, along with periods of rediscovery, throughout the twentieth century. It is a notable achievement.

STANLEY CAVELL
July 19, 2004

THE GLEAM OF LIGHT

ONE

IN SEARCH OF LIGHT IN DEMOCRACY AND EDUCATION

Deweyan Growth in an Age of Nihilism

... when the intervals of darkness come, as come they must,—when the sun is hid, and the stars withdraw their shining,—we repair to the lamps which were kindled by their ray, to guide our steps to the East again, where the dawn is. (Emerson, "The American Scholar")¹

Indifference is the evidence of current apathy, and apathy is testimony to the fact that the public is so bewildered that it cannot find itself . . . What is the public? If there is a public, what are the obstacles in the way of its recognizing and articulating itself? (Dewey, *The Public and Its Problems*)²

In *The Public and Its Problems* John Dewey criticized the democracy of American society in the 1920s. The "eclipse of the public" that he warns against is not only a matter of political participation but also a moral issue that has a bearing on one's way of living. Dewey captured the ethos of his times in terms of a sense of "hollowness." This is the sense that one cannot articulate one's feelings or even that, in the loss of one's own taste, one does not know "what one really wants."³ In Dewey's view, the weakening of the personal sense of being is tied up with the loss of a sense of the common good in the public realm. When one's voice is released simply as a matter of superficial self-presentation, it cannot genuinely contribute to the common good. In *Individualism Old and New*, published in 1930, Dewey describes this state in terms of the "tragedy of the 'lost individual.'"⁴ In the crisis of an American society afflicted with the rugged individualism of capitalism and the mass culture of standardization and uniformity, conformity is a debased condition of democracy, a condition

{ *1* }

that robs human beings of their capacity to be "captains of their own souls" (*ION*, 67). Dewey speaks of the loss of one's integrity—in effect, of the light one lives by, with its power to illuminate the darkness of the political. His call for democratic participation and the rebuilding of the Great Community is driven by the sense of crisis over the spiritual void of democracy, a void created in the rift between the private and the public.

In his idea of the "tragedy of the 'lost individual'" Dewey is prophetic about the fate of democracy and education in late modernity, where material affluence and political freedom do not assuage a burgeoning spiritual degeneration. With the loss of what Dewey called the dimension of the personal way of life, democracy itself is threatened.[5] With the tendency toward selfish individualism has come the loss of a sense of responsibility toward others and toward the future, and a general thinning of the ethical life. We would like to reach out our hands to others beyond the narrow confines of our private lives, but we do not know how. The denial of others is a tragic phenomenon in our ordinary lives. Apathy among young people displaces the inclination to learn and grow.[6] In these contexts, for many young students school is not necessarily a place for experiencing the joy of learning, for reconfirming their sense of existence, or for that matter for finding their own voices. Education, which is so often driven by assumptions of gaining and raising (whether this takes the form of the appeal to raise standards, or to achieve excellence, or to teach right and wrong, or to increase the understanding of other cultures), often aggravates, ironically, the ubiquitous sense of loss or irrelevance that afflicts teachers and students. As if to combat this, however, or to cover over the pervasive sense of loss with something else, the quest for absolute goals gains momentum in recent educational reforms. Such limitations are symptoms of nihilism and cynicism in democracy and education. The loss of intensity of life among young people simultaneously darkens the culture as a whole.

Dewey calls philosophy a "general theory of education."[7] He claims that our task of reconstructing democracy involves the endeavor of *philosophy as education*, the critical reexamination and transformation of the moral and spiritual basis of our living. The challenge to Dewey's philosophy today is how to sustain his hope for democracy and education, while resisting its familiar reduction to a naive optimism of progressive growth; how to make best use of his pragmatism as a wisdom for living with and beyond the incipient nihilism of our times, to address the spiritual crisis of the "tragedy of the lost individual"; and how to summon it to the task of revitalizing and bridging the disjoined private and public realms. To do so we require another mode of education—a kind of education that cannot be fully grasped in the language of standardization, quantification, and moralization, but one whose significance may well be recognized by many educators in their daily struggles. We need to reclaim a lost dimension in education, one in which we can inspire the invisible, patient transformation of the spirit—education as the constant process of conversion, turning away from loss toward the rekindling of light.

As an attempt to respond to such a call, this book tries to revive and critically to reconstruct the contemporary significance of the Deweyan task of democracy and education, in dialogue with *Emersonian moral perfectionism*[8]—a perfectionism without final perfectibility through which the spiritual and aesthetic dimension, and the tragic nature, of Deweyan growth can be reclaimed. To be engaged in critical dialogue with Dewey in the light of the changing situation of our times, this book attempts to show that Cavell's Emersonian moral perfectionism is a standpoint in light of which the recessive, Emersonian dimension in Dewey's pragmatism can be illuminated. As a philosopher of growth, Dewey never gave up his faith in democracy. His struggle to reorient American society toward liberal-communitarian democracy—the reconstruction of a public space in which individual freedom is realized within community—can be understood as an expression of his hope for democracy. That democracy can always fall into a state of conformity means that it must never be allowed to settle down in some fixed telos; it is a state forever to be worked toward, never finally to be achieved. In our age when a simple faith in growth cannot suffice, we need to reclaim this spirit of perfection, which is, so I shall argue in this book, no less than the amelioration, liberation, and reconstruction that Dewey shares with Emerson and Cavell; but we must do this in such a way as to be in touch with, to start from within, a sense of loss and powerlessness.

It is in response to the nihilistic crisis of democracy and education in our times that this book develops, and it does this around a figure that is sustained in Emerson and developed by Dewey. Emerson writes: "A man should learn to detect and watch that gleam of light which flashes across his mind from within."[9] This is an image that symbolizes the sense of being and becoming in the path of perfection. It is an idea that Emerson explicitly discusses in his "Self-Reliance," and that Dewey appropriates in *Construction and Criticism*. The gleam of light is a guiding metaphor for the themes, in Emersonian moral perfectionism and Deweyan growth, of the tragedy of the lost individual and the rebirth of the new. It illuminates also other Emersonian connections with Dewey—growth as the unending expansion of circles, self-transcendence in the here and now, impulse as the crucial beginning and directional force in intelligence. It indicates also perhaps a way to the critical reconstruction of that intelligence. The orientation it suggests points also to the possibility of "reconstruction in philosophy"—Emerson's and Dewey's common project in reconfiguring philosophy as involving our ways of living and as inseparable from our aesthetic and religious experience of the ordinary. It points also, therefore, to the process of education as conversion. Crucially related to Emerson's ideas of self-reliance and self-transcendence, the gleam of light is recaptured as a symbol not of isolated individualism but of receptivity to otherness. Furthermore, in a way characteristic of American philosophy, Emerson and Dewey together show that the gleam of light represents nothing substantive, but an ongoing process (or, say, stream) with its power of prophesy in discontinuity. Cavell rehearses Thoreau's words that morning comes after mourning: we come to rejoice in the arrival of the light only through undergoing and leaving the darkness. It is in relation to this imagery that the later chapters in the book follow the thematic development from loss toward rebirth, concluding by offering a vision and theory of perfectionist education.

The Need for Reconstructing Deweyan Growth

The reconstructing of Deweyan growth in the light of Emersonian moral perfectionism is needed, especially in view of the criticism that has been directed toward it. The idea of growth underlies Dewey's philosophy of democracy and education. He proclaims: "Education is all one with growing; it has no end beyond itself" (*DE*, 54). The aim of education, for Dewey, is to produce more growth in a child, to foster a continuous reorganization of a child's experience in his or her interaction with the adult world. To the question, "What is the criterion of growth?" his answer is the "principle of the continuity of experience."[10] This we might call *growth without fixed ends*.

Dewey developed this notion of growth in the wake of his conversion from Hegelian absolutism to Darwinian naturalism. Unlike his former concept of self-realization directed toward a final end-point, Hegel's Absolute, growth came to be seen later as a contingent and endlessly evolving natural process. It is a form of development that takes place in the interaction of an organism and its environment without the positing of a single, eternal resting point outside that process.

Dewey's moral vision for a democratic community is based upon this naturalistic philosophy of growth. Growth is an ongoing interaction between the innovation of the younger generation, on the one hand, and the wisdom and cultural heritage of the older, on the other. To liberate the full potential of a child, the mechanism of naturalistic growth necessitates constraints given by culture and through other human beings. At the same time, the immaturity of a child is not, and should never be considered to be, a mere preparatory step to the mature state of an adult. Each stage of growth has its own intrinsic value as part of the ongoing process of grow*ing* (*DE*, 56). This interactive process of growing is an essential condition for the healthy and flexible reconstruction of any democratic society.

Dewey's idea of growth without fixed ends has been controversial from his time to ours. It raises the perennial question, "Growth towards what?" The question has been raised mainly by those who firmly believe that there must be definite ends for education. In Dewey's time, Boyd H. Bode phrased the question as "Growth whither?" and pointed out that Dewey's progressive view of growth could not provide a democratic principle in "a topsy-turvy world."[11] I. L. Kandel also criticized Dewey's child-centered view of education for its lack of clear values and, hence, for promoting the development of children without a sense of direction, responsibility, or ideals. He condemned Dewey for fostering nihilism and anti-intellectualism in America.[12] Randolph Bourne, who opposed Dewey's support of America's entry into World War I, criticized his pragmatism for lacking definite ends beyond the principle of adjustment.[13] A concern over the relativism possibly entailed by Dewey's idea of growth has resurfaced again in our times. Allan Bloom, worried by the nihilism and cultural relativism of contemporary American youth, criticizes the lack of moral virtues and fundamental principles in Dewey's pragmatism.[14] And John Patrick Diggins sees him as refusing to define any specific ends toward which education should aspire.[15] Still today those who claim a need for "moral" education attack Deweyan "child-centered" education as a cause of the degeneration of education.[16]

These criticisms might well encourage skepticism about Dewey's Darwinian naturalistic philosophy of growth. They present him as not having any fixed ends, or more particularly, *moral* values, principles, or ideals that can guide children in the right direction. They worry, therefore, that Dewey's philosophy of education and its principle of growth will lead children to moral relativism, uncertainty, and chaos—all insidious forms of democratic freedom. "Growth towards what?" expresses the kind of worry that many educators still feel. It is this worry that points education in the direction of more stable, conservative solutions, either by reinforcing moral discipline and inculcating moral restraints on unbridled freedom, or by fixing measurable standards for student achievement.

It is against this background that another related sense of anxiety is expressed, now more than ever: that Dewey's pragmatism is overly optimistic, that it lacks perhaps a sense of tragedy.[17] In Dewey's times, Bourne attacked Dewey's progressive good will, raising doubts over whether the method of intelligent control and its instrumentalist attitude toward life could deal adequately with the crises of human life.[18] Richard Hofstadter argued that Dewey's assumptions regarding the pre-established harmony between individual growth and the interests of a democratic society were optimistic, if not utopian.[19] Even contemporary Deweyan scholars who are basically sympathetic to Dewey share similar concerns. Steven C. Rockefeller, though a staunch defender of Dewey's spiritual vision of democracy, thinks that he fails to develop a convincing account of human evil.[20] Cornel West asserts that Dewey does not fully escape an "Emersonian theodicy" of optimism, robust individualism and the enshrinement of power.[21] Raymond D. Boisvert argues that Dewey's pragmatism, in so far as it equates scientific advancement with moral progress, is typical of naive nineteenth-century modernity. As a result, his empiricism lacks a tragic sensibility, a sensitivity to a limitation inherent in the nature of things, what Boisvert calls "the Nemesis of Necessity."[22] Such criticism demands that the implications of Deweyan progressive growth be reconsidered, especially in the light of the nihilistic tendencies of our times delineated above.

From Rorty to Cavell and Emerson: Another Way toward the Antifoundationalism of Deweyan Pragmatism

Reconstructing Deweyan growth in the light of Emersonian moral perfectionism can also make a new contribution to other ways of interpreting Deweyan pragmatism, in particular one that is offered by Rorty. In response to the question, "Growth towards what?" Richard Rorty's reconstruction of Deweyan pragmatism is a significant contribution. From his *Philosophy and the Mirror of Nature* (1980) to his most recent writings, Rorty sheds light on the cogency of Dewey's pragmatism. In *Truth and Progress* (1998) his "hypothetical" reading of Dewey's position as situated between Hegel and Darwin elaborately and explicitly demonstrates the potential of Dewey's Darwinian concept of growth.[23]

This book, however, takes the stance not only that Rorty's approach to reconstruction in philosophy omits an internal tension hidden between the Hegelian and Darwinian components in Dewey's concept of growth, but also that Rorty's proclivity toward demystifying Dewey's pragmatism as a philosophy of power and progress discloses his blindness to the sense of the tragic implied therein—Dewey's keen sense of the "tragedy of the lost individual." It is claimed that Rorty is subject to a limitation common in Hegelian and Darwinian philosophies, and therefore common to any thinker positioned on a continuum drawn between them: these are philosophies of totality; that is, philosophies characterized by the view that reality is in principle understandable in terms of a coherent whole, the price of which is a tendency toward the reductionism of difference to the same.[24] I shall argue that, behind Rorty's relativist approach and antifoundationalism, Rorty's Dewey, in its concentration on power and progress, masks a tragic and spiritual dimension latent in Dewey's idea of an unending process of growth: the metaphysics of ongoing growth that can be captured only by paying close attention to its process; and the sense of attained and unattained perfection, a process symbolized by the flickering of the gleam of light. Rorty's antifoundationalism makes it harder for Deweyan pragmatism to be appreciated among those who persistently raise the question, "Growth towards what?"

Besides Rorty, there are a number of other scholars who have contributed to the revival of Dewey's pragmatism whose thoughts I shall discuss in the book. Their interpretations, however, which are again based mainly upon the framework of Dewey between Hegel and Darwin, similarly fail to elucidate the suppressed dimension of Deweyan growth. Ironically, the tendency to sanctify Dewey casts his philosophical outlook in more optimistic terms, despite claims to the contrary, and in so doing exposes a kind of naivete in the face of the real challenge posed by the contemporary democracy and the continuing criticism that Dewey lacks the tragic sense. Consequently, Deweyan progressive education, tainted as it has become with the aura of naive optimism, has been enthusiastically taken up by conservatives as the scapegoat for the decline of academic achievement and morality.[25] As educational policy and practice around the world illustrate, however, absolutist tendencies in education muffle and dispel the sense of loss and the invisible in their drive toward fixation and articulation.

A part of the aim of this book, therefore, is to search for an alternative way to reclaim Dewey's ateleological notion of growth through a recognition of its perfectionist spirit—without falling either into Rortian antifoundationalism or a reactionary turn to absolutism and the quest for certainty in democracy and education; it is to show that, if the meanings of these terms are salvaged from their typical misunderstanding, the "ateleological" concept of growth and the "antifoundationalism" of Deweyan pragmatism can enable us to transcend the tragic toward hope.

To bring this about, however, Dewey's pragmatism must be reconstructed. By giving a serious ear to the conservative's worry, "Growth towards what?" it is necessary to redefine carefully the meaning of progressive growth. The reading of Dewey needs to recount why growth without fixed ends is still important today and to demonstrate the significance of his naturalistic view of moral life. In so doing there is a need to overcome a limitation in interpreting Dewey's idea of growth solely from the perspective of "Dewey between Hegel and Darwin," and to reconstruct Dewey's concept of progressive growth in such a way as to make it a viable philosophy of democracy and education in response to nihilism. To this end, this book explores Emerson's perfectionism and the idea of the gleam of light as a third standpoint, *beyond* Hegel and Darwin—as a recessive dimension in Deweyan growth.

Dewey has called Emerson "the Philosopher of Democracy,"[26] and a careful examination of his writings reveals an undeniable presence of Emerson throughout Dewey's career. With the recent resurgence of American pragmatism, the connection between these thinkers has become one of the focal points of philosophical discourse. While a majority of the defenders of Dewey not only find a connection between Dewey and Emerson but claim that Emerson is the fountainhead of American pragmatism, Cavell remains firmly opposed to this placing of Emerson. He takes a powerful minority position by claiming that Dewey is not Emersonian and that Emerson is not a pragmatist. The defenders of Dewey respond by charging that Cavell misunderstands Dewey. The issue remains unresolved.

Within the context of this debate, I shall highlight Cavell's idea of Emersonian moral perfectionism—a philosophy that I shall argue taps a latent dimension in Dewey's concept of growth, the idea of the attained and unattained perfection. It is in Dewey's emphasis on this, I shall argue, that some connection can be explored between his view on growth and Emerson's sense of human perfection. The Emerson represented by Cavell is a social (as opposed to an individualistic) and a democratic (as opposed to an elitist) figure. Further, as Hilary Putnam points out, it is Dewey who "anticipated Cavell's identification of philosophy with education."[27] At the heart of Cavell's Emersonian moral perfectionism lies the idea of philosophy as education, philosophy as "education of grown-ups."[28] Rereading Dewey through Emersonian perfectionism, and connecting impulse with the gleam of light, elucidates the spiritual and aesthetic dimension of Deweyan growth. This helps us envision a conception of growth that is altogether richer than the one evident in his characteristically scientific discourse with its associated notion of intelligence. But it is important to resist too quick a reading of the imagery here. The lambent illumination that is implied must be understood in terms of the necessary, faltering discontinuities of growth—the leap that is the very dynamic of expanding circles, of which Emerson speaks. It is with this in mind that Dewey's language, in dialogue with Emerson and Cavell, is critically reexamined and reclaimed as the language of education, a language sensitive to the experience of the child, to the child's necessary interaction with the adult, and to the child within any adult who continues to grow.

I shall try to show that Dewey's pragmatism can provide an antifoundationalism different from Rorty's in what might be called the

Emersonian middle ground – going beyond the dichotomy of no ground and the absolute ground, and enabling a searching for and cultivating of the ground through which private and public lives come to be related. Emerson's idea of perfection, because of its similarity to *and* difference from Dewey's growth, and because of *and* despite Cavell's criticism of Dewey, has the capacity to reconstruct Dewey's pragmatism *from within*. In this sense, I shall side with Cavell but draw a conclusion different from his. Namely, I shall agree to the effect that the internal tensions, ambiguousness and precariousness of Dewey's thought can, when elucidated in the Emersonian gleam of light, offer that thought the momentum to transcend with its prophetic force the common limitation in his Hegelian and Darwinian horizons—the limitation that, in its proclivity toward totalities of power and progress, tends to expel the tragic from the understanding of the human condition. In a three-sided conversation among Emerson, Cavell, and Dewey, I shall attempt to draw out possibilities to which we are sometimes deafened by the sonorous proclamation of Deweyan pragmatism and progressive growth. Lending our ears to this quieter, muted Emersonian voice—in Dewey and in us—can, I believe, guide the lost individual in this age of nihilism out of tragedy and toward hope.

Inevitably, Deweyan growth reconstructed in the light of Emersonian moral perfectionism will turn our eyes into philosophy as education—education as the continuous process of conversion, metamorphosis, and internal transformation, toward the rebirth of one's lost light. It guides us to the Emersonian passage from the inmost to the outmost as a way of bridging the private and the public. Among all there are three distinctive contributions of Emerson's and Dewey's perfectionist education. First, it presents us with a secularized or naturalized notion of conversion in place of the Christian notion of conversion. In Emerson's and Dewey's process-oriented idea of perfectionism, conversion does not take place once and for all, but is taking place in the here and now, and again and again. Second, Emerson and Dewey show us that the process of cultivating the gleam of light requires the encounter with the other—one that helps us remember and recover our gleam of light. The gleam of light in their American thinking is released from the isolated inner soul back to life as a whole including social relationship with others. Third, Emerson and Dewey in their idea of the cultivation of the gleam of light point us to the significance of aesthetic education, one in which poeisis is at the heart of political democracy.

The Structure of the Book

In subsequent chapters, the project takes the following steps. Chapter 2 initiates the reexamination of Rorty's revival of Dewey's pragmatism within the framework of "Dewey between Hegel and Darwin." In response to the perennial question, "Growth towards what?" and the concomitant criticism directed at Dewey's claim of the continuity of the moral and the natural that is made possible through the application of intelligence, Rorty presents a way of rereading Dewey's pragmatism in a relativist and antifoundationalist direction. While Rorty's position is criticized by other inheritors of Dewey's pragmatism, including Hilary Putnam, both Rorty and its critics stand within the framework of Dewey between Hegel and Darwin. In this common framework, their defense as well as their criticisms, and their debate itself, disclose a totalizing tendency latent in Dewey's philosophy of growth, especially his concept of the scientific method—a tendency that frustrates the kind of reading of Dewey's pragmatism that might best meet the anxiety of our times.

To find a way out of this impasse, chapter 3 takes a radical turn and sheds new light on a latent dimension in Dewey's naturalistic philosophy of growth. This is done by putting Emerson in dialogue with Dewey. Scholarship on the connection between Dewey and Emerson within the recent revival of American pragmatism confirms again the plausibility of this direction of thought. At the same time, however, the opposing interpretations of the relationship between contemporary pragmatists and Cavell cautions against making any easy connections. Yet the paradoxical relationships between Dewey and Emerson, and between the defenders of Dewey and Cavell, are themselves a rich source for reconstructing Dewey's philosophy in its Emersonian direction, *beyond* Hegel and Darwin. Cavell's dissenting voice must be more attentively listened to in order that the strongest possible reconstruction in Dewey's philosophy of growth might be achieved.

Chapter 4 introduces Cavell's idea of *Emersonian moral perfectionism* (hereafter abbreviated as EMP) and offers it as a critical base from which to reexamine Dewey's naturalistic philosophy of growth. Despite Cavell's refusal to call Dewey an Emersonian perfectionist, his celebration of Emerson's idea of perfection bears similarities, in certain respects, to the way Dewey celebrates Emerson as a philosopher of democracy and of education. An overview of some of Dewey's writings in the light of EMP provides further evidence for this claim. On the strength of this, I shall tentatively hold Cavell's criticism in suspension, taking the view that Cavell's refusal to call Dewey Emersonian does not do full justice to Dewey.

Chapter 5 presents a reading of Dewey's metaphysics of growth reinterpreted in the light of EMP as a middle way beyond relativist abrogation of foundations and their maintenance in absolutism. I shall represent his concept of habit reconstruction in the naturalistic process of growth as transactional holism: the notion of a never-complete unity that is composed of ongoing processes of interaction between ever-changing factors. Dewey's idea of the ends-means relationship, along with Emerson's ends, takes the perfection of life to be understood solely as perfecting in the present participial form. Dewey and Emerson do not deny the concept of telos per se, but their philosophy of the attained and unattained self rethinks teleology. Challenging the very foundation for the question, "Growth towards what?" Dewey and Emerson shift the focus of the question to *how*: How shall we continue to create and recreate better ends on the path of further growth?

Turning away from the proximity of these writers, chapter 6 emphasizes the distance that Dewey creates in his paradoxical relationship with Emerson. Dewey's writings, challenged further, still want to seek a response to the question concerning the criteria for growth:

how can a good end be determined at each moment of perfecting? Dewey's answer is his pragmatic and evolutionary concept of socially revised criteria. At this point, Deweyan growth starts to deviate from EMP. The way Dewey describes a recalcitrant child in the classroom illustrates this. In contrast, Cavell's description of the Emersonian child represents the unconventional voice that unsettles convention. In comparison with the literary brilliance of both Emerson and Cavell, and the simultaneous energizing and destabilizing of thought that this enables, Dewey's writing is famously prosaic, lacking the capacity itself to illustrate the processes through which criteria are socially revised. This is not merely a stylistic difference, but one that affects and is affected by the contents of their philosophies. Cavell's criticism of Dewey's inadequate use of language is now heard anew as a voice of warning against a totalizing tendency in Dewey's philosophy of growth, a tendency at odds with the Emersonian direction toward infinity.

Chapter 7 endeavors to redirect Dewey's idea of growth to EMP, and to rescue it from this totalizing tendency. It attempts to draw his idea of naturalistic impulse into a nexus with Emerson's notion of *the gleam of light*. As a symbol of our aesthetic and spiritual impulses, the gleam of light originates in the undivided condition of nature, embodying our aspiration for fulfilling life. A link between Dewey's idea of impulse and Emerson's gleam of light offers a promising clue to reconstructing Deweyan growth in the light of EMP. It also brings Dewey's transactional holism closer to Emerson's idea of growth in expanding circles. Dewey's aesthetic and quasi-religious concept of directive criteria represents this holistic growth. Closely related to the prophetic impulse and imagination, this shows the way to a better vision of life, by initiation, projection, and discontinuitity. Directive criteria embody the moment of perfecting, the nexus point of the attained and the unattained self.

In response to the question of whether his progressive notion of growth can still be viable in times marked by uncertainty and the sense of loss, chapter 8 reexamines the sense of the tragic that is implied in Dewey's reconstructed view of growth as EMP. This is shown in his resistance to the "tragedy of the lost individual" in the spiritual crisis of democracy and education. This side of Dewey is given a further depth by Emerson's second sense of the tragic as beyond mere mourning over loss: this is the tragic understood in terms of the proximity of evanescence and luminosity in the gleam of light, and of the double condition of democracy attained and unattained. In response to the standard criticism that Dewey lacks a sense of the tragic, I shall argue that Deweyan growth is peculiarly attuned to the sense of the tragic that we must face today: it can be reread as a warning against our obliviousness to the double condition of human beings, that is, the threatening force of nihilism, the obliviousness that flattens our ethical lives. Resisting the abrogation of hope in our times, Dewey, after Emerson and Cavell, helps us re-see and re-assess the tragic sense of democracy and education in postindustrial society. Here Emerson's "antifoundationalism," which is to be distinguished from Rorty's, guides us to a way of transcending the tragic—a middle way of living beyond the restricted, fixed choice between no ground and absolute ground.

In chapter 9, as conclusion, I adumbrate a vision and theory of Deweyan-Emersonian perfectionist education: education as the constant process of conversion, epitomized by the rekindling of the gleam of light. The chapter will try to show how perfectionist education can engender the aspiration for creative democracy, reconstituting the private and the public. Such a rereading of Dewey is important today, not only because of his huge influence on education in the last hundred years, but also in the light of the recurrent misreading of his views, both by progressive educators and in conservative reactions to them.

In the aesthetic turn of his later years, Dewey tells us that reawakening the intensity of living by cultivating the prophetic impulse—in effect, the gleam of light—is a crucial step to creative democracy. I shall show how this connects with Emersonian self-transcendence, which calls not only on the art of communication, but also that of translation. It is in this context that the *poiesis* that Dewey calls creative intelligence plays a significant role. A broader concept of intelligence than the scientific method of thinking, this is the art of remaking the self and the world, and a condition for the criticism and (re)construction of democracy.

Inevitably, perfectionist education puts an emphasis on friendship. In the education of the gleam of light, we are not engaged in isolated or secluded meditation, or in a kind of aesthetic self-indulgence. It is in the patient process of the conjoint metamorphosis of the self and the culture that the human soul is reborn: this requires receptivity, detachment, and the orientation toward the other. Such a line of thought will contribute to a pervasive reconstruction of the ethics of education, beyond the existing teleological concepts of moral education and in favor of an ethics before moral imperatives and moral reasoning. Such an approach has implications also, it should be clear, for citizenship education and education for global understanding. The spiritual and aesthetic dimensions of Deweyan-Emersonian perfectionist education are preconditions of political education. Perfectionist education can, thus, provide a third way, beyond progressivism and traditionalism: it is liberal learning in dialogue between the innovation of impulse and initiation into culture.

TWO

DEWEY BETWEEN HEGEL AND DARWIN

One criticism directed against Dewey's concept of growth, "Growth towards what?" is caused by an ambiguity entailed in his position between Hegel and Darwin, two main philosophers who influenced the formation of his view on growth. Dewey asserts that the moral ends and ideals of growth can be explained solely on the basis of Darwinian naturalism and the scientific method. Indeed, the major part of the interpretation of Dewey's pragmatism, whether being defense or attack, has been made within this framework of Dewey between Hegel and Darwin—an evolutionary naturalist who has not completely abrogated ethical ideals.

Richard Rorty has shown us one possible direction to which this controversial philosophy of growth can turn. As Richard J. Bernstein points out, Rorty in his *Philosophy and the Mirror of Nature* sheds light on pragmatism's move away from traditional epistemology, "the accurate representation of reality" or the foundational view of the world.[1] From this antifoundationalist position, Rorty, in what he calls his "hypothetical" rereading of Dewey, presents us with one possible picture of Dewey from the standpoint of "Dewey between Hegel and Darwin," but reorienting this notoriously toward the relativist direction. His controversial reinterpretation of Dewey can act as a window through which we can further penetrate into the quarry of Dewey's naturalistic philosophy of growth. Indeed, the debate over Dewey's naturalistic ethics and its concomitant concept of the scientific method of thinking discloses the limitations of the very framework of Dewey between Hegel and Darwin—its totalizing tendency geared toward power and progress that masks the subtle implications of the life of growth without fixed ends.

Dewey from Hegel to Darwin

In *Democracy and Education*, Dewey presents his Darwinian manifesto: "Life is a self-renewing process through action upon the environment."[2] This is the essence of Deweyan growth, the theory of the interaction between an organism and its environment through functional and purposeful activities in specific situations. An emphasis is put on growth as grow*ing* in the present participial form, a "culminative movement of action toward a later result" (*DE*, 46), not "a movement toward a fixed goal" (55). Its distinctive feature is "immaturity," which he calls "the possibility of growth" (46), "a positive force or ability, the power to grow" (47). According to Israel Scheffler, Darwinian evolutionary theory, with its claim of continuity between mankind and the lower animals, and its emphasis on process in nature, had a significant impact on American pragmatism. In contrast to British empiricism, which divides mind from world in a static and analytical way, American functional psychology stresses the notion of "*dynamism, utility, and organism*" with "biological, social, and purposive considerations."[3] This is a major turn from his old Hegelian, teleological view of self-realization: a movement directed to and measured by the ultimate end, the ultimate harmony of self and social realization, and "the perfection of personality."[4] In *Psychology* (1887), Dewey writes: "The self, in its true nature, is universal and objective.... The self always confronts itself... with the conception of a universal or completed will towards which it must strive."[5] It is this teleological dimension of Hegelian self-realization, or in his words, "the absolute goal" or "whole" that Dewey came to reject later (*DE*, 62).

His naturalistic idea of growth is not restricted to his earlier educational writings; it continues to prevail in his succeeding works. In *Reconstruction in Philosophy* (1920), for example, the growth metaphor backs up his claims for the moral reconstruction of the world: "Growth itself is the only moral 'end.'"[6] In *Human Nature and Conduct* (1922), growth is a key not only for the education of children in schools, but also for the renewal of democratic society as a whole.[7] In *A Common Faith* (1934), growth is given a religious tone as "a higher value and ideal than is sheer attainment."[8] It is a spiritual process that involves "intense realization of values" (*CF*, 53). In *Experience and Education* (1938), in defending progressive education as something different from a laissez-faire, child-centered education, Dewey restates his belief: "educative process can be identified with growth when that is understood in terms of the active participle, growing."[9] As Sidney Hook says, Dewey is a "philosopher of growth" throughout his career.[10]

Dewey's naturalistic view of growth represents his claim of *continuity* between the human world and the natural world:

> A morals based on study of human nature instead of upon disregard for it would find the facts of man continuous with those of the rest of nature and would thereby ally ethics with physics and biology. (*HNC*, 11)

This epitomizes his naturalistic ethics of the "desirable." Dewey claims that a morality originates in the empirical facts of the "desired," and that this acquires the moral status of what "*should* be desired."[11] Growth can be considered to be a process in which the desirable traits of a moral life are cultivated. Here, the scientific method plays a crucial role—the procedure of practical judgment in a particular situation based upon the consequences of one's conduct.

It is a method for *"judgments about the conditions and the results of experienced objects; judgments about that which should regulate the formation of our desires, affections and enjoyments."*[12] Namely, the scientific method is a means to mediate the moral and the natural, man and nature, and to bridge the desired to the desirable. Dewey's scientific method is not the positivist's notion of science, but a more Peircian, experimental method of inquiry based upon the procedures of hypothesis, observation, and control, and a critical habit of mind. Through the scientific method, Dewey claims, humans can reach the facts and laws of nature[13]; it is an avenue for "effective moral renewal" (*RP*, xxxvii).

With the concept of scientific method, Dewey tries to offer an alternative picture of naturalism as a way to overcome the bifurcation of the "is" and the "ought": *an antireductionist naturalism*. On the one hand, he is opposed to the materialist view of nature as it reduces "all distinctive human values, moral, aesthetic, logical to blind mechanical conjunctions of material entities.[14] On the other hand, he is opposed to the antinaturalism claimed by supernaturalists, theologians, and philosophers who deny nature as the basis of morality. What Dewey means by nature covers physical and animal nature, but this also includes humanity, and the human use of intelligence. The ethical is continuous with, not the same as, nature. The ethical grows out of the physical universe as an extension of nature. Values are part of nature. Thus,

> Naturalism is often alleged to signify disregard of all values that cannot be reduced to the physical and animal. But so to conceive nature is to isolate environing conditions as the whole of nature and to exclude man from the scheme of things.[15]

Dewey's antireductionist naturalism constitutes not only the basis of his pragmatism, but also his ideal of democratic humanism:

> [N]aturalism finds the values in question, the worth and dignity of men and women, founded in human nature itself, in the connections, actual and potential, of human beings with one another in their natural social relationships. ("Anti-Naturalism," 54)

For Dewey, moral authority resides exclusively in mankind's natural and social life. The social ideal of democracy is founded on human nature, not on some preconceived, fixed nature, but on human nature in growth.[16] Dewey's naturalistic ethics also represents the antimoralism and antiauthoritarianism of his thought—his struggle against "the escapism and humanistic defeatism inherent in antinaturalism" ("Anti-Naturalism," 61). He opposes any hierarchical distinction that relegates man's nature to a lower realm, while placing morality in a higher one.

In his naturalistic philosophy of growth, however, Dewey has left us with a certain ambiguity. In drifting from Hegelian absolutism to Darwinian experimentalism, Dewey's naturalistic philosophy of growth retains a strong sense of idealism. In his autobiographical essay, "From Absolutism to Experimentalism," Dewey describes the path of his intellectual development as "drifting" in an imperceptible movement, which took as long as fifteen years. He acknowledges that "acquaintance with Hegel has left a permanent deposit in my thinking."[17] Much research on Dewey's philosophy emphasizes this point. As Israel Scheffler says, Dewey continues to retain Hegelian emphases on continuity, wholeness, on development, and on the power of ideas.[18] Richard Bernstein expresses this as "Hegel's organicism."[19] Steven C. Rockefeller offers an interpretation to the effect that even after Dewey had left Hegelianism, he did not lose his faith that life is full of ideal meaning.[20] Alan Ryan also argues that Greene's influence on Dewey's ethics was continuous with his later pragmatist ethics.[21] Similarly, Russell B. Goodman argues that "Dewey never ceased to be an idealist" and that "there are many traces of Hegel even in Dewey's later writings."[22]

As these scholars demonstrate, even if the absolute end point disappears from the path of growth, Dewey's faith in the power and progress of humanity—his Hegelian quest for the whole, the active development of human potential, and ethical idealism—continues to be an integral part of his naturalistic philosophy of growth. In his Hegelian period, Dewey describes his ethical ideal as follows:

IN THE REALIZATION OF INDIVIDUALITY THERE IS FOUND ALSO THE NEEDED REALIZATION OF SOME COMMUNITY OF PERSONS OF WHICH THE INDIVIDUAL IS A MEMBER; AND CONVERSELY, THE AGENT WHO DULY SATISFIES THE COMMUNITY IN WHICH HE SHARES, BY THAT SAME CONDUCT SATISFIES HIMSELF.[23] (Capitalized in the original text)

This stance is retained in his later naturalistic period. In *Ethics* (1908), Dewey claims: "The good for any man is that in which the welfare of others counts as much as his own."[24] In *Democracy and Education* (1916), he argues that the democratic way of living involves the "full development of private personality [and] is identified with the aims of humanity as a whole" (*DE*, 102). This Dewey calls "*a common good*" (E1908, 338), or "a good shared by all."[25]

In western ethics, the type of continuity claim that Dewey makes has been a target of criticism. As G. E. Moore says, in his famous claim against the naturalistic fallacy, the good in itself has its own intrinsic status and can never be identified with the natural.[26] According to W. K. Frankena, the criticism of the naturalistic fallacy has its historical root in Hume, who bifurcates the "ought" of value and the "is" of fact, and who claims that any attempt to reduce the former to the latter is doomed to failure.[27] The bifurcation of facts and values is still dominant in contemporary western ethics. For example, Charles Taylor, in opposition to reductionist versions of naturalism, including utilitarianism and the behavioral sciences, considers goods as having their own intrinsic claim apart from natural facts. He considers the "sources" of these moral ends to be "independent of our own desires, inclinations, or choices." And thus, he claims that the "real growth" of the self is a journey toward these higher sources of the ultimate goodness.[28] Likewise, Bernard Williams holds the view that the realm of the moral life is independent of the world of empirical, natural science.[29]

An attack on Dewey's naturalistic ethics of the desirable is in the same vein as these arguments against the naturalistic fallacy. Morton White claims that a relationship between the de facto condition of something "appearing red" and the de jure condition of something being "objectively red" is equivalent to a relationship between the desired and the desirable in Dewey's argument. Based upon this analogy, White asserts that just as something objectively being red does not impose any moral obligation, Dewey's concept of the desirable based upon the scientific method does not have an obligatory force; and therefore, the "ladder" from the desire to the desirable in Dewey's empirical approach "cannot lead us from the descriptive to the normative." At the bottom of White's criticism lies his own desire for "a rock that is more substantial than mere desire" as a source of moral obligation. Based upon this observation, White argues that Dewey fails in his attempt to "take a middle course between transcendentalism and extreme naturalism," suggesting a possible vacillation on Dewey's part between Hegelian idealism and Darwinian naturalism.[30] Walter Feinberg also impugns Dewey's continuity claim, asserting that Dewey "muddied the distinction between [the natural and ethical]."[31] Similarly, Ryan is skeptical, claiming that the evolution of complex ideas, moral ideals, and aesthetic taste *are different* from the evolution of animal species, and that the latter cannot explain the former. Dewey says nothing about "the grounds for preferring Einstein to Newton, Beethoven to Bach, or the life of an ascetic to the life of a Wall Street banker."[32]

Nel Noddings, though Dewey's sympathetic supporter, thinks that Dewey does not provide specific criteria for moral judgment. She is particularly doubtful of Dewey's scientific and instrumental method, pointing out that his moral theory based upon the scientific method cannot deal with *all* moral judgment. She claims that in our moral decisions involving should-claims, we need *moral* criteria as distinguished from *non-moral* ones—criteria based upon "certain universals in the human condition," ideas that are "very nearly absolute."[33] On this point, Noddings seems to join White's search for the "rock" that is the foundation of morality. Her criticism implies that Dewey's naturalistic view of growth, based as it is upon the scientific method, can be applied only to that limited realm of our lives where absolute criteria of moral judgment are not involved.

All these critics imply that the comprehensive and distinctively moral dimension of the human life of growth—its ends, ideals, and criteria for good or bad growth—cannot be fully supported by Dewey's claim of a continuity between the natural and the moral. They are especially doubtful about the transferability of the scientific method employed in the natural realm of "is" to the moral realm of "should."

Rorty's "Dewey between Hegel and Darwin"

It is this bifurcationist worldview presented by those critics of Dewey's naturalistic ethics, and their quest for a foundation that Rorty wishes to rebut. Rorty attempts to reconcile a tension between Hegel and Darwin evident in Dewey's naturalistic view of growth. On the one hand, because of his Hegelian background, Dewey does not give final authority to natural science despite his commitment to the scientific method. On the other hand, he is "sufficiently naturalistic" to think of human beings in Darwinian terms.[34] Dewey is "a pragmatist without being a radical empiricist, and a naturalist without being a panpsychist."[35]

Based upon this interpretation, Rorty supports the implications of Dewey's naturalism for his American democratic vision in terms of his antimoralism and antiauthoritarianism—pragmatism's revolt against a bifurcationist's worldview. Dewey carried with him a "lifelong distaste for the idea of authority—the idea that anything could have authority over the members of a democratic community save the free, collective, decisions of the community."[36] This is founded on Dewey's naturalism, "a metaphysic of the relation of man and his experience in nature."[37] Rorty compares Dewey's vision of democracy to Whitman's "democratic vistas"—the significance of natural human experience, "something that can be loved with all one's heart and soul and mind." Unlike Plato, with his idea of "eros," or Kierkegaard with his concept of the "Wholly Other," but not unlike Nietzsche and his "polytheism," Dewey brings the authority of the moral life back to humans on earth, "an indefinitely expansible pantheon of transitory temporal accomplishments, both natural and cultural."

Thus, Rorty concludes that Dewey's God, the "symbol of ultimate concern," is the sublime diversity seen through human eyes, and created by human experimentation. This supports Dewey's vision of a democratic community that treasures the potential of each individual.[38] Rorty inherits an asset of Dewey's naturalistic ethic that opposes a hierarchical distinction between morality and nature—a democratic faith made possible by Dewey's continuity claim.

Rorty, however, turns Dewey's naturalistic philosophy of growth in the direction of relativism and antifoundationalism—a direction that disturbs those who express concern about the allegedly ateleological view of Deweyan growth. He does so with his "hypothetical" rereading of "Dewey between Hegel and Darwin," by means of a very Hegelian synthesis of the Hegelian and Darwinian aspects he finds in Dewey.[39] As for Dewey's Hegelian roots, Rorty's interpretation is as follows:

> Teleological thinking is inevitable, but Dewey offers us a relativist and materialist version of teleology rather than an absolute and idealist one. Whereas Hegel held that the study of history brings over from philosophy the thought that the real is rational, the Hegel-Darwin synthesis Dewey proposes must de-ontologize this claim and make it simply a regulative, heuristic principle.[40]

As for the implication of Dewey's Darwinian naturalism, Rorty claims:

> If one asks why flexibility, articulation, variety, and interestingness are worthy ends to pursue—why they are morally relevant ends for individuals or societies—Dewey has nothing more to tell you than "so act as to increase the meaning of present experience".... Squirrels do what is best by their lights, and so do we. Both of us have been moving in the direction of what seems, by our respective lights, more flexibility.[41]

Thus, by synthesizing his deontologized Hegelian historicism and relativized Darwinian naturalism, Rorty represents Dewey's pragmatism as socio-cultural relativism.

The claim he makes on behalf of Deweyan growth is this: "Growth itself is the only moral end."[42] For Rorty, naturalistic growth is merely an expedient activity of an organism's adjustment to environments—nothing more or less. Beneath his relativist approach, however, the way Rorty explains how Hegel and Darwin join hands in Dewey represents a faith in power and progress typically common to these thinkers—the "teleology" of freedom in the image of infinite expansion that groundlessness enables humans to obtain.

One dominant criticism is directed at Rorty's Darwinian linguistic behaviorism and his rejection of Dewey's "metaphysical" account of experience and nature. Against the representation theory of language—the idea that language mirrors the ultimate reality, reality "out there"—Rorty asserts that human beings are simply engaged in contingent language games in which linguistic activities are social and cultural functions. There is no ultimate foundation on which we can rely. From this perspective, Rorty criticizes Dewey's underdeveloped theory of language: "[Dewey] should then have gone on to note that the development of linguistic behavior—of social practices that used increasingly flexible vocal cords and thumbs to produce longer and more complex strings of noises and marks—is readily explicable in naturalistic, Darwinian terms."[43]

Rorty is particularly critical of Dewey's *Experience and Nature*. In this book, Dewey, in Cornel West's words, scratches a "metaphysical itch," an itch that Rorty thinks Dewey should not have scratched.[44] This position of Rorty is elaborated in his explicit criticism of "Dewey's Metaphysics."[45] While Rorty acknowledges the contribution of Dewey's pragmatism as it serves as a philosophy for social and cultural criticism, he is impatient with what he considers the residue of the old metaphysics of experience, the "generic traits" of experience, in Dewey's *Experience and Nature*. Rorty attacks the traces of old metaphysical concepts in such phrases as "prime matter" and "thing-in-itself," found in Dewey's account of "qualities of interaction."[46] In Rorty's view, naturalistic growth as presented by Dewey must be merely an expedient activity of an organism's adjustment to environments, without any link between experience and nature. Nature is anything but that which gives a deep or spiritual meaning to the activity, as in transcendental idealism or panpsychism. Nor does nature give a moral end, a telos in the Greek sense. Rorty brings Dewey's naturalism much closer to a mechanical view of nature, a unification of man and nature by means of "behaviorism and materialism."[47] The following remark by Rorty encapsulates this:

> Every speech, thought, theory, poem, composition, and philosophy will turn out to be completely predictable in purely naturalistic terms. Some atoms-and-the-void account of micro-processes within individual human beings will permit the prediction of every sound or inscription which will ever be uttered. There are no ghosts.[48]

Here Rorty is making a reductionist (eliminative materialist) criticism of Dewey.[49] The subtleties of the moral life are subsumed again in the totalizing force of reductionism. This is a "consequence of pragmatism" that Rorty produces out of Dewey's claim of a continuity between the moral and the natural.

Rorty's linguistic behaviorism and the breakage of a link between experience and nature are criticized by other Deweyan scholars. They express concern that something crucial in Dewey's original account of human experience is missing from Rorty's reinterpretation, and therefore that Rorty's claims, in James Gouinlock's words, "undo Dewey's work, rather than carry it forward."[50] Ralph W. Sleeper claims that Dewey's theory of communication is supported by generic traits of nature, or its "transformative ontology"—"the transformational character of discourse that is recognized only when the signs of language are seen as works of a social art invented to turn the powers of nature to account."[51] Gouinlock also claims that Dewey's metaphysics is the attempt to provide "a generic characterization of the human involvement with the nature of things." That is to say, such features of our surroundings as trees, rivers, fish, animals, friends, enemies, the earth, and implements of all kinds enter into the shared activities of human beings. It is Dewey's rich account of nature that gives an orchestrated and intelligible account of life experience, man's intimate continuity with the plural, ever-changing processes of nature. It is this dimension, Gouinlock points out, that is missing from Rorty's Dewey.[52]

Likewise, West gives a positive interpretation to what Rorty criticizes as Dewey's "metaphysical itch." In West's view, it serves as "the principal cultural motivation for various scientific and artistic forms of redescriptions and revisions of the world."[53] Robert B. Westbrook expresses a similar concern that in Rorty's Dewey the rich account of the nature of selfhood, the motive of moral behavior, and the meaning of human life disappear—all of which Westbrook claims are the central concerns of Dewey as a philosopher of reconstruction. Westbrook identifies a major difference between Dewey and Rorty in terms of the latter's lack of the "ground-maps" that philosophers can provide in the course of their cultural criticism, the basis of moral and cultural commitments. Due to this lack, according to Westbrook, Rorty refuses to accept the heart of Dewey's ethical postulate of democracy, the communitarian view of the unity of self-realization and the social good, and consequently presents his alternative idea of a "liberal utopia" in which private and public spheres are split.[54]

These critics suggest that Dewey's naturalistic philosophy of growth can support his democratic ideal and that it can offer a far richer, ethically thicker account of human experience than Rorty's Dewey. They imply that Rorty's reinterpretation of Dewey is an inadequate response to the bifurcationist criticism of Dewey's naturalistic ethics. Rorty's full-fledged negation of the foundation and directionality in Deweyan growth and his mechanization of nature aggravate the concerns of those who need clear, definite moral ends outside the realm of nature.

As much as being loyal to Dewey's original philosophy, however, his defenders reveal a tendency, to borrow Rorty's words, to "stick so closely to the letter that they can make no concessions to current audiences . . . They maintain purity of doctrine at the price of having to explain disagreement with Dewey, or refusal to take Dewey seriously."[55] As a result, they have not yet responded adequately to the questions that have been continuously addressed to Dewey's idea of growth: What specifically does it mean to keep growing without fixed ends? What is ethical about such a naturalistic stance? How can we obtain a moral source for continuing growth? What is going on in the moment of growing? And perhaps the most challenging question is: How first of all can we commit ourselves to such an apparently progressive, optimistic view of growth in this age of cynicism? These questions can be understood as those that are directed against the affirmation of the nature of power and progress that runs through Deweyan growth and his pragmatism as a whole—a philosophy that is supported by its Hegelian and Darwinian background. The answers to these questions demand more than a literal interpretation of Dewey's idea. The sympathetic and critical mapping of Dewey's position stands in need of a new vocabulary.

Such need is found especially in Dewey's defenders' account of his idea of intelligence, or the scientific method of thinking. For example, Gouinlock, in his defense of Dewey against Rorty, shows his own position to be based upon Deweyan "scientific intelligence"— experimental inquiry, a willingness to question, investigate, and learn, a determination to search for clarity in discourse and evidence in argument. Gouinlock writes: "These virtues embrace novelty, innovation, growth, regard for the concerns of others, and scientific discipline. They reject the blind following of custom, authority, and impulse. They preclude not only dogmatism and absolutism, but deliberately hurtful conduct as well."[56] Though he acknowledges that such a positive stance is supported by Dewey's awareness of nature's limitations as much as its possibilities, Gouinlock's language is characterized by his faith in the "scientific-democratic virtues"[57]—a faith in the democratic freedom of power and progress. It is about such vocabulary or way of speaking that critics of Dewey express their concern, particularly in this age of uncertainty and precariousness.

More recently, Larry Hickman has offered a richer account of Dewey's concept of intelligence and scientific method through his positive evaluation of Dewey's views on science and technology. Hickman defends Dewey from the charge of positivistic scientism made by the Frankfurt critical theorists. While scientific realism presupposes objective truth and static structures, Hickman says, Dewey's conception of scientific method is his instrumentalism: a view that science *works* to improve tools to resolve problems in life. Facts are not objective truth, but "facts-of-the-case." Facts cannot be value-free as in positivistic scientism. Dewey's is the experimental method of inquiry typically utilized in scientific-technical disciplines but also applicable in other fields. This does not mean, however, Hickman emphasizes, that the scientific-technical method should serve all forms of inquiry, including art, for example; rather, along with other forms of inquiry, scientific method enriches the general pattern of human intelligence by improving the tools and artifacts that we have at our disposal when we seek to overcome difficulties. Intelligence is not static but is in the process of constant refinement and change. Further, Hickman claims that the community of inquirers endorses the desirability of the case as distinct from the subjective state of the desired. In all of these respects, Hickman argues, Dewey's pragmatism cannot be identified with enlightenment scientism.[58]

Still, this strand of the defense of Dewey's concept of intelligence and the scientific method of thinking cannot expel the radical doubts of the critics. In their eyes, the defenders of Dewey faithfully inherit his Hegelian and Darwinian assumptions of power and progress. Particularly in the context of the far more advanced state of science and technology in our times, the defense of Dewey's idea of intelligence as the human capacity to employ the scientific method to the solution of problems sounds weak. Hickman's trust in the power of "the community of inquirers" to endorse the desirability of a case invites the kind of question that Andrew Feenberg addresses. In response to Hickman's defense of Dewey's pragmatism in the age of technology, Feenberg responds:

> [Dewey] lacked the dystopian sensibility that would have brought him face-to-face with the threat of science and technology... The constant talk about experimental method, for example, extended into every aspect of life, suggests a narrowly manipulative and intellectualist attitude toward the world. Perhaps Dewey's thinking is belied by his language as his defenders claim, but it is difficult to overlook nevertheless.[59]

In the twenty-first-century world, the threat of this dystopian aspect of technology is so much a part of our daily lives, and in this age of nihilism we can become so easily blind to this danger.[60] The call to overcome this danger merely through the power and desirability of human intelligence and will, from Dewey and Deweyan scholars, sounds naively utopian.

Putnam's Defense: A Step Forward

Hilary Putnam shows us a way beyond Rorty's Dewey, but in such a way as to be sensitive to those voices of anxiety over Dewey's pragmatism and naturalistic philosophy of growth. On the one hand, in defense of Dewey's antibifurcationist claim of the moral and the natural, and against Rorty's relativist interpretation, Putnam shows us Dewey's third position beyond foundationalism and antifoundationalism—another sense of "objectivity" that Dewey's pragmatism points towards. On the other, he elucidates a certain limitation entailed by Dewey's philosophy of growth based upon the scientific method of thinking.

As a pragmatist, Putnam agrees with Rorty that it is futile to talk about objective reality in terms of "things in themselves." In his negation of traditional ontology and epistemology in western philosophy, however, Putnam points out that Rorty flatly rejects the addressing of this objectivity in an either-or way—whether there *is* or *is not* such a reality "out there." This dualistic scheme of Rorty's thinking ignores the undeniable sense of objectivity that is so much a part of our everyday, common experience: our belief that there is a reality of objects in the world that are not the products of thought or language, and that, in the light of this, it behooves us to "get the facts right"; our solid sense that "outside of our skins," even after we die, events will continue; and the fact that we can still sympathize with the experience of others as something real. In Putnam's view, these factors in our common sense demonstrate the kind of objectivity that needs to be accounted for, in what might be called "the ordinary notion of representation." In a way different from traditional representational theory, we are still able to "represent" a certain kind of "objectivity" in the world of human beings, within a third realm that lies between the world with the absolute ground and one with no ground. Putnam claims that: "Rorty has failed to explore the sort of 'impossibility'" that we still have to deal with beyond absolute guarantees; that he fails to "inquire into the character of the unintelligibility" of certainty that is entailed in the metaphysical realism that he wishes to attack. In other words, Putnam suggests that Rorty has avoided venturing into an intricate third realm of human experience that lies beyond the either-or choice of metaphysical realism or relativism—a third way that is implied in Dewey's pragmatism.[61]

In place of Rorty's relativist approach, Putnam presents his "realist" defense of Dewey's pragmatism and antireductionist, nonbifurcated naturalism.[62] In Putnam's view, Dewey is engaged in "the search for a middle way between reactionary metaphysics and irresponsible relativism," while avoiding both Aristotle's metaphysical essentialism and early modern realism.[63] Putnam acknowledges Dewey's invaluable contribution toward the idea of the "entanglement of fact and value."[64] Putnam opposes the bifurcated view of the relationship between fact and value that has dominated analytical philosophy: a division between "the true world" composed of objective facts that are "really there," on the one hand, and a separate realm of value belonging to the world of appearance, on the other.[65] Against this dichotomous view, Putnam agrees that there is a continuity between the moral and the natural in Dewey's naturalism. He claims that Dewey, along with other classic pragmatists, incorporates "the first-person normative point of view" as an essential component in the constitution of facts.[66]

He also points out that Dewey's scientific method of inquiry is a way of discovering what is warrantedly assertible about both facts and values.[67] It is a method of hypothesis, testing, and experimentation through cooperative inquiry and free communication: what Putnam calls "the *democratization of inquiry.*"[68] In this social procedure, "ethical objectivity" is made possible, even without relying on "a universal set of 'criteria'" applicable to all situations. He calls this pragmatist concept of objectivity "justification without foundations."[69] This idea of objectivity is an application of Dewey's concept of "warranted assertibility," his pragmatic view of objectivity as being that which is being discovered and revised in the continuous process of inquiry in each specific situation.[70] By tapping this potential in Dewey's antireductionist naturalism, Putnam shows that Dewey's pragmatist concept of objectivity presents a third way beyond essentialist realism or positivist objectivism, on the one hand, and beyond subjectivism, idealism or "irresponsible relativism," on the other. His realist interpretation of pragmatism's third sense of ethical objectivity helps us better to understand how Dewey's naturalistic idea of growth, despite its Darwinian basis, can present growth as still capable of having a moral end. As James Conant claims, Putnam's philosophy has "an overall guiding vision,"[71] and this distinguishes Putnam's Dewey from Rorty's.

The implications of Putnam's realist position are illustrated by his account of Dewey's philosophy of education. He claims that education for Dewey is the continuous reorganization of the child's experience for increased connections of meaning. It is conducted with the aim of cultivating children who will be members of a pluralistic, but not relativistic, democratic society—a society that involves cooperative interactions among individuals possessing diverse values. Dewey's democratic philosophy, Putnam argues, aims to maintain the ideal of cultural interdependence against the fragmentation of society, and suggests a mediated position for multicultural education in America: an alternative way beyond the choice between a relativistic, separationist stance and an assimilationist call for a common "American culture" (or "the submerging of all our differences"). The educative process conducted in smaller, intermediate-level communities is a way of cultivating a larger democratic community based upon the "sufficiently strong bonds of shared interests."[72] Thus if we follow Putnam's Dewey, growth without fixed ends does not end up with chaos, but rather, being supported by the method and attitude of democratic inquiry and dialogue, with the *search* for common ground. To sustain this overall guiding vision, which Putnam argues for on Dewey's behalf, instead of teaching children merely "facts and skills," with virtues added alongside, schools should teach children to test continuously both facts and values through inquiry and experimentation by "*applying intelligence to value questions.*"[73]

There is, however, a catch. Despite his help in the defense of Dewey's naturalistic philosophy of growth, and despite his realist espousal of this third objectivity made possible in Dewey's theory of inquiry, Putnam has to acknowledge limitations inherent in Dewey's pragmatism: what he calls "the limits of intelligence as a guide to life."[74] In other words Putnam restricts the realm of moral life over which Dewey's scientific method of thinking, or his concept of intelligence, is able to have effect. While he defends Dewey's concept of social intelligence as exercised in the realm of "social goods," he asserts that there are other situations in the moral life where Dewey's naturalistic ethics, insofar as it is based upon scientific method, is powerless. In Putnam's words, "While Dewey's social philosophy is overwhelmingly right, as far as it goes, his moral philosophy is less satisfactory when we try to apply it to individual existential choices." To illustrate this point, Putnam cites Sartre's character Pierre who makes an existential choice between joining the Resistance and taking care of his mother. Here no generalized method or social perspective, with their totalizing tendencies, applies, but "[i]ndividuality is at stake."[75] This is the moment when "the limits of intersubjectivity" in Deweyan pragmatism are disclosed.[76]

Putnam suggests that there is a limitation inherent in Dewey's naturalistic philosophy of growth, one that tries to explain the moral dimension of human life solely based upon the concept of growth associated with the scientific method of thinking. Acknowledgment of this limitation rather than full endorsement of Dewey's position may mollify the attack from the critics of Dewey. If Putnam is right, however, it means that there is something in Dewey's pragmatism that makes it inevitable for the private ethical life and the public life to be divided. The method of scientific inquiry and Dewey's concept of intelligence turn out to be inadequate to serve the moral vision of democracy and education to which he aspires. This not only contradicts Dewey's own claim of reconciling these two realms, but also undermines the basic line of his pragmatism.

Putnam's critical defense of Dewey shows us the nature of this limitation—or perhaps the internal tension—in Dewey's pragmatism, both by being true to his claim of a continuity of the moral and the natural and by disclosing the danger that follows if we simply pursue it: that is, the limit in the scientific method of thinking exposed in a certain dimension of the moral life.

Neither Rorty's relativist reinterpretation nor Putnam's realist one can present an adequate defense of Dewey's naturalistic philosophy of growth in such a way as to save the basic line of his pragmatism. In different ways, Rorty, the Deweyan scholars, and Putnam all disclose the limitations of a totalizing tendency inherent in Dewey's philosophy of growth where this is interpreted within the framework of "Dewey between Hegel and Darwin." It is a philosophy of power and progress that stifles the delicate sense of an ethical reality exceeding the dichotomy of foundationalism and antifoundationalism, and the sense of the impossible and the infinite entailed by the path of growth without fixed ends. Dewey's naturalistic philosophy of growth, when strictly interpreted within the framework of Dewey between Hegel and Darwin, and in the language of scientific method, cannot respond to the concerns of critics steeped in the context of our times. Is this a limitation embedded in the structure of Dewey's own thought, or is it possible to overcome this impasse from within the structure of his own philosophy?

It is the latter potential that the rest of this book aims to explore. Following on from the contributions made by Rorty, Putnam, and other Deweyan scholars, I shall try to explore another possibility of reconstruction in philosophy in Dewey's naturalistic philosophy of growth—seeking a way toward Dewey *beyond* Hegel and Darwin, beyond the philosophies of totality. I shall attempt to show the ethical reality of the possible and impossible that humans undergo in the passage of continuous growing by navigating a middle way beyond foundationalism and antifoundationalism. This I believe is a call from our times, a call to which the task of reconstruction in Dewey's pragmatism must be dedicated. The task will inevitably require the critical reconstruction of Dewey's concept of intelligence, for this has been too much associated with the scientific method of thinking.[77]

THREE

EMERSON'S VOICE
Dewey beyond Hegel and Darwin

The debate surrounding Rorty's reinterpretation of Dewey has shown a limitation of defending Dewey's naturalistic philosophy of growth solely within the framework of "Dewey between Hegel and Darwin." A way out of this impasse is suggested by Ralph Waldo Emerson, whom Dewey calls the "Philosopher of Democracy." Historical and textual evidence as well as recent scholarship on their connection demonstrates Dewey's undeniable connection with Emerson. Among those who today consider Emerson to be the source of American pragmatism, however, Stanley Cavell stands out in virtue of his eloquent resistance to any easy connection between Emerson and Dewey. He is at pains to stress profound differences in their thought. The defenders of Dewey respond by arguing that Cavell misrepresents Dewey. The debate itself suggests that Emerson offers another framework of critical reconstruction in Dewey *beyond* Hegel and Darwin.

"Emerson—The Philosopher of Democracy"

Though the basis of Dewey's philosophy was formed, first under the influence of Hegel, and then Darwin, it has another facet: the influence of Ralph Waldo Emerson. The presence of Emerson in Dewey's thought is not always perspicuous or constant, and his influence is not necessarily direct. Still, Dewey, from the early to the later period of his career, disclosed a hidden identity, or perhaps a spirit that he inherited from Emerson.

In the earliest formation of his thought, even before he read Hegel, Dewey encountered Emerson, though indirectly, via Vermont Transcendentalism. This constitutes one of the underlying streams in Dewey's philosophy throughout his philosophical career. Dewey spent the years from 1859 to 1879 in Vermont, attending the University of Vermont from 1875 to 1879.[1] He rebelled against the prevailing intellectual milieu of Lockean empiricism and Scottish realism, dissatisfied with their dualism and their conception of the human mind as passive. Especially concerning the intuitionism associated with Scottish realism which he studied under H. A. P. Torrey, Dewey found himself ill at ease with its metaphysical dualism of intuition and reason, where intuition gave direct spiritual insight and was the ultimate source of truth about God.[2] George Dykhuizen points out that Dewey believed that intuition was not the final source of truth, but that it must be verified by the intellect.[3] As Alan Ryan puts this, Dewey found that "intuitionism did little more than affirm a trust that ideas accepted with a sufficient degree of unshakability must reflect reality."[4] He felt that intuitionism was intellectually "timid" "FATE," 148). Dewey was, however, affected by and found hope in the thought of James Marsh and Samuel Taylor Coleridge, especially after reading Marsh's edition of Coleridge's *Aids to Reflection*, which was published in America in 1825. It was via the influence of Marsh and Coleridge, though indirectly perhaps, that Dewey came to encounter Emerson. It occurred in the following manner.

In 1826, Marsh was appointed as the fifth president of the University of Vermont and became the leader of the Vermont School of

Transcendentalism.⁵ His "Preliminary Essay" and his edition of Coleridge's *Aids to Reflection*, as well as writings of the German idealists that he introduced to America, had a significant impact upon New England transcendentalists, including Emerson, in the 1830s and 1840s.⁶ As a revolt against Lockean empiricism and Scottish realism, Marsh and Coleridge, in the spirit of German idealism, emphasized the mind's growing process, the regenerating power of the human will in its continual striving, and the capacity for individual self-realization and affirmation. Based upon a distinction between reason and understanding, they claimed that reason as a higher faculty based upon intuitive judgments enables mankind to understand the world. In the words of Marsh's "Preliminary Essay": "The Christian belief is the perfection of human reason."⁷ Furthermore, American transcendentalists shared the organic metaphor of German idealism which asserted the ultimate unity of both mind and the world, and of the individual and the universal in a dynamic and creative process of growth. Marsh inherited and spread Coleridge's liberal and radical view of religion as that which was tested by the power of reason, an idea, in Marjorie H. Nicholson's description, that bought about "the reconciliation of religion and philosophy."⁸ Philosophy became a religious and moral affair that involved the living of life itself; and vice versa, religion became a philosophical affair that involved the rational power of the human mind.

These views of Marsh and Coleridge had a significant impact not only on Emerson and other New England transcendentalists, but in terms of the strain of German idealism that persisted in American intellectual history. According to Steven C. Rockefeller, after the influence of New England transcendentalism subsided with the advent of the Civil War, the idealist tradition in America was inherited by the St. Louis Hegelians, including William T. Harris, a founder of *The Journal of Speculative Philosophy*. It was through this journal that the young Dewey was introduced to American neo-Hegelianism. Rockefeller also suggests that there was "some cooperation between the old leaders of New England Transcendentalism and the Midwestern Hegelians," especially concerning an organic view of the universe.⁹ As an illustration of such common ground, Rockefeller indicates that George Sylvester Morris, Dewey's Hegelian teacher at Johns Hopkins, shared with Coleridge and Marsh the notion of ethical self-realization, or self-determination, based upon self-conscious intelligence and free will.[10]

Dewey's philosophy developed in this intellectual milieu. In 1941, reflecting upon Marsh's influence, he tells us how Marsh and Coleridge liberated his thought and inspired his spirit—their trust in the higher faculty of Reason and the Will of man, their holistic view of the universe in the correlation of objects and mind, the spirit of "a challenge to the existing state of belief and action" in "the radicalism of Coleridge," and the necessity of educative community for the full development of individual power.[11] Rockefeller points out that Dewey was particularly sympathetic to their idea of "the art of reflection," the art of self-knowledge by means of reason or intelligence. According to this view, spiritual intuitions are not merely passive or ultimate but are themselves "the operations of reason or intelligence," in which heart, will, and emotion play significant roles. A faith in the rational power of mind, according to Rockefeller, was the common ground on which Dewey later came to commit himself to neo-Hegelianism. In fact, Rockefeller points to the fact that Dewey's first book, *Psychology* (1887), offers philosophy as the "practice of reflection," with his ideas about the "search for self-knowledge" echoing those found in Marsh's "Preliminary Essay."[12]

Thus, surprisingly at this early stage, Marsh and Coleridge could have helped Dewey to find a religious, moral, and spiritual starting point for his later philosophical vision. To illustrate their profound and lifelong impact upon the development of Dewey's philosophy, Rockefeller cites the following remarks by Dewey himself:

> All I can do on religion is to say again what I learned from Coleridge way back in my childhood, and this *A Common Faith* is, as far as I am concerned, just a restatement of my early faith that I got at the University of Vermont through Marsh and Coleridge.[13]

This statement, made after the publication of *A Common Faith* in 1934, suggests that, as early as the 1870s, Dewey had already acquired something of the spiritual dimension that was to characterize his later pragmatic and naturalistic religious views. Likewise, Ryan claims that, though Marsh's influence on Dewey's thoughts was obscure, "the concerns he grew up with and the intellectual resources he brought to them were a plausible starting point for his later ideas."[14] These comments help to reveal the extent to which Dewey, *before* he read Hegel and Darwin, shared this background with Emerson. And he retained until the end of his career this original vision—a voice from his childhood to which he always wished to return.

In 1903, Dewey published his essay, "Emerson—The Philosopher of Democracy."[15] Ever after his conversion from absolutism to experimentalism, the strain of thought that had originated in Vermont transcendentalism persisted in his work. In this essay, Dewey, though now a Darwinian naturalist and pragmatist, still displays his admiration of Emerson as a spiritual naturalist and a poet philosopher set firmly in the American grain. The way that Dewey approaches Emerson's thought throws light on his idea of growth.

The essay starts with the statement: "It is said that Emerson is not a philosopher. I find this denigration false or true according as it is said in blame or praise" ("Emerson," 184). Dewey tries to demonstrate that Emerson is a philosopher in a rather distinctive sense. In highlighting the role of perception in Emerson's thought, and expressing an appreciation for the poetic mode of his language, Dewey invites the reader to reconsider the meaning of thought, reason, or logic as they have dominated Western philosophy. In Dewey's view, Emerson takes philosophical thinking to be "paths by which truth is sought" rather than "truth" itself (ibid., 186). Most importantly, on Dewey's view, he brings philosophy back down to earth by speaking of "the facts of the most real world in which all earn their living." Philosophy serves "the common experience of everyday man" (188), and "all nature exists for the education of the human soul" (189). In Dewey's view, Emerson shifts the locus of truth from the "mountain high" to the "deposit that nature tolerates" at the bottom (191), where each and every individual represents the truth of mankind (189).

Dewey finds in Emerson's thinking a direction of reconstruction in philosophy and calls him "the Philosopher of Democracy" (190).

This essay indicates that even after his shift away from Hegelian idealism, Dewey holds on to Emersonian "idealism" (187)—a faith in and an ethical drive toward the ideal vision of democracy—democracy for the everyday experience of the common man and the universal community of mankind. Dewey does not, however, base that ideal on a fixed, absolute Reality. In Emerson's transcendentalism, Dewey finds a form of idealism that is made possible on a natural basis—ideals realized in "the Here and Now" rather than the "Beyond and Away," or "the There and Then." This Dewey takes to be the essence of Emersonian "spiritual democracy" for everyday experience (189–90). Although it was Darwin and James who helped Dewey reconstruct his philosophy towards naturalism and experimentalism, a close reading of this essay suggests that Emerson was perhaps a similarly, or perhaps even, more profound influence. Through Dewey's connection with Emerson, beyond the framework of Dewey between Hegel and Darwin, we may find a rich metaphysical implication of his idea of continuous growing without fixed ends.

Is Dewey an Emersonian? Is Emerson a Pragmatist?: The Debate between Cavell and the Defenders of Dewey

There is a good reason to take this connection with Emerson as a starting point for reconstruction in Dewey's pragmatism. In the recent resurgence of American pragmatism, a number of researchers have found the origins of classic American pragmatism in Emerson's thought. Cornel West, in his "genealogy of pragmatism," finds the common root of various branches of pragmatism in Emerson, and traces this influence to and beyond Dewey. West's central claim is that American pragmatism rebels against modern Western philosophy which has been dominated by the Cartesian and Kantian models of epistemology: philosophy as a matter of knowing truth through Reason characterized by "abstract dualisms, philosophic absolutisms, autonomous discourse, professional divisions, and academic differentiations." In place of this tradition, pragmatists return philosophy to common sense, and transform it into cultural, social, and political criticism.[16] West finds the roots of this project in Emerson's thought, whose motif is "power, provocation, and personality—permeated by voluntaristic, amelioristic, and activistic themes.[17] In West's interpretation, Dewey inherits Emerson's evasion of philosophy and takes up his idea of the moral development of individual personality and self-creation through communal participation.[18] Dewey, however, situates the Emersonian motif within the historical context and social concerns of his times, and develops pragmatism, understood as a philosophy supporting critical intelligence, as the most effective means of good social practice. Ideas are not copies of the world; they are, rather, means for action. Thus West concludes: "Dewey is first and foremost an Emersonian evangelist of democracy."[19] West's interpretation of the connection between Emerson and Dewey and his appreciation of pragmatism is based upon the assumption that the foremost task of philosophy is to work for sociocultural change. From this perspective, West claims, Dewey is more a "full-fledged democrat" than Emerson, for Dewey fights against the social miseries of the age. West is critical of Emerson's political inactivism.[20]

Russell B. Goodman makes another major contribution in rediscovering the connection between Dewey and Emerson, focusing on the thread of Emersonian romanticism to be found in Dewey's pragmatism. Following Cavell's Emersonian theme of the "marriage of self and world," Goodman presents the romantic tradition of American pragmatism that originated in Emerson's thought. He claims that Emerson is at once "an empiricist," "a transcendental idealist" and "an experimentalist," and that Dewey takes up this Emersonian position.[21] Dewey's view of the "deeper and richer intercourse" of experience and nature is an Emersonian one in which "experience itself reveals an objective world."[22] In Goodman's view, Dewey continues to be an Emersonian romantic idealist while being an empirical realist even after his parting with Hegelianism in the 1890s.[23] Goodman calls Dewey a naturalistic spiritualist who considers the ideal and the spiritual both to be part of the natural world. Likewise, Richard Poirier finds Emerson at the root of "the pragmatist-poetic line."[24] He interprets Dewey's essay on Emerson as showing that the Emersonian pragmatist theme prevails throughout—the theme of self-creation "in movements, in transits and the abandonment of order," and the emphasis on "the Here and Now" as the essence of Emerson's "spiritual democracy."[25]

More recently, Lawrence Buell has taken the position that there is a connection between Emerson and pragmatism. Citing a phrase from Emerson, "the transformation of genius into practical power," Buell says that "this is the proto-pragmatist Emerson," and that "[t]he late-twentieth-century revival of interest in Pragmatism has given new prestige to the Emerson-to-Pragmatism story." Buell claims, however, that Dewey, despite his admiration of Emerson, lacks interest in "Emerson's thought about God." In his view, Dewey's connection with Emerson is limited to the aspect of "the Philosopher of Democracy," and, in virtue of this, he implicitly separates religion from democracy.[26]

Stanley Cavell, himself a writer in the Emersonian tradition, has been one of the few philosophers to go against the currents of this mainstream of thought. He refuses to call Emerson a pragmatist, or to call Dewey an Emersonian philosopher, first in *Conditions Handsome and Unhandsome* (1990)[27] and subsequently in "What's the Use of Calling Emerson a Pragmatist?" (1998).[28] The gist of Cavell's criticism is that Dewey's idea of intelligence is based upon scientific method. He views Dewey's pragmatism as a form of thinking which moves in action from a problematic situation to its solution "by the removal of an obstacle" (*Conditions*, 21), and as means of the enlightenment from "superstition, bigotry, gullibility, and incuriousness," and as "intellectual preparation for a better future" ("Calling Emerson," 78–79). As a result, he claims, the main emphasis of pragmatism is on social change through action with profound political implications. If these are what Dewey considers the characteristics of pragmatism and the role of intelligence, then Emerson is not, Cavell claims, a pragmatist, since for Emerson, "the success of science is as much a problem for thought as, say, the failure of religion is" (*Condi-*

tions, 15). While Dewey is "an enlightened child" (16), Emerson is an antienlightenment figure who recognizes the necessity of passion and patience as ingredients of ordinary experience and sources of transformation. Emersonian thinking, as Cavell represents it, finds its incentive not in action or solving problems, but in "living"—living as being "total" and "strong" (42–43). Criticizing Dewey's concept of scientific method, Cavell addresses the fundamental question of the meaning of intelligence, and eventually of philosophy.[29] In Cavell's view, philosophy is different from that kind of polemical or political discourse in which we "take a side in argument." With Wittgenstein, he claims that philosophy takes place "after all scientific arguments are over."[30] Thus, Cavell maintains that calling Emerson a pragmatist is a serious "repression" of Emerson's voice in American culture ("Calling Emerson," 79).

Cavell is also critical of Dewey's use of philosophical language. In his view, Dewey's language does not, as Emerson's does, help us understand and deepen the meaning of our experience (73). It is too general and abstract, and lacks concreteness:

> In Dewey's writing, the speech of others, whose ideas Dewey wishes to correct, or rather to replace, especially the speech of children, hardly appears—as though the world into which he is drawn to intervene suffers from a well-defined lack or benightedness. (75)

This is a serious betrayal of Emerson's investment in ordinary words as he assiduously attempts to return philosophy to ordinary life, "from metaphysical to everyday" (*Conditions*, 22). Cavell sees ordinary words as inseparable from self-discovery and self-transformation in moral relationships, in those relationships where one's position is at stake in confrontation with others.[31] Thus, Cavell concludes: "Are these different responses to language not philosophically fundamental? They seem so to me" ("Calling Emerson," 75). Cavell objects to Dewey's essay on Emerson because it "reads like a poignant wish to find something in Emerson's achievement that [Dewey] could put to use in his own work" (*Conditions*, 16).[32]

In a more recent book, *Emerson's Transcendental Etudes* (2003), Cavell restates his position on the relationship between Emerson and Dewey's pragmatism. There is a slight change in Cavell's tone with regard to "Dewey's textual debt to Emerson's transcendentalism": he finds it an "interesting and promising turn of events." Cavell does not deny either that "Emerson was a muse of pragmatism." His basic position, however, is unchanged. This is that, to his mind, "the assimilation of Emerson to pragmatism unfailingly blunts the particularity, the achievement, of Emerson's language, in this sense precisely shuns the struggle for philosophy . . . that Emerson sought to bequeath." While keeping "an old and continuing respect for John Dewey," Cavell continues to express some frustration with Dewey's language and with his concept of intelligence: for Emerson the essential predicate of "intellect" is "dissolves," whereas for Dewey the function of "intelligence" is to "solve problems." Cavell finds a lack of concreteness in Dewey's language of the middle way between extremes, making him feel "empty-handed, abstracted from thinking." In contrast, Cavell claims that, though Emerson's idea of "resolving" points to a "middle way," and in his idea of a thinking that requires "conversion or transfiguration," there is "no middle way between, say, self-reliance and self- (or other-) conformity"; for Emerson, the question of thinking occurs "before" these are resolved into practical problems.[33]

Cavell's criticism of Dewey and his opposition to comparing Dewey with Emerson has created a stir among the defenders of Dewey. Douglas R. Anderson's article, "American Loss in Cavell's Emerson," raises a direct criticism of Cavell's interpretation. He charges Cavell with missing "an Emersonian vein" in Dewey's philosophy and its significant contribution to American culture and democracy. Cavell misrepresents both Emerson and Dewey by viewing them through his own "un-Emersonian and un-American" lens, and in his "elitist Emersonian style" deforms Dewey's philosophy of experience for the common man which, in Anderson's view, is a very Emersonian aspect of Dewey's thought.[34] More specifically, Anderson criticizes Cavell for misreading Dewey's concepts of science, knowing, and intelligence. He asserts that Dewey's idea of knowing is far richer than suggested by Cavell's interpretation of Dewey's scientific method of problem-solving, since for Dewey "knowing is thoroughly environed by 'havings' and 'valuings'" beyond any narrow sense of empiricism.[35] According to Anderson, Dewey's concept of intelligence cannot be reduced to a kind of "technologism" as Cavell attempts to do, but rather, is closer to Emerson's "intellect"—thinking that involves human action, or a sense of "phronesis" that works for "empowerment in the world."[36] In this regard, Anderson sides with West who says that for both Emerson and Dewey, intellect is "a distinctive function of and inseparable from the doings, sufferings, and striving of everyday people."[37] Thus, Anderson maintains that Dewey's idea of intelligence is not merely one of problem-solving in the narrow sense, but instead, "an appeal to the funded experience"; genuine science as Dewey sees it is "infused with wisdom."[38] As a general orientation of philosophy, Dewey's idea of democracy as a way of life, so Anderson thinks, complements Cavell's presentation of Emersonian moral perfectionism: it is not by differentiating but rather by connecting the two that we can redeem not only Dewey but also Emerson. By doing so, we can enrich American democracy.

Anderson criticizes not only Cavell's misunderstanding of Dewey, but also Cavell's own philosophical assumption, which he claims is characterized by European "intellectualism," an elitist style, and an "impolitic" proclivity.[39] He is particularly critical of Cavell's "linguistic project," which focuses on "an intellectualist realm of language: words, voice, sign, conversation, reason, sentences, and so on."[40] In Anderson's view, Cavell is more a traditional professional philosopher than "an Emersonian American scholar."[41] The stance of Anderson seems to represent well the position of Dewey in the sense that he considers practice and action to be inseparable from thinking and intelligence. Anderson points out that "for Emerson, the intellect itself is both receptive and constructive," and refuses "Cavell's implicit claim that 'receiving' and 'acting' are exclusive."[42] Moreover, for Anderson, Dewey's "inadequate literary means" does not mean an inadequacy of "philosophical means."[43] The "difference in style" between

Emerson and Dewey "should not blind us to the importance of the similarities."[44]

More recently, Hilary Putnam has raised the question of Cavell's interpretation of Dewey in connection with Emerson.[45] Despite his appreciation of Cavell's contribution to philosophy, Putnam cannot accept Cavell's argument in "What's the Use of Calling Emerson a Pragmatist?" since he thinks that in this specific essay Cavell misrepresents Dewey. Putnam, like Anderson, is opposed to Cavell's understanding of Dewey's concept of intelligence as scientific methods of thinking in relation to experience. Concerning Cavell's citation of the phrase from *Experience and Education*, "the significance of our everyday experiences," Putnam argues that what Dewey has in mind here is precisely a matter of *connections* in experience. In opposing Cavell's decontextualized comparison of Emerson's "mourning" in experience and Dewey's problem-solving concept of experience, Putnam tries to elucidate Dewey's emphasis on everyday experience with the claim that everyday experiences mean for Dewey *everyday* experiences—not the death of one's own child which Cavell discusses in regard to Emerson. Putnam highlights the richness entailed by Dewey's concept of experience by saying that for Dewey human life is composed of "the dialectical relationship between consummation and inquiry." Inquiry is not purely an intellectual matter, but involves the diverse activities of human practice.

Further, in opposition to Cavell's attempt to differentiate Emerson's concept of thinking from Dewey's intelligence, Putnam instead finds common ground between the two: "[Emerson's] route to the universal is compatible with [Dewey's] scientific method." Dewey's call for the use of intelligence in moral life includes a respect for trial and error in experiment and discussion, which Putnam considers as significant fortification against "subjectivism." Rejecting Cavell's characterization of Dewey as a child of the Enlightenment, Putnam emphasizes the fact that Dewey does not merely accept the Enlightenment, but also criticizes the *way* it took place—a situation in which science and technology did not lead to the application of intelligence to our moral and political life.[46] In response to Cavell's criticism of

Dewey's pragmatism as too much associated with action and social change, Putnam defends Dewey in two related respects. First, Dewey does not, despite his faith in social science, propose control by scientific experts, but rather claims, in his vision of "participatory" or "deliberative" democracy, the need for *social* sciences for the benefit of working people.[47] Second, his aim of social reform is not just a matter of economic, redistributive justice. Instead, Putnam says, Dewey in his ethical writings shares an Emersonian vision of democracy both when he speaks of "setting free to the fullest extent possible the powers and capacity of all individuals," and in his use of such Emersonian expressions as "human flourishing," "pursuit of moral happiness," and "self-transformation."[48] Like Anderson, Putnam implies that Dewey has an Emersonian faith in democracy—the unity of self-realization with social intelligence. In conclusion, Putnam acknowledges Dewey's contribution towards ethics beyond subjectivism in his call for solidarity with fellow human beings. Though not as explicitly as Anderson, Putnam suggests that Cavell has a romantic, subjective proclivity in his overemphasis on self-transformation.

Cavell and the defenders of Dewey seem to remain apart concerning how we should best understand the Dewey-Emerson connection. Their distance in the debate raises a series of questions. First, it makes us wonder if there is any one "true" Emerson or Dewey whose position either camp best represents. Second, the debate addresses not only the issue of the relationship of two American thinkers, but also puts in question the identity of pragmatism as an American philosophy. It is undeniable that both Cavell and the defenders of Dewey share a common stance in the "American evasion of philosophy," their quest for a philosophy that serves for the ordinary experience of common men, practice being a crucial component of philosophical thinking. Cavell and the defenders of Dewey, however, show a different understanding of what they think Emerson and Dewey mean by such concepts as "practice," "action," "social," "change," or "experience." With their respective images of Emerson and Dewey, they diverge in what they consider to be the identity of *American* philosophy and American *philosophy*. Cavell and the defenders of Dewey have contrasting views on Dewey's concept of scientific methods of thinking, which turn upon what they expect of "intelligence" in philosophy. They adopt different stances towards Dewey's use of language, and the role of language in philosophy.

While Dewey's connection with Emerson seems to offer a promising framework, beyond Rorty's "Dewey between Hegel and Darwin," of reconsidering his naturalistic philosophy of growth, the debate over whether Dewey is an Emersonian thinker and Emerson is a pragmatist suggests still an unresolved, or even a flexible border in their relationship. It is this very precarious border in which we might be able to find a key to enhancing a potential as well as articulating the limitation entailed in Dewey's pragmatism and its naturalistic philosophy of growth. It is Cavell's dissenting voice that suggests a need to further disclose this yet fully unexplored realm of Dewey's relationship with Emerson, and by so doing to destabilize and reconstruct his philosophy *from within*.[49]

FOUR

EMERSONIAN MORAL PERFECTIONISM
*Gaining from the Closeness between
Dewey and Emerson*

In the debate that we have been examining, Cavell represents a dissenting voice. The majority of pragmatists think that Cavell misunderstands Dewey, which is, in Anderson's words, an "American loss." I believe, however, that leaving this gap within American philosophy unexamined will be a greater loss. We might be able to learn something from Cavell's sense of resistance for the sake of further enhancing the contributions made by Dewey's pragmatism in connection with Emerson's thought. Instead of keeping the two camps apart, therefore, I will try to engage his voice more fully in dialogue with neo-pragmatists and Deweyan scholars.

A crucial factor that splits Cavell from Deweyan pragmatists in the debate is his interpretation of *Emersonian moral perfectionism* (EMP)[1] Deweyan scholars who find a connection between Dewey and Emerson suggest that Dewey can be an Emersonian moral perfectionist; whereas Cavell, though acknowledging that Dewey is "some sort of perfectionist," maintains that he is *not* an *Emersonian* perfectionist.

Cavell asks us to "see how close and far they are to and from one another" (*Conditions*, 15). In order to find a source of Cavell's dissenting voice in the debate, and lead toward a more penetrating analysis of Dewey's relation to Emerson, a closer examination of EMP is essential.

To this aim, this chapter first examines Cavell's interpretation of EMP. In the light of its key features I shall then go over some of Dewey's text in which he echoes Emersonian voice. It shows that the preoccupations that run through Cavell's discussion of EMP are, in fact, very close to Dewey's central concerns with democracy, education, and growth. The chapter concludes that EMP can constitute an alternative framework to reevaluate Dewey beyond Hegel and Darwin.

Cavell's Emersonian Moral Perfectionism

Cavell introduces the concept of perfectionism as "a dimension or the tradition of the moral life" in Western thought—a stream of philosophy as a quest for the good life that originated with Plato and Aristotle (2). It puts weight on the question, "How do we live?" as a matter of the state of one's soul rather than of theoretical argument in such moral theories as utilitarianism or Kantianism (6). Perfectionism is concerned with "the plane on which the issue arises 'before' questions of the good and the right come to occupy moral reasoning."[2] As examples of perfectionist thinkers, Cavell includes a broad range of writers such as Plato, Aristotle, Emerson, Nietzsche, Kant, Mill, Kleist, Ibsen, Matthew Arnold, Oscar Wilde, Bernard Shaw, Heidegger, Wittgenstein—and even the Dewey of *Experience and Nature* (5). By naming them, however, Cavell does not offer us a "closed list of features that constitute perfectionism," since perfectionism, as "an outlook or dimension of thought embodied and developed in a set of texts," refuses to be defined for some "theoretical purpose" (4, 6).

The perfection of the self is a process of transformation, or perhaps, more conventionally, self-realization. Aristotle's words capture the gist of this:

> [W]e must not follow those who advise us . . . but must strain every nerve to live in accordance with the best thing in us. . . . This would seem, too, to be each man himself, since it is the authoritative and better part of him. It would be strange, then, if he were to choose not the life of himself but that of something else.[3]

Cavell's idea of perfectionism has a similarly strong ethical and moral drive in the pursuit of a better state of the self: "Perfectionism is the dimension of moral thought directed less to restraining the bad than to releasing the good" (*Conditions*, 18). Cavell here uses a thematic metaphor of "the soul's journey" (32)—or "the myth of the self as on a journey (a path in Plato's image, a stairway in Emerson's, a ladder in others'), a journey to, let us say, the truth of itself (not exhausted by its goods and its rights" (*Pitch*, 142). Cavell implies that although perfectionism is concerned with the self, it does not treat it as the object of knowledge in an epistemology or of the subject of moral judgment in ethical theories. It alters the perspective on the self by centering on the question of how "I" should live. Here, some sense of a "dialogue" between the "I" and the voice of the text to which "I am invited" is crucial in Cavell's idea of perfectionism. In other words, the state of one's soul has a stake in how readers participate in the "city of words" built in a text (*Conditions*, 8)—how their "I" confronts and responds to the perfectionist author that they read. As Cavell tells us: "The moral force of perfectionism does not collect in judgments but is at stake in every word" (32); and more recently: "Writing from self-reliance is thus simultaneously an emblem or instance of the self-reliant in word and in deed, in words that are deeds."[4]

The transformation of the self, however, is not merely a matter of self-interest. It is inseparable from the betterment of society with the spirit of amelioration seen through the state of one's soul. In this regard, Cavell echoes the sentiments and the expression of Matthew Arnold:

> Culture, which is the study of perfection, leads us . . . to conceive of true human perfection as a harmonious perfection, developing

all sides of our humanity; and as a general perfection, developing all parts of our society.[5]

The "inward operation" and the total development of society are inseparable in perfectionism.[6]

In this broad framework Cavell presents his view of *Emersonian* moral perfectionism. It has three main characteristics: (1) perfection as perfect*ing* with no fixed ends; (2) as a distinctively American democratic ideal; and (3) with significant implications for education emphasizing conversation and friendship. First, it presents a distinguishably American version of perfectionism—a view of human perfection that is located in the ordinary and that sharply contrasts with the teleological form of Plato's and Aristotle's perfectionism.[7] The essence of *Emersonian* moral perfectionism, as Cavell presents it, is the endless journey of self-overcoming and self-realization whose central focus is on the here and now in the process of attaining a further, next self, not the highest self. Drawing on Emerson's idea of the "unattained but attainable self" in "History," Cavell states: "The self is always attained, as well as *to be* attained" (12) and *"each state of the self is, so to speak, final"* (3).[8] The self that is attained now is immediately connected to the next state that is as yet the unattained, and therefore, the attainable. There is no one unattained/attainable self, but rather, Cavell says, "'having' 'a' self is a process of moving to, and from, nexts" (12). The direction of Emersonian perfection is "not up but on ... in which the goal is decided not by anything picturable as the sun, by nothing beyond the way of the journey itself" (10). *Emersonian* perfectionism is characterized by "goallessness" (xxxiv); it refuses final perfectibility.[9]

If Cavell retains the name of perfection for self-realization, it might be asked how that self-realization is to be characterized, what self-realization consists in. Cavell's suggested response is secular, which is to say naturalistic. A direction for perfection is not given by theology or moral lessons. Rather perfection is firmly rooted in our natural sense of *shame* as a driving force and the quest for happiness. Cavell calls Emerson's "Self-Reliance" "a study of shame" (*Conditions,* 47).

He states: "One way or the other a side of the self is in negation—either the attainable negates the attained or vice versa" (12). Indeed Emerson, in his call for cultivating the self-reliant American Scholar, expresses his sense of shame over the "degenerated state" of the American society: "Public and private avarice make the air we breathe thick and fat."[10] This contrasts with Thomas Hurka's omission of natural pleasure or desire from his concept of perfectionism. Or in comparison to Russell B. Goodman's and George Kateb's writings on Emerson, Cavell's language most intensely echoes Emerson's sense of shame or "disdain" (*Conditions*, 49)[11] In this regard, Cavell is more Freudian than Aristotelian. This sense of shame is specifically directed against the fallen state of democracy, what Emerson calls "conformity"[12]—the state in which we subject ourselves to "our given opinions, learning nothing new" (*Conditions*, 12), being "subject to an oppressive helplessness" with "a sense of compromise and of cynicism."

Second, EMP represents an ideal of *American* democracy.[13] At the very beginning of the introduction to *Conditions Handsome and Unhandsome*, Cavell raises the question: "Is Moral Perfectionism inherently elitist?" (*Conditions*, 1). Since perfectionism involves the matter of excellence, this is an inevitable question. Hurka points out that some perfectionisms are antiegalitarian, including that of Nietzsche, which limits the idea of perfection to the few best individuals.[14] Contrary to Anderson's criticism of Cavell's Emerson as an "un-American," intellectual elitist, Cavell presents Emerson as a democratic philosopher. Responding to John Rawls' opposition to an elitist version of perfectionism, Cavell says:

> My direct quarrel with *A Theory of Justice* concerns its implied dismissal of what I am calling Emersonian Perfectionism as inherently undemocratic, or elitist, whereas I find Emerson's version of perfectionism to be essential to the criticism of democracy from within. (*Conditions*, 3)

Cavell's project resists the charge of elitism. Emersonian perfection is a call to the potential nobility of the self, what might be called an aristocracy of the self, rather than the endorsement of political inequality. He represents EMP as not only "compatible with democracy, but its prize."[15]

The democratic way of life, as Cavell sees it in Emerson, involves the continuous illumination of the state of "my" compromise with society in which I find myself and "my" response to society in "my" own voice of criticism; self-criticism and social-criticism are conjoined. On this Cavell says: "The necessity of our (a citizen's, one whose consent is invested) participation in a democracy is not expressed by saying, as Kateb insists, that we 'must' act." The "political" implication of EMP is our participation in the "democratic city of words." It is the matter of our "thinking and acting aversively" (*ETE*, 190). Cavell's thought here can be traced back to *The Claim of Reason* where he writes:

> [I]n the political, the impotence of your voice shows up quickest; it is of importance to others to stifle it; and it is easiest to hope there, since others are in any case included in it, that it will not be missed if it is stifled, i. e., that you will not miss it. But once you recognize a community as yours, then it does speak for you until you say it doesn't, i. e., until you show that you do.[16]

Although Emerson does not make an appearance here, what Cavell says presages his later Emersonian idea of the "criticism of democracy from within" (*Conditions*, 3). Siding with Emerson, who claims that "genius" is not the privilege of a few individuals, but the "sound estate of every man" ("AMS," 41), Cavell takes a position that Emersonian perfectionism is not elitist.[17] Responsibility of criticism is "universally distributed" among each of us as a "capacity" and "an opportunity" as well as "a threat" (*Conditions*, 9, 26).

Cavell revives Emerson's spirit of nonconformity not for the cause of isolationism, but for the sake of the betterment of self and society, as a form of social participation.[18] In resonance with Emerson's voice, "I do not see how any man can afford, for the sake of his nerves and his nap, to spare any action in which he can partake" ("AMS," 43), Cavell resists a "shrinking participation in democracy" (*Conditions*, 51). EMP calls for a response without cynicism in conjunction with a reaffirmation of consent to the society in the light of one's "constitution." The social contract is realized in a "responsiveness to society." The pursuit of happiness not only satisfies the self; it involves the "public" quest as that for which the self searches and to which it necessarily attests. Liberty is "my liberty as a matter of my voice." Justice, whose adequacy is the mark of goodness, is sought not only in one's soul, but constantly tested in "the conversation of justice" in which the fate of all is shared (27–28). Cavell finds in Emerson "the democratic aspiration" (1). Against the dominant, conventional image of Emerson as a representative of American individualism, Cavell shows us the *social* Emerson.[19]

Third, EMP offers a view on the education of the self in dialogue with others based upon friendship. While emphasizing Emerson's praise of "the infinitude of the private man," with its stress on the process of individuation, Cavell reminds us that "we need not, we should not, take [Emerson] to imagine himself as achieving a further state of humanity in himself alone" (*Conditions*, 10–11). Recognition of "my attained perfection (or conformity)" requires "the recognition of an other—the acknowledgment of a relationship" (31). Cavell shows us that the relationship of acknowledgment is at the heart of Emerson's idea of friendship, and that it involves Emerson's idea of representativeness: the "friend (discovered or constructed) represents the standpoint of perfection" (58–59). As Emerson says: "the private life of one man" can represent and animate all men ("AMS," 49)[20] Cavell elaborates on the idea of representativeness as follows:

> [T]his another of myself—returning my rejected, say repressed, thought—reminds me of something, as of where I am, as if I had become lost in thought, and stopped thinking.[21]

The presence of another is Emerson's transfiguration of Kant's idea of "the reception of the moral law, the constraint as Kant names the relation, by the moral imperative, expressed by an 'ought'" (*Passages*, 26). Cavell highlights the fact that for Emerson, this constraint is not a matter of "ought," but that of "recognition and negation." A friend reminds us of the sense of shame, that of "aversion to our selves in our conformity." By so doing, a friend invites us "beyond ourselves" (or not) (*Conditions*, 58–59). It is illustrated by Cavell's Emersonian idea of the conversational act of reading. Emerson the writer is "this other for his reader" who confronts the reader with her attained state with a sense of shame, and by doing so guides her on the soul's journey (32).

As Emerson himself suggests from time to time, friendship is the relationship that is featured by inspiration and awakening.[22] "[T]he friend permits one to advance toward oneself" (*Passages*, 26). The perfection of one's self requires the process of education as Cavell sums up: "As representative we are educations for one another" (*Conditions*, 31). In Kateb's words, it is a matter of "achievement."[23] Thus with an emphasis on friendship in EMP, Cavell again projects the image of the *social* Emerson, not Emerson as an individualist, or the proponent of a solipsistic, subjective, or autonomous self.

In sum, EMP has shown diverse dimensions of Cavell's interpretation of Emerson that have not been fully recognized in the debate. He presents Emerson as a democratic figure, not an "elitist," who is fully participatory and responsive. Although Cavell distances himself from political and polemical issues, a stance for which he is sometimes criticized as being apolitical, he is not simply insensitive to these imatters; rather he takes a different approach to the democratic concepts of justice, liberty, and equality as those that concern the noble condition of each state. Although it is true that Cavell treasures language, this is not merely a matter of linguistic play, as Anderson criticizes. Instead EMP has shown that language is a necessary route to his Emersonian democratic vision. Furthermore Cavell's strong concern for education is a factor that marks his account off from many other interpretations of Dewey's connection with Emerson. The standpoint of EMP can now be used to bring into focus Dewey's relationship with Emerson and reexamine his philosophy of growth in a new light.

Reviving Dewey's Muted Voice: Gaining from the Closeness between Dewey and Emerson

> The one thing in the world, of value, is the active soul. This every man is entitled to; this every man contains within him, although, in almost all men, obstructed, and as yet unborn. The active soul sees absolute truth; and utters truth, or creates. In this action, it is genius; not the privilege of here and there a favorite, but the sound estate of every man. (Emerson, "The American Scholar")

> That every individual is at once the focus and the channel of mankind's long and wide endeavor, that all nature exists for the education of the human soul—such things, as we read Emerson, cease to be statements of a separated philosophy and become natural transcripts of the course of events and of the rights of man. (Dewey, "Emerson—The Philosopher of Democracy"[24])

Dewey is in tune with Emerson's vision of "spiritual democracy" ("Emerson," 190). He responds to the voice of Emerson who calls for the "upbuilding" of the American Scholar, the private individual whose central fire "animates all men" ("AMS," 49). For Dewey, spiritual democracy involves the "education of the human soul" for the sake of rebuilding the public in America. It is the responsibility and the right of *each* individual. And like Emerson, Dewey is aware that democracy is never a perfected state, but that it needs to be attained; it requires the patient process of education in "the Here and the Now" ("Emerson," 189).

Despite the apparently common ground that Dewey's essay on Emerson suggests, Cavell claims that this represents merely Dewey's "poignant wish" to *sound like* Emerson. Are these words of Dewey above merely his passing remark, as Cavell implies? Or is there something here that reveals Dewey's authentic voice and that might help us tap the potential of his idea, of democracy, education, and growth? To find a valid answer to these questions, and as an initial step in untangling the implications of Cavell's request to "see how close and far [Dewey and Emerson] are to and from one another" (*Conditions,*

15), it is worth rexamining Dewey's text—his words, tone, and spirit—this time in the light of distinctive features of EMP.[25]

Dewey's writing style typically lacks a personal or emotional tone and it often creates a barrier between him and his readers. Steven C. Rockefeller claims: "Dewey's writing style tended to be dry, and his books and essays left many readers feeling that something to do with the emotions, the heart, and values was missing." Although Dewey was a man of strong feeling, "his passions to a large extent had been channeled into a rarefied form of philosophical discourse and social idealism."[26] Likewise, in connection with his "self-effacing" personality and abhorrence of "psychobiography," Alan Ryan characterizes Dewey's writing as "impersonal" and "reticent."[27] His characteristic writing style, however, has a positive side. Ryan cites the remark by Justice Holmes that Dewey wrote the way God would have "if he had been terribly anxious to tell us something of great importance but had found himself temporarily at a loss for words." When he read Dewey's *Experience and Nature*, Holmes felt that "he had for the first time seen the universe 'from inside.'"[28] Raymond D. Boisvert claims that, in trying to present new metaphysical theories, Dewey is "a pioneer breaking new ground" with "philosophical courage" and "honesty," a philosopher who breaks away from old dualistic assumptions.[29] Similarly, Rockefeller finds Dewey's way of addressing philosophical problems difficult to comprehend "in part because it runs counter to traditional ways of thinking." Once it is understood, however, "it emerges as a convincing and profound expression of one of the major alternative ways of being religious open to modern men and women."[30] These scholars agree that Dewey's apparently muddy language is a sign of his innovative philosophical thinking, a language that requires a reader to be actively and imaginatively engaged in the interpretation of his text.

In fact, Dewey does not necessarily sound dry or unemotional, particularly when his writing touches upon some common themes with EMP. His autobiographical essay, "From Absolutism to Experimentalism" (1930), which was written late in his career, illustrates this.[31] The essay presents Dewey's philosophical conviction that a philosopher's thought, to the very end, should stay on the road to perfection. By calling himself "unstable, chameleon-like" ("FATE," 155), he suggests his Emersonian sensitivity to inconsistency, and tells us: "I have, I hope, a due degree of personal sympathy with individuals who are undergoing the throes of a personal change of attitude" (153). His drifting from absolutism to experimentalism is accompanied by the EMP sense of the attained and the unattained self—that of "wandering in wilderness" aiming at "the promised land" (160). The language that he uses in this essay conveys "an intense emotional craving." Such a craving comes from a vital life experience, "from persons and from situations more than from books." His philosophical search is his honest response to a call from life, a call that refuses to be constrained by "a final consequence," or "some set of convictions," or some "hard-and-fast dividing walls" (153). In order to return philosophical thought to experience, Dewey dares to shoulder "all the inconveniences of the road [he has] been forced to travel" rather than treating experience as "the germ of a disease" (156). Dewey as a philosopher speaks like Emerson the perfectionist—Emerson who calls for "power and courage to make a new road to new and better goals."[32]

The undeniable spirit of EMP expressed here is not merely a matter of language; it suggests a possibility that Dewey's naturalistic philosophy of growth may be reread as one that is related to the distinctive features of EMP. There are two of Dewey's writings that distinctively suggest this direction: *Democracy and Education* (1916) and *Human Nature and Conduct* (1922). These are the books that were written after Dewey drifted from Hegelian into naturalist, but that still maintain his Emersonian idealist language and vision. In *Democracy and Education* Dewey makes it explicit that his naturalistic concept of growth differs from the idea of "perfection" as an unfolding of latent powers toward "a final unchanging goal," as "completion."[33] In place of the idea of the telic perfected state, Dewey is close to Cavell in claiming that "the perfect or complete ideal is operative here and now" (*DE*, 62). Dewey thus criticizes Hegel's view of perfection as the concept of development that aims at "the Whole, or perfection" (63), "an absolute goal" on "a stepladder of ascending approximations" (64). In its absolute institutionalism and historicism, "the Hegelian theory swallowed up concrete individualities," allowing "conformity" to become a principle of education (65). The naturalist Dewey's rejection of this Hegelian concept of perfection can be reread as his solidarity with Emersonian perfectionism—the American voice of democracy.

Human Nature and Conduct is also filled with opportunities for rereading Dewey within the framework of EMP. As a book on human *nature* based upon the theory and vocabulary of Darwinian naturalism, it discusses the "ethical import of the doctrine of evolution,"[34] presenting the naturalistic theory of habit reconstruction as a basis of growth. Among biological, scientific, and naturalistic, as well as pragmatist discourse, however, we can find throughout the text the Emersonian message. It is permeated by the nonconformity and antimoralism of EMP. Thoroughly rejecting the fixed end point of growth, "a static perfection" (*HNC*, 122), Dewey proclaims: "Perfection means perfecting, fulfilment, fulfilling" (200). Growth as perfection is an ideal to be attained at each moment. And it is a process in which we are not allowed to "rest upon attained goods" for "[n]ew struggles and failures are inevitable" (199).

Thus, *Democracy and Education* and *Human Nature and Conduct* offer promising signs that show a striking similarity between Dewey's concept of growth and Emerson's view of perfection. Against the common foe of teleological perfectionism, Dewey and Emerson create solidarity for what might be called an American version of perfectionism—a philosophy that puts weight on the here and now, and therefore questions sincerely how we can live a better life in this moment, rather than focusing on goals that we strive to achieve. In this minimum sense, Cavell unintentionally offers a hopeful bridge between Dewey and Emerson.

Based upon this original intuition, let us explore further other texts of Dewey. *Reconstruction in Philosophy* (1920) presents a philosophical vision in tune with the central theme of EMP. Responding to the chaos and uncertainty of American society in the postwar period,

Dewey calls for a reconstruction of philosophy in order to throw light upon the issues troubling mankind in the here and now.[35] Reconstruction is neither a complete rejection of the heritage from the past, nor the mere application of ready-made intelligence (*RP*, ix, xxxvi). Rather, it is a sustained criticism of the crises and tensions arising from new human situations. The means of this reconstruction he calls "intelligence" or "scientific knowing," as distinct from "reason" or "pure intellect" (viii). Philosophy can no longer be conducted under the old doctrine of immutable, ultimate truth. Dewey's idea of *reconstruction* in philosophy echoes the idea of EMP in its resistance to fixity, insofar as fixed standards, norms, and ends cannot be "the only assured protection against moral chaos" (xiii). A philosophical endeavor should be a response to ever-changing situations and an endless effort to fulfill "what we have as yet attained only partially" (xxxix).

Dewey in this book explicitly uses the term "perfection" in an Emersonian way.

> The end is not longer a terminus or limit to be reached. . . . Not perfection as a final goal, but the ever-enduring process of perfection, maturing, refining is the aim in living. . . . Growth itself is the only moral "end."(177)

Growth is perfection; and perfection is perfecting. This echoes Emerson's message, "Success treads on every right step" ("AMS," 46); and his use of the natural metaphor of a rose: "There is simply the rose; it is perfect in every moment of its existence . . . [Man] cannot be happy and strong until he too lives with nature in the present, above time" ("SR," 141). Like Emerson and Cavell, Dewey does not reject our natural sense of happiness (and shame) as the ingredient of such perfection. He does, however, emphasize that happiness is not "a fixed attainment" but resides in the process of searching—"succeeding, getting forward, moving in advance" (*RP*, 179–80).

Further, as in EMP, Dewey makes it clear that perfection is not merely a matter for the individual self, but is accompanied by the melioration of society as a whole. Democracy in this moral vision aims at "the all-round growth of every member of society," and *a fortiori* the education of the child (186). The book concludes with a symbolically religious expression of perfectibility: "The wind of the spirit bloweth where it listeth and the kingdom of God in such things does not come with observation" (212). Dewey restates Emerson's perfectionist message that it is "every man," each of us, who creates—or to put it more correctly who will gradually and hopefully create—the kingdom of God on earth.

In the late 1920s and the 1930s, Dewey's language becomes richer, which enables us to hear more acutely his Emersonian voice, particularly involving the theme of the rebuilding of the public in American democracy and the rebuilding the individual. Among the works of this period, four writings deserve attention: *The Public and its Problems* (1927), *Individualism Old and New* (1930), *Construction and Criticism* (1930), "Creative Democracy—The Task Before Us" (1939). In each, Dewey's language conveys his sharp recognition of the obstacles to the progress of democracy, given the difficulties of the age, and in that sense, he becomes more realistic and less optimistic about the attainability of his democratic ideal.

The Public and its Problem is a book in which he criticizes the "eclipse of the public":

> Indifference is the evidence of current apathy, and apathy is testimony to the fact that the public is so bewildered that it cannot find itself... What is the public? If there is a public, what are the obstacles in the way of its recognizing and articulating itself?[36]

A sense of struggle permeates the text, with its recognition that a democratic community "does not occur all at once nor completely," and that "it sets a problem rather than marks a settled achievement" (*PP*, 331). Dewey's concern with the eclipse of the public, the disintegration of American society, resonates with Emerson's criticism of the fallen state of democracy in "The American Scholar":

> The state of society is one in which the members have suffered amputation from the trunk, and strut about so many walking monsters—a good finger, a neck, a stomach, an elbow, but never a man. ("AMS," 38)

Emerson's powerful call for the rebuilding of Man Thinking in the name of "Culture" originates in his sense of shame, as Cavell suggests, over what degrades society into the meaningless mass. Dewey shares this sense of shame.

Concerning the question of "how far" we will succeed in reestablishing "the void left by the disintegration of the family, church and neighborhood," Dewey tells us: "We cannot predict the outcome" (*PP*, 369). Still, his vision of participatory democracy is unflagging. To create a democratic public, Dewey renews his faith in education, "not just in the sense of schooling but with respect to all the ways in which communities attempt to shape the disposition and beliefs of their members" (360). He also emphasizes the significance of face-to-face communication between self and others (371). In intimate social relations, democracy as a way of life is the process of mutual education—learning how to think, communicate, and act together. The book concludes with Dewey's allusion to Emerson : "We lie, as Emerson said, in the lap of an immense intelligence" (372). Intelligence here connotes broader implications that include the capacities, habits, and attitudes that are needed for the recreation of the public. The citation can be interpreted as Dewey's restatement of the Emersonian task of democracy—democracy that necessitates the education of "Man Thinking" in order to attain "true union" ("AMS," 51).

Individualism Old and New also addresses the task of creating a democratic community, but here it is with sharper focus on the individual. The tone of Dewey's text is more severely realistic, being permeated with a sense of shame for the degraded condition of American democracy as it becomes more and more materialistic and defined by a more uniformly corporate culture. Dewey says that he does not have in mind here "an 'optimistic' appeal to future time and its possibilities"[37]; and that the "promise of a new moral and religious outlook has not been attained" (*ION*, 49). He is warning particularly of the crisis of the "lost individual" (66) who is "divided within himself" by conformity (65). In Emersonian vein, Dewey describes the crisis as one of "the human soul" (52), for democracy is a matter of the "spiritual" (49). This echoes Emerson's critical voice: "How many individuals can we count in society? How many actions? how many opinions? So much of our time is preparation, so much is routine, and so much retrospect, that the pith of each man's genius contrasts itself to a very few hours."[38]

Despite all these difficulties, Dewey proposes the creation of a new type of individual, an "integrated individuality." This is not a proposal for isolated individualism. Rather, as if to follow Emerson's faith that "man is one" ("AMS," 48), and indeed by alluding to Emerson, Dewey concludes the book with the Emersonian vision of democracy—the vision of a universal community of mankind, and "the connection of events" (from Emerson's words in "Self-Reliance"), in which alone an integrated individuality is realized:

> To gain an integrated individuality, each of us needs to cultivate his own garden. But there is no fence about this garden: it is no sharply marked-off enclosure. Our garden is the world, in the angle at which it touches our own manner of being. By accepting the corporate and industrial world in which we live, and by thus fulfilling the pre-condition for interaction with it, we, who are also parts of the moving present, create ourselves as we create an unknown future. (*ION*, 123)

This is a manifesto of Dewey's ideal vision of democracy with the metaphor of cultivation as a matter of "Culture" as Emerson proposes: "Each philosopher, each bard, each actor, has only done for me, as by a delegate, what one day I can do for my self" ("AMS," 49). Since this is a state of democracy that is yet to come, it is the creative task of democracy, and hence, the task of education in the broadest sense. And if this is the task of perfection, perfection is not the monopoly of selected individuals; it is the task, the responsibility, that is assigned to each individual. This is the perfectionist theme that will be passed down and taken up again in his later essay, "Creative Democracy."

Construction and Criticism is a continuation of the theme of *Individualism Old and New*, a search for a new individual, one engaged in the critical reconstruction of democracy from within—the theme that Cavell finds in Emerson's perfectionism. Dewey here discusses various themes relating to individuality—the creative mind, individual responsibility, freedom, and criticism. The vocabulary that he uses, however, becomes more elaborate and subtle. He does not write only *about* the individual, but passionately speaks *for* the individual, *as* an individual with the Emersonian anticonformist spirit. Along these lines, Dewey cites words from Emerson's "Self-Reliance": "A man should learn to detect and watch that gleam of light that flashes from within."[39] By citing these words of Emerson, Dewey recognizes the significance of the education of the "active soul" as Emerson says— the activities of critical and creative individuals. He concludes the essay by saying: "Creative activity is our great need; but criticism, self-criticism, is the road to its release" ("CC," 143). This resonates with Cavell's idea of the "criticism of democracy from within" and with the Emersonian passage towards true union, a road that is being rebuilt from the private to the public. Emerson writes: "[Man Thinking] is one, who raises himself from private considerations, and breathes and lives on public and illustrious thoughts" ("AMS," 46).

The 1939 essay, "Creative Democracy—The Task Before Us," highlights Dewey's philosophical endeavor to articulate his spiritual vision of American democracy.[40] He reiterates his claim: "Democracy is the faith that the process of experience is more important than any special result attained." What gives this impetus is the "[n]eed and desire" that make us "go beyond what exists, and hence beyond knowledge, beyond science," for "[t]hey continually open the way into the unexplored and unattained future" ("CD," 229). Attaining an unattained future—we are plainly close here to Cavell's description of the "journey" of perfection that Emerson recurrently takes.

What is at the heart of creative democracy is, according to Dewey, the cultivation of the "capacity of human beings" to be engaged in "free inquiry, free assembly and free communication" (227). Hence he declares: "faith in democracy is all one with faith in experience and education." As one of the conditions of such an educative process of democracy, Dewey highlights the significance of friendship—the practice of mutual learning and the "habit of amicable cooperation" (228).

To sum up the theme of perfection, the essay concludes with the following statement:

> The task of this release and enrichment is one that has to be carried on day by day. Since it is one that can have no end till experience itself comes to an end, the task of democracy is forever that of creation of a freer and more humane experience in which all share and to which all contribute. (230)

This statement can be complemented by Emerson's strong call for the rebirth of the American Scholar: "In self-trust, all the virtues are comprehended. Free should the scholar be, free and brave. Free even to the definition of freedom, 'without any hindrance that does not arise out of his own constitution'" ("AMS," 47). For both Dewey and Emerson, democracy is the ongoing and endless task of perfection. It is also the ongoing task of creation as it is related to newer and better experiences of each and all individuals, and hence, constitution of culture itself. The central fire of the private man cannot be "enshrined in a person" (49); it is the matter of inspiration and sharing that is at the heart of Emerson's and Cavell's perfectionist idea of the public, and with which Dewey's thought resonates. "Creative Democracy" can be considered Dewey's mature restatement of the EMP proclaimed thirty-six years before in "Emerson—The Philosopher of Democracy." These writings of Dewey reinforce the view that he is an Emersonian idealist even after he has parted company with Hegel and in spite of his joining hands with Darwin.

In view of these striking similarities between Dewey and Emerson, it is understandable why Dewey praises Emerson as the "Philosopher of Democracy"; why he associates the task of creative democracy with Emerson's idea of the education of the human soul; and why the defenders of Dewey find a connection between the two. Despite Cavell's refusal to call Dewey an Emersonian moral perfectionist, the present rereading of Dewey's text in dialogue with Emerson has revived Dewey's muted voice; it has shown that his idea of naturalistic growth has too much in common with Cavell's EMP just to be ignored. Just as Rorty's framework is inadequate, so too is Cavell's criticism not wholly fair to Dewey; but Cavell's unfairness can, in fact, be helpful in directing us toward a metaphysics of growth. Though the limitation of stylistic range that Cavell criticizes in Dewey needs to be acknowledged, and indeed, though there is still a need to conduct a more thorough critical reading of his work, something I shall undertake in later chapters, the standpoint of EMP can now be seen to disclose more about the recessive, rich dimension of Dewey's naturalistic philosophy of growth than is achieved by Rorty's "Dewey between Hegel and Darwin." The account thus far may then enable us to find what it means to live a life of growth without fixating its ends, and to create the passage of the attained and unattained self in continuous growing.

Let us move on and see what we can gain from considering the closeness between Dewey and Emerson, and then come back again to Cavell's sense of distance.[41]

FIVE

DEWEY'S EMERSONIAN VIEW OF ENDS

"Education is all one with growing; it has no end beyond itself."[1] As this statement of Dewey represents, growth in his evolutionary view of the world is the contingent and endlessly evolving natural process. It takes place in the interaction of an organism and its environment without relying on the eternal resting point outside that process. This is the essence of Dewey's idea of *progressive* growth. How can we save this challenging worldview from a persistent voice of anxiety that asks, "Growth towards what?" and from the stigma of optimism filled with trust in power and progress? In view of the common ground between Emerson and Dewey, does Emerson help Dewey respond to these questions? In the project of rereading Dewey in light of EMP, the task is to articulate further the Emersonian "ethical import" implied in the natural process of growth. This is to be done by showing a richer metaphysics of growth with an Emersonian sense of the attained and unattained perfection.

As an initial attempt, this chapter reexamines Dewey's idea of *habit reconstruction*. It presents his Emersonian view of ends for growth, and even gestures toward an Emersonian holistic view of growth in ever-expanding circles.

Habit Reconstruction: Growth as Transactional Holism

Dewey says: "Man is a creature of habit, not of reason nor yet of instinct."[2] Habit is Dewey's fundamental tool for understanding human nature and the basis for growth (*HNC*, 51). It represents his Darwinian functional theory of "active adjustments" as they are achieved by means of the interaction of an organism and its environment (*DE*, 52). Dewey's idea of habit is not mere habituation as "accommodation," but habituation as active control of the environment (51–52). While he rejects the idea of "repetition" as the essence of habit (*HNC*, 66), Dewey considers some mechanism or pattern to be indispensable to habit (51). Habit as social custom, or "the form of life," is the basis for the formation of individual habits, which Dewey calls "secondary and acquired" (43, 65). The latter, however, modify the former by a distinct force. This interactive modification of habits is the mechanism of habit reconstruction—a gradual transformation of culture and society from within.

There are two specific aspects of habit reconstruction: impulse and intelligence. Impulse is the innate tendency that plants the seed of novelty and breaks the grasp of old custom. Dewey defines the function of impulse as follows: "Impulses are pivots upon which the reorganization of activities turn, they are agencies of deviation, for giving new directions to old habits and changing their quality" (67). There is, however, a catch. Although impulse is a natural source of novelty, it is only the beginning of the new habit. As soon as it comes into the world, it is under the influence of the preexisting habits of social relationships. In this sense, impulse is an acquired novelty; as Dewey says, "Impulses, although first in time are never primary; in fact they are secondary and dependent" (65). Therefore, impulses must be redirected by the function of intelligence, that is, the responsibility "to observe, to recall, to forecast," and the courage "to go deeper than either tradition or immediate impulse goes" (118). Through the guidance of intelligence, impulse becomes "incarnated in objective habit" (62). Impulse and intelligence are not metaphysical distinctions but functional ones in the cycle of habit reconstruction. The following statement recapitulates the point:

> Thought is born as the twin of impulses in every moment of impeded habit. But unless it is nurtured, it speedily dies, and habit and instinct continue their civil warfare. (118)

The mechanism of habit reconstruction encapsulates Dewey's antidualistic, holistic view of growth. It represents his battle against the "privacies of inner life" that are so much a part of Cartesian rationalism and British empiricism (9). It also reflects his opposition to instinct theories, including those of Freudian psychoanalysis that were popular in his day.[3] Alan Ryan argues that Dewey's aversion to the introspective emotion is derived from his early experience with Puritanism.[4] Dewey fears the "moral pathology" of "a sickly introspection" (*HNC*, 109, 140). Thus, in his theory of habit reconstruction, Dewey flatly rejects the concept of "separate instincts" (104) or any substantial "psychic causes" (106), and tries to return human nature to "the public open out-of-doors air and light of day" (6).

In his rejection of the inner psyche as separate from the outer world, Dewey aims to build an antidualistic, holistic view of the world. Dewey's views on nature, Thomas M. Alexander tells us, are based upon the principles of continuity, transaction, and potentiality within the medium of the *situation*, which makes possible his claim about the relationship between nature and experience. Dewey, he argues, presents a rich concept of experience "in" nature.[5] Russell B. Goodman also defends Dewey's view of a "deeper and richer intercourse" of experience and nature in which "experience itself reveals an objective world."[6] As these scholars point out, Dewey's views on the transactional relationship between man and world are basic to his naturalism and represent his holistic view of the universe, his attempt to overcome the subject-object dualism. As Dewey says:

> In experience, human relations, institutions, and traditions are as much a part of the nature in which and by which we live as is the physical world. Nature . . . is in us and we are in and of it.[7]

In this holistic view of the world, Dewey's idea of habit reconstruction is filled with apparently paradoxical concepts that create the image of his merely wavering between, or even obscuring, the distinction between opposites: the inner and the outer, mind and body, subject and object. On the one hand, for example, an impulse that originates in our natural and biological disposition is a kind of inner urge originated in each individual being. Yet, on the other hand, an impulse is anything but a subjective feeling or a mind composed of sense data. Impulses manifest themselves as "active tendencies" in observable, shared public situations (*HNC*, 144). Thus, he says: "'It thinks' is a truer psychological statement than 'I' think." (216). In this regard, Dewey has a behavioral tendency, though not in the sense of the reductionist behaviorism of B. F. Skinner or J. B. Watson. Rather, Dewey is a social behaviorist like G. H. Mead. Dewey's behavioral theory of habit reconstruction falls also under the influence of Frederick M. Alexander's physiological approach, an approach that strives to unite body and mind.[8]

The truth is that Dewey tries to speak in the middle ground between the in and out in his situational, decentralized, and developmental concept of human nature. In place of an either-or way of thinking[9], Dewey presents an alternative, holistic worldview in "a middle term" (*HNC*, 51). Indeed, this pragmatic wisdom, as Israel Scheffler suggests, is the unique contribution of Peirce's idea that "we begin in the middle of things."[10] In his idea of habit reconstruction, Dewey tries to capture the "intermediate" realm (*EE*, 17) between mind and body, stability and change, the old and the new, conservation and renovation, dependence and independence, formation and deviation. In his idea of the "middle" or "intermediate," however, Dewey does not posit a static middle point between two static opposites; he instead envisions a path of development rather than a series of fixed points. This is a continuous regeneration of a moving middle in an ongoing transaction between ever-changing factors. The path of the middle is a historical and progressive stream of time within the context of practice, what Dewey calls "events."[11] It is in this distinctive sense that we might call Dewey's view of the universe *transac-*

tional holism.[12] It is the worldview of pragmatism that we always start, live, and grow in the middle—in the process of interaction and in an intermediate, indeterminate situation.[13]

It is this transactional holism that constitutes Dewey's naturalistic idea of growth, and that reinforces its common ground with EMP— the mechanism for the reconstruction of culture from within, a reconstruction made possible by the interaction of the novel impulses of the young and established habits of adults. A change that takes place through habit reconstruction is not a radical revolution nor the destruction of the old; rather it is a gradual renewal of habits from within the culture. It is "reconstructive growth" (*HNC*, 68). Since habit reconstruction is always taking place in the middle, the reconstructive process of growth is best understood as a participle perfection—as "perfecting" (200).

Reconstructive growth in this middle ground, however, does not mean opportunism or non-commitment. Sharing Cavell's idea of the criticism of democracy from within as it is found in EMP, Dewey's transactional holism is permeated by the Emersonian spirit of nonconformity and criticism. For example, in his Emersonian voice, Dewey criticizes the "inert stupid quality of current customs" that suppresses the plasticity of the young (47). It is particularly demonstrative in his claim of treasuring the innovative impulse of the young as the essential condition of habit reconstruction—a reflection of his solidarity with Emerson's "respect for immaturity" (*DE*, 57).

Dewey's Emersonian View of Ends

Dewey's Emersonian spirit of nonconformity is supported by and supports his thorough refusal to be contained by fixed ends. Dewey, with Emerson, reconstructs the concept of ends in opposition to the classical Greek teleology—the teleology of "fixed, eternal ends" (*HNC*, 159).

This naturalistic idea of habit reconstruction is not unlike Aristotle's functional and action-oriented view of human nature—the view that moral virtue is acquired as a second nature through habit and practice.[14] Dewey also agrees with Aristotle that contingency and particularity are an integral part of nature; in this respect they share a "pluralistic" view of the universe (*EN*, 48). Despite these similarities, however, Dewey criticizes Aristotle's (and Plato's) concept of telos as final cause, with its accompanying mentality of "the craving for the passage of change into rest, of the contingent, mixed and wandering into the composed and total" (78). In Dewey's view, it was Aristotle who gave credibility to the Western idea of perfection as a complete, fixed, end-state of self-realization (*HNC*, 154–55):

> In Aristotle this conception of an end which exhausts all realization and excludes all potentiality appears as a definition of the highest excellence. It of necessity excludes all want and struggle and all dependencies. It is neither practical nor social. Nothing is left but self-revolving, self-sufficing thought engaged in contemplating its own sufficiency. (122)

The way Dewey criticizes the fixed end of perfection is reminiscent of the way Cavell distinguishes Emersonian perfectionism from Plato's teleological perfectionism.

Dewey calls this view the Greek "love of perfection" (*EN*, 162) and criticizes it for the following reasons. First, in his view, Greek perfectionism and its teleology are "fatalistic." It involves "a limiting position, a point or goal of culminating stoppage, as well as an initial starting point" (279–80). It molds a pessimistic temperament that tends toward the view "every endeavor [one] makes is bound to turn out a failure compared with what should be done, that every attained satisfaction is forever bound to be only a disappointment" (*HNC*, 199). Second, the Greek view of perfection is hierarchical, with a distinction between a lower realm of contingent and unstable nature, and the highest realm of contemplation in "pure and unalloyed finality" (*EN*, 89, 192). The former stage is merely a point from which to climb toward the latter. A dichotomy between "knowing and doing" is created as a result (*HNC*, 130). On the path toward perfection, the elements of the temporal and accidental in nature are to be gradually eliminated as obstacles to the achievement of the highest end, as "recalcitrant, obdurate factors" (88-89). As a result, Dewey feels, what is significant in the ongoing process of the here and now is excluded from the picture of perfection. "[S]truggle, suffering and defeat" in natural human life are viewed as limits to human perfection (88). Thus, he says:

> We long, amid a troubled world, for perfect being. We forget that what gives meaning to the notion of perfection is the events that create longing, and that, apart from them, a "perfect" world would mean just an unchanging brute existential thing. (58)

As in EMP, in which the natural sense of shame plays a crucial role, there is a strong sense that the negative phases of our experience are a significant source for our drive for human perfection.[15] Hence, he declares: "Happiness is not something to be sought for, but is something now attained, even in the midst of pain and trouble" (HNC, 182). Third, Dewey thinks that the Aristotelian view of perfection creates a "deficiency" model of development that views the immature child as being "incomplete" and "imperfect" in the context of the faultless perfect state of "sufficiency" (EN, 48, 78, 84, 162). A sharp dichotomy is produced between the immature and mature. Dewey thinks that the significance of perfection can never be measured against a perfected state, but is solely experienced and communicated through the ongoing process of perfecting.

In place of Greek perfection and teleology, Dewey presents an alternative concept of an end that aligns with Emerson's perfectionism. This is his idea of the means-ends relationship as a fruit of his transactional holism. In Dewey's view, a distinction between means and ends is not metaphysical, but functional. They are "two names for the same reality," a reality which is composed of the series of "intermediate acts" (HNC, 28). Ends function as a means by serving as the perspective from which we anticipate the next act. In turn, a means is the name for the next immediate action to be taken as "a temporary end" (DE, 113). "Means are means; they are intermediates, middle terms" (HNC 28).[16] Ends are being reconstructed at each moment of action. "Ends grow."[17] They are not static points, and cannot be "located at one place only" (*AE*, 63). Rather, ends are "ends-in-view" that represent a whole series of acts (*HNC*, 155; *EN*, 88): "the terminal outcome when anticipated ... becomes an end-in-view, an aim, purpose, a prediction usable as a plan in shaping the course of events" (*EN*, 86). Dewey's idea of the means-ends relationship is a mark of growth as growing in the middle.[18]

Dewey's idea of the means-ends relationship supports the direction of rereading Deweyan growth in the light of EMP. He reconstructs the concept of end as being pluralistic and dynamic, ends loyal to the Emersonian view of perfection. As with Cavell's Emersonian idea of the endless attainment of the unattained self, Dewey's transactional holism claims that "nothing in nature is exclusively final" (*EN*, 99). He transforms the concept of end from a mere finishing point to a tentative, consummatory closure that simultaneously constitutes a new beginning, opening "a further state of affairs" (85). "A natural end" is not a "de facto boundary" (86) but a "fulfilling close" (*AE*, 62). Ends liberate one action for the next; they do not contain it. Hence, Dewey says: "Every closure is an awakening, and every awakening settles something" (174). Thus, paradoxically, "[e]nds are literally endless" (*HNC*, 159); ends are open-ended. Dewey's view of ends resonates with Cavell's remark that "'having 'a' self is a process of moving to, and from next," and that "*each* state of the self is final."[19] Dewey, along with Cavell and Emerson, proposes the concept of end in the ongoing act of "endings" (*EN*, 84). We perfect our life with each moment of action, and we do this always starting anew in the middle of experience. As Dewey says, "travelling is a constant arriving" (*HNC*, 195).

Growth in Expanding Circles

Showing a striking similarity to the basic feature of EMP, Dewey's concept of end in his transactional holism represents his innovative view of growth—the trajectory of growth not as a linear, goal-directed route but as one of an infinite expansion of the whole whose ends are open to all directions. In his description of habit reconstruction, Dewey suggests a quasi-Hegelian quest for "an enveloping whole" (180–81). This whole, however, is not of an absolute totality, but a whole that always leaves room for infinite space, the realm of the unknowable and the uncertain beyond the existing reach of our knowledge. In this regard, Dewey's quest of the whole is closer to Emersonian whole in the attained and unattained path of perfection.

Goodman, who connects Emerson, Dewey, and Cavell to the American romantic tradition, points out that a common thread running through their thought is what Cavell calls the "marriage of self and world." In Cavell's view, according to Goodman, Emerson overcomes "a metaphysical fixture" posed by Kant: the universe being composed of the subjective world of experience and the objective world in itself, beyond the grasp of human understanding.[20] Indeed, Cavell maintains that Emerson, with his "epistemology of moods," transforms the meaning of "experience," and is thus able to "destroy the ground" upon which the metaphysical distinction between the subjective and the objective is situated. Thus, Cavell says, Emerson's view of the universe is neither one of "realism" nor "solipsism." Moods "color" the world in "succession." The meaning of the world is "revealed" by moods (*Senses*, 125–28). Cavell argues that the relationship between the self and world is that of reciprocal responses. This corresponds to Dewey's transactional holism – the idea that neither self nor world is something to be known as a fixed entity, but that their meaning is revealed only in a transactional process.

Emerson's contribution, however, does not end merely with this transactional concept. Emerson's "ever-widening circles," Cavell suggests, make possible an "onward" movement that resolves the antinomy of subjectivity and objectivity, the private and the public, or the inner and the outer (128, 137–38). The Emersonian view of perfection moves in "endless, discontinuous encirclings" (*Conditions*, xxxiv). Emerson himself describes the idea of expanding circles as follows:

> Our life is an apprenticeship to the truth, that around every circle another can be drawn; that there is no end in nature, but every end is a beginning; that there is always another dawn risen on mid-noon, and under every deep a lower deep opens. This fact, as

far as it symbolizes the moral fact of the Unattainable, the flying Perfect, around which the hands of man can never meet, at once the inspirer and the condemner of every success, may conveniently serve us to connect many illustrations of human power in every department.[21]

This passage implies that endlessly expanding circles, which Emerson calls "a self-evolving circle" ("Circles," 167), is the metaphysics of perfection, "the flying Perfect." It makes possible his view of ends as new beginnings. On the circumferences of expanding circles, ends to be attained exist in all directions, not only in one, upward direction. Everything in nature is in flux, including the state of perfection. In striking similarity to Dewey's transactional holism, Emerson writes: "Permanence is a word of degrees. Every thing is medial" (176). This explains why Cavell says, "*each* state of the self is final," and why perfection is perfecting. Once we think we have completed a circle, another yet unattained horizon awaits us. When Emerson says, "People wish to be settled; only as far as they are unsettled is there any hope for them," he implies that settlement and unsettlement, perfection and imperfection, and the attained and unattained are facets of "the total growths" (174). Emerson's metaphysics of growth in expanding circles implies the theme of EMP as a journey of self-overcoming.

Emersonian holistic growth suggests the sense of infinity, with his sense of wonder over an unknowable realm always awaiting in the path of human perfection: "The last chamber, the last closet, he must feel, was never opened; there is always a residuum unknown, unanalyzable. That is, every man believes that he has a greater possibility" (168). In contrast to the Aristotelian concept of perfection enclosed by its final limit, Emerson's idea of growth in expanding circles is open-ended. Or to put it in other words, Emerson is closer to Dewey than Aristotle when he declares: "I simply experiment, an endless seeker, with no Past on my back" (173).[22] Thus, for Emerson, "[t]he only sin is limitation" (169), and "[l]ife is a series of surprises" (174).[23]

Dewey's idea of growth as transactional holism, its accompanying concept of end, and his quest for "an enveloping whole" may be reread in the light of the Emersonian view of growth in expanding circles. In his description of habit reconstruction, Dewey conjures up the image of new horizons opening ahead with the metaphor of the port:

> Activity will not cease when the port is attained, but merely the present direction of activity. The port is as truly the beginning of another mode of activity as it is the termination of the present one. (*HNC*, 156)

In the compensatory and circular rhythm of nature (*EN*, 66–67), Dewey says, growth is in "the ever-recurring cycles" (*AE*, 152). In this path, what is midway between apparently paradoxical and contradictory opposites becomes thinkable. Possibilities for growth are opened in all directions. Dewey's "expanded whole" may share common ground with Emerson's infinitely expanding circles—holistic circles that combine the notion of unity with the idea that unity is not complete (171.) Dewey's perfectionism with its ethical import of Darwinian naturalistic growth is much closer to Emerson's perfectionism than to Aristotle's or Hegel's. His Darwinian worldview is surely progressive, but it is permeated by the sense of "humility" over the ever unattainable nature of perfection—"the sense of our slight inability even in our best intelligence and effort" (*HNC*, 200). Dewey's idea of growth reread in the light of EMP, in place of Dewey between Hegel and Darwin, gestures toward Emersonian holism beyond the philosophy of power and progress.

Dewey's Emersonian holistic, expanding, and changeable view of the universe, but with its humble sense of infinity and imperfection, transforms the very question that we must address on growth. Since an end can never be fixed on a point in a limited direction, and since an end is infinitely growing with the sense of the unknowable, it cannot be questioned in such forms as "Growth towards *what*?" or "*What* is the end of growth?" as if the content of growth were knowable and identifiable. These questions themselves reflect a presupposition that there are certain definable moral sources and foundations that we can ultimately strike. Just as Cavell says that the goal of Emersonian perfection is "nothing beyond the way of the journey itself"

(*Conditions*, 10), so too does Dewey's growth as EMP demand a new set of questions addressed to the way of the journey, to the ongoing process of growing. These must be questions that ask "how." *How* are we to endlessly create and recreate ends in the here and now in particular situations of our lives? *How* can each of us learn to articulate and realize ends-in-view as our ways of life? *How* do we bring forth a "fulfilling close" in "each doing"? (*AE*, 62).[24]

SIX

GROWTH AND THE SOCIAL
RECONSTRUCTION OF CRITERIA
*Gaining from the Distance between
Dewey and Emerson*

Cavell urges us to see how close and far Dewey and Emerson are. Having discussed the common ground between them, we turn now to attend more closely to Cavell's voice of criticism. One of the challenging questions that Cavell addresses to Dewey is the lack of concreteness in his language. Especially, he cannot hear "the speech of children" in Dewey's writings on education.[1] To take up this line of criticism, we now invite Dewey, the how-philosopher, to respond to the following question: *How* can a good end be determined at each moment of perfecting? A more concrete picture of growth is needed in order to show what it means to live the life of growth as growing without relying on fixed ends, and what is going on in this very moment when we are perfecting our lives with the sense of finitude and infinitude. An attempt to answer this question involves Dewey's idea of the social reconstruction of criteria.

In the face of the challenge, Dewey starts to disclose his distance from Emerson. It is Cavell and Emerson, his critical conversational partners, who confront Dewey with this distance. The distance becomes apparent in the form of the inadequacy of his language to narrate, or itself to exemplify, the process of growth as perfection. The distance is a matter of not only *linguistic* means, but also of *philosophical* means, which affects Dewey's theme of EMP. An internal gap that lies between the horizons of EMP and the scientific horizons in his naturalistic philosophy of growth is suggested.

How Do We Know a Good Ending of Growth? Growth and the Social Reconstruction of Criteria

In response to the question of how he distinguishes "educative" growth from its "mis-educative" counterpart, good growth from bad, Dewey states: "When and *only* when development in a particular line conduces to continuing growth does it answer to the criterion of education as growing."[2] To elaborate further the meaning of this "principle of continuity," however, it remains incumbent upon Dewey to respond to the question of the *how*, to demonstrate the way in which the principle applies in determining each ending of growth as a good one or bad one.

Dewey's idea of the social reconstruction of criteria partially responds to this question. He takes an evolutionary position with respect to the good, a view that everything is in flux and medial. The good is a matter of degree, as Dewey says:

> Reflection upon action means uncertainty and consequent need of decision as to which course is better. The better is the good; the best is not better than the good but is simply the discovered good. Comparative and superlative degrees are only paths to the positive degree of action. The worse or evil is a rejected good. In deliberation and before choice no evil presents itself as evil. Until it is rejected, it is a competing good. After rejection, it figures not as a lesser good, but as the bad of that situation.[3]

This represents Dewey's pragmatist position since it allows the process and consequence of an action in a particular situation to determine its value. He rejects the idea of fixed, pre-given criteria as the definitive measures.[4] The significance of growth as perfection can never be measured by "standardization, formulae, generalizations, principles, universals."[5] As an alternative, Dewey presents the concept of revisable criteria in connection with the idea of "warranted assertibility." Criteria are not "fixed first principles as ultimate premises or as contents of what the Neo-scholastics call *criteriology*."[6] Rather, they emerge from the ongoing process of cooperative inquiry in a particular situation.

The way to bring forth a good ending for perfection hinges on what kind of social interaction takes place in the process of revising criteria. Dewey says that it is conducted through a cooperative action in experimentation and dialogue. Hilary Putnam discusses this concept by claiming that what guarantees Dewey's pragmatist concept of "justification without foundations" is the procedure of "the democratization of inquiry"—the scientific method of hypothesis, testing, and experimentation through cooperative inquiry and free communication.[7] This is a democratic procedure by means of social intelligence. The acquisition of the capacity for an equal and free exercise of social intelligence is a condition of growth, and it requires education (*EE*, 56).[8] Moral standards of culture and custom are being questioned and reconstructed through reflective and experimental intelligence in interaction between and among the young and the adult. The ways they interact with each other in their daily lives determine the production of good ends for growth.

As a more specific characteristic for such social interaction, Dewey presents the idea of "intimate contacts between the mature and the immature" (21). This represents his idea of face-to-face dialogue and friendship. Dewey claims that moral standards cannot be found in a choice between control given by the adult, as a representative of social custom, on the one hand, and freedom exercised by the young in their rebellion from custom, on the other (ibid.). In his idea of habit reconstruction, criteria for a good end of growth are continually sought and reconstructed in the middle realm between the lives of adults and the young, through the flexible interaction of their perspectives. In such shared activity, Dewey says, "the teacher is a learner, and the learner is, without knowing it, a teacher" (*DE*, 167). The young and adults mutually educate and grow as friends and equal partners.

Dewey puts the idea of interaction as follows:

> The word "interaction," which has just been used, expresses the second chief principle for interpreting an experience in its educational function and force. It assigns equal rights to both factors in experience—*objective and internal conditions.* Any normal experience is an interplay of these two sets of conditions. Taken together, or in their interaction, they form what we call a situation. (Emphasis added) (*EE*, 42)

By "objective conditions," Dewey means such external factors in the classroom as the teacher, books, and equipment, which constitute the environment of the young. By "internal conditions" he means the impulse and the immediate inclinations of the young (41). Interaction is the process that mutually modifies the two. Dewey further elaborates:

> [W]hen it is said that they live in these situations, the meaning of the word "in" is different from its meaning when it is said that pennies are "in" a pocket or paint is "in" a can. It means, once more, that interaction is going on between an individual and objects and other persons. (43)

The key word here is "between." To live in a situation and thereby participate in interaction means to live in the middle realm between the internal and the external, a realm that is being created between individuals and their surrounding objects. Dewey does not reject the concept of the "in" or the "internal" as a unique attribute of an individual being; as he says: "Experience does not go on simply inside a person. It does go on there, for it influences the formation of attitudes of desire and purpose. . . . But this is not the whole of the story" (39). There is no such thing as "something purely 'inner,'" or "an 'inner' personality" to be perfected (*DE*, 129). The "inner" is given its meaning solely in the matrix of our life situation. The impulse of a child finds and realizes its meaning only in its manifestation in action in a shared situation. This is probably what Dewey means when he speaks of the unity of "action and soul" in his theory of habit (*HNC*, 52). And, as the sole meaning of human life is found out in "intimate contacts," adults are compelled to observe, interpret, and engage themselves carefully with the life of the young in the middle realm of interaction.[9]

The social reconstruction of criteria takes place in this process of intimate interaction. The relationship of face-to-face dialogue is a dynamically but subtly constructed practice of revising criteria among diverse perspectives. In addition to the child's life, and his or her "present inclinations, purposes, and experiences," a situation encompasses a wide range of objective conditions,[10] including:

> What is done by the educator and the way in which it is done, not only words spoken but the tone of voice in which they are spoken. It includes equipment, books, apparatus, toys, games played. It includes the materials with which an individual interacts, and most important of all, the total social set-up of the situations in which a person is engaged. (*EE*, 45)

At each moment of interaction, our ways of thought, action, and speech are at stake for the social reconstruction of criteria. In this sense, bringing forth a good ending for growth without relying on fixed criteria is a task that demands rigor. It must involve an urgent sense that "the good is now or never" (*HNC*, 200).

The Case of the Recalcitrant Child

Dewey's idea of the social reconstruction of criteria and its concomitant idea of the intimate contacts between the young and the adult, however, pose a question concerning the how. Israel Scheffler, criticizing Dewey, puts this as follows:

> How, one wants to know, is an instance of *flexible* remaking of habits to be recognized, in contrast with a *non-flexible* sort? How is one to establish a balance between thought and energy? How is one to determine when a piece of thinking embodies a "balanced arrangement of propulsive activities," or reflects a "proportionate

emotional sensitiveness?".... In sum, if the balance between reflection and impulse turns on the avoidance of their respective vices, the very notion of such balance turns out to be empty, or virtually empty, without additional specification. One can interpret the desired balance in various ways, depending upon how one independently reads the situation.[11]

Here Scheffler maintains that Dewey's theory of situation is viciously circular, allowing us arbitrary choices. In addition to this general difficulty, he points to a confusion involved in Dewey's concept of impulse as the pivot for reconstruction. Dewey's "psychological" account asserts that impulse is released only when habit breaks down. Scheffler claims that this cannot, however, explain Dewey's moral imperative that habits should be *continuually* reconstructed, since he does not show any energizing source for impulse prior to a habit breakdown.[12] Scheffler raises the question of how the impulse of the young can be released continually. He implies that the principle of continuing growth alone is not enough.

Robert B. Westbrook raises similar questions. He asks "how impulses could be employed to break the cake of custom if they required adversarial habits to redirect them." Westbrook's interpretation is that Dewey offers two responses. One is the education of children for "habits of flexible response." When customs are rigid but when there is nevertheless a need to educate children for the acquisition of flexible and creative habits, however, a second solution presents itself: adults should locate "the source of a disposition for reform in the conflict among prevailing habits."[13] At such a general level of explanation as Westbrook gives for Dewey, however, it is not clear how the social reconstruction of criteria is being flexibly and continually conducted in the interaction between the young and the adult; nor how the rigid custom of the adult can be prevented from suppressing the plastic impulse of the young, when they are already embedded in custom. If the existing standards of a culture function smoothly, and if there is no disturbance or conflict among habits or institutions in a well-regulated state, how can the young obtain the source for the release of their impulses? They may not even feel the need to change the status quo. These are the questions concerning the process of growth that Dewey is obligated to answer as the philosopher of the how.

There is also a more specific case that challenges Dewey concerning how loyal he is to his own claim of the social reconstruction of criteria: the case of the recalcitrant child in the classroom. Dewey exhibits an Emersonian perfectionist spirit of nonconformity and criticism. He criticizes conformity in the following manner:

> Natural instincts are either disregarded or treated as nuisances—as obnoxious traits to be suppressed, or at all events to be brought into conformity with external standards. Since conformity is the aim, what is distinctively individual in a young person is brushed aside, or regarded as a source of mischief or anarchy. Conformity is made equivalent to uniformity. Consequently, there are induced lack of interest in the novel, aversion to progress, and dread of the uncertain and the unknown. (*DE*, 55–56)

This is the Dewey who shows the Emersonian courage to venture, with the immature young, into the uncertain realm of growth. He does not fear the innovation of the young as a potential source of anarchy. And he is critical also of the tendency of the adult to "regard novelties as dangerous, experiments as illicit and deviations as forbidden" (*HNC*, 159). Dewey allows for deviancy as a necessary element of experimental growth. He writes:

> The justification of the moral nonconformist is that when he denies the rightfulness of a particular claim he is doing so not for the sake of private advantage, but for the sake of an object which will serve more amply and consistently the welfare of all. The burden of proof is upon him. In asserting the rightfulness of his own judgment of what is obligatory, he is implicitly putting forth a social claim, something therefore to be tested and confirmed by further trial by others.[14]

Dewey's view of nonconformity presents a notion of courage that is demonstrated not in the mode of nonjoining or estrangement, but more thoroughly in the attitude of participation—the courage to accept others' criticism from them face-to-face, and to shoulder the responsibility of one's own counter-claim. This may well remind us of the following passage in Emerson:

> It is easy in the world to live after the world's opinion; it is easy in solitude to live after our own; but the great man is he who in the midst of the crowd keeps with perfect sweetness the independence of solitude.[15]

With Emerson, Dewey presents a middle path by overcoming the dichotomous choice of either not joining or participating, of being solitary or being social. He offers a view of the nonconformist *within* a society. Dewey as an Emersonian moral perfectionist is not a mere proponent of social guidance; he recognizes a space for the unique and deviating perspective of the young in the social reconstruction of criteria.

It is perhaps surprising then that Alan Ryan criticizes Dewey for never sufficiently emphasizing "ethical individualism," the "ability to stand out against the crowd" as "the introspective nonjoiner" in "estrangement." He thinks that Dewey does not allow for an "imaginative, quirky, original" child.[16] To a certain degree, however, Ryan is correct that Dewey limits the concept of deviancy. Dewey, in his social theory of self, consistently shows his caution with the "recalcitrant" individual. In *Democracy and Education*, he condemns the "aloofness and indifference" of "self-sufficient" individuals. He thinks that it is an illusion to think that one can "stand and act alone" (*DE*, 49). In *Human Nature and Conduct*, he distinguishes the "independence" that is "subjected to severe, experimental tests" from "cranky eccentricity" (*HNC*, 47). His avoidance of extreme deviance becomes most conspicuous in the later book, *Experience and Education*, especially in the chapter "Social Control." There Dewey's attitude toward the "exceptional" individual seems to become less tolerant, or even inflexible. True to his respect for nonconformity, he tells teachers to deal with "exceptional" children who are "bumptious," "unruly," or "downright rebellious," by doing their best to discover "the causes for the recalcitrant attitudes." He maintains, however, that "authority" resides in "the moving spirit of the whole group," not in "personal will." The "normal, proper conditions of control" take over the exceptional, since "[e]xceptions rarely prove a rule or give a clew to what the rule should be." Teachers should not allow "the unruly and non-participating pupils to stand permanently in the way of the educative activities of others." In this context, Dewey cites the example of the rules of a game, and emphasizes the importance of the "conventional" in the formation of rules (*EE*, 54–59).

In interpreting these remarks, we must take into consideration the historical context of the late 1930s. Dewey had to emphasize the importance of social control in order to save liberal progressive education from the charge of being permissive and chaotic, the stock response of conservative critics to the emerging left. He inspires, however, such criticism as Ryan's because he ducks the challenge of articulating any specific, persuasive account that might give substance to his Emersonian claim for nonconformity. The way Dewey speaks *about*—and does not speak *for*—the recalcitrant child suggests his tendency to muffle the voice of a single child in the confidence of an adult who, from an overintellectualized distinction between the conventional and the exceptional, attempts to discover and judge the benefit of a whole group in the light of the "normal" standards. The inner life of a recalcitrant child—or her first-person standpoint—seems to be subsumed in the clear, established minds of adults.

In the light of his theory of interaction between internal and objective conditions, it is not clear how Dewey would handle the internal (or invisible) condition (and process) of the life of the visibly antisocial, recalcitrant child. Dewey may call Emerson's "nonchalant boy" recalcitrant—a child who gives judgment on the passersby in "unaffected, unbiased, unbribable, unaffrighted innocence," and hence, who "put[s] them in fear" ("SR," 33). The ambiguity in Dewey's description of the social control of the recalcitrant child may, in spite of his intentions, endorse a prevailing conformity. If this is what Dewey envisions as "face-to-face" dialogue in social reconstruction of criteria, and if this is how we measure the moment of perfecting, it seems to defeat the Emersonian perfectionist spirit. It is here that

Cavell's criticism of Dewey comes back to us—his frustration with the lack of concreteness in Dewey's language and with the inaudibility of voices of children in his text.

Lending an Ear to the Emersonian Child: Cavell's Idea of Criteria

These doubts are augmented when compared with Cavell's handling of the Emersonian child in *The Claim of Reason*, the book in which he most fully interprets Wittgenstein's concept of criteria. Though Emerson does not appear at center stage, Cavell's words presage his later claims for EMP and present the voice of Emerson's child.[17] He discusses the relationship between adult and child as creating an "asymmetry between teaching and learning"—where there is a discrepancy between an adult's and a child's perspectives.[18] This asymmetry is most evident in the moment when an adult, in the face of a child's novel and unexpected questions about the facts of life, feels that his or her reason comes to an end. He describes such a moment as follows:

> When my reasons come to an end and I am thrown back upon myself, upon my nature as it has so far shown itself, I can, supposing I cannot shift the ground of discussion, either put the pupil out of my sight—as though his intellectual reactions are disgusting to me—or I can use the occasion to go over the ground I had hitherto thought foregone. If the topic is that of continuing a series, it may be learning enough to find that I *just do*; to rest upon myself as my foundation. But if the child, little or big, asks me: Why do we eat animals? Or Why are some people poor and others rich? Or What is God? Or Why do I have to go to school? Or Do you love black people as much as white people? Or Who owns the land? Or Why is there anything at all? Or How did God get here? I may find my answers thin, I may feel run out of reason without being willing to say "This is what I do" (what I say, what I sense, what I know), and honor that. (*Claim*, 124–25)

The specific questions that Cavell asks with and for the voice of a child represent his view of growth, as filled with puzzles and uncertainties. Faced with the natural reactions of a child (or, to borrow

Dewey's term, the impulse of the young) the adult cannot simply rely on her conventional criteria. This is the crucial moment when "attunement" between adult and child becomes "dissonant" (115). The adult is forced to question the ground of her reason in wonder. She poses the question: "When? When do I find or decide that the time has come to grant you secession, allow your divergence to stand, declare that the matter between us is at an end?" (ibid.). Cavell speaks with the voice of an adult who submits the limitation of his reason to the novel, perhaps disturbing, perhaps threatening, impulse of a child.

Behind this attitude lies Cavell's idea that both normality and abnormality constitute a "fundamental unity" in civilization (112). For Cavell, a child often represents the voice of the abnormal, or "lunatic" (122), something that unexpectedly betrays our conventional views. It is easy for an adult to pretend not to see the abnormal, and to continue to live in the conventional view. As Cavell says:

> Children's intellectual reactions are easy to find ways to dismiss; anxiety over their "errors" can be covered by the natural charms of childhood and by our accepting as a right answer the answer the child learns we want to hear, whether or not he or she understands what we think of as the content of our instruction. (124)

This captures the crucial moment when a mismatch occurs between the adult's expectation and the child's learning. There is a humble sense of the unknowable that is expressed by an adult who tries to see the invisible beyond the visible. In connection with the theme of EMP, Cavell later discusses the similar issue of the exclusion of the newcomer from society: "If the child is separated out, treated as a lunatic, this shows at once society's power and its impotence—power to exclude, power to include" (*Conditions*, 76). For Cavell, a child is "our familiar stranger" who sometimes forces us to acknowledge abnormality itself as "the other's separateness from me" (*Claim*, 122, 124). The child is the other within ourselves. Cavell's tolerance for and inclusion of a novel but abnormal child reflects his Emersonian perfectionist sense of imperfectability in the knowledge of the other.

For an adult to open his or her mind, beyond his or her conventional views and cognitive understanding, to the child's unexpected and unknowable horizon of life is not a nostalgic romanticization of childhood; rather it is a tough obligation assigned to us to remember and confront "the prospect of growth and the memory of childhood" within and without ourselves (125). Cavell offers the perspective of mutual growth for adults and children as the endless process of perfection.

Cavell reveals the process of the dynamic search for criteria in a confrontation between the young and the adult. In interpreting Wittgenstein's concept of criteria, he emphasizes that an agreement among different perspectives is not a matter of knowing with absolute certainty in an absolute "correlation" between "some inner stuff" and its outward manifestation, all as a matter of epistemological knowledge (91–92). Rather, it is "the fact of agreement itself" (32), namely, the "coincidence of soul and body, and of mind (language) and world *überhaupt*—an attunement of the inner life and outward behavior in the effort of "placing-oneself-in-the-world" (108–09).[19] This empirical fact he calls "mutual attunement," or "the attunement of one human being's words with those of others" (32). Mutual attunement involves what Cavell calls "regions of the soul" (101). He interprets "soul" not as referring to something "inaccessible, hidden (like a room)," but as something "pervasive, like atmosphere, or the action of the heart" (99). When we successfully find a match between the inner and the outer, it is not that "I move from uncertainty to certainty," as if we identify the absolute location or existence of the inner that matches the outer behavior. Rather, it is a fact of our achievement in which we move "from darkness to light" (102).[20] It is such criteria, rather than the calculated measurement of success or failure, that are integral to moments of mutual perfection. Criteria embody the sense of attainment that can at any time defeat us, bordering on the sense of unattainment and uncertainty. Cavell's EMP is foreshadowed by the sense of the proximity of attainment and unattainment.

Cavell's account of criteria, however, is no celebration of irrationality or luck. Instead, he suggests that mutual attunement requires a particular type of reasoning. Contrasting the realm of morality to the playing of a game, Cavell says:

> Our way is neither clear nor simple; we are often lost. . . . What alternatives we can and must take are not fixed, but chosen; and thereby fix us. What is better than what else is not given, but must be created in what we care about. Whether we have done what we have undertaken is a matter of how far we can see our responsibilities, and see them through. . . . Here we cannot practice the effects we wish to achieve; here we are open to complete surprise at what we have done. (324–25)

In chaotic, uncertain, and ever-surprising moral struggles, a "moral reason can never be a *flat* answer to the competent demand for justification." We cannot simply rely on "the rules of an institution," or social convention (303), nor can we remain "within clear lines" (325).[21] The search for the mutual attunement of criteria in the interactions between the young and the adult can be considered a good example of those moral struggles in which the adult's reason is faced with its limitations, or in which, as Cavell says, "the paths of action, the paths of words, are blocked" (125). He does not, however, consider this to show "the irrationality of morality," but rather to "help to articulate what gives it the rationality it has" (325). We are at a "crossroads" when our reason is tested through the confrontation between our "culture's criteria" and our words and life (125).

Thus, Cavell's idea of mutual attunement in search of criteria embodies his view of human reason as that which confronts and assimilates the facts of uncertainty, disappointment, and surprise posed by life—expressed by the voice of an Emersonian child. Cavell's early discussion of Wittgenstein's idea of criteria not only presages his later EMP, but also sows the seed for his criticism of Dewey—a criticism that he cannot hear the speech of children in Dewey's text.

Gaining from the Distance between Dewey and Emerson

The contrast between Dewey's treatment of the recalcitrant child and Cavell's Emersonian child indicates their different stances toward a child in growth—a child whose immaturity and novel perspective poses a challenge to social convention and the adult's intelligence, on the one hand, and a child whose natural life of growth is more or less carefully molded, even if not tightly confined, into the adult's convention, on the other. Simultaneously, the difference affects how criteria of good growth can be socially determined in each moment of growth in the process of interaction.

In comparison to Cavell's description of the process of growth, the way Dewey presents his theory of situations, notwithstanding what he says about a unity of "soul and action," does not quite seem to integrate the inner soul and outer action. Despite his Emersonian call for face-to-face dialogue between adult and child in the social reconstruction of criteria, the way he describes the relationship obscures the subtle realm in which the self and the other meet in the here and now. Despite his claim of the flexible concept of revised criteria, how he describes it is in reality gives us an impression that it is less flexible, demanding some definite, clear point of reference. Despite the Emersonian sense of expanding circles in Dewey's transactional holism, any sense of infinite expansion disappears in Dewey's straightforward, clear-cut description of growth. In other words, compared to Cavell's idea of reason, Dewey's notion of intelligence seems to function within a carefully delineated regime of clarity, organization, and stability, avoiding or even suppressing the senses of the invisible, the infinite, and the imperfect. Such an intelligence appears at times not courageous enough to guide the young to grow without relying on fixed ends.

Though it could never have been his intention, in comparison to Cavell, the way Dewey describes the guidance of youthful impulse by adults suggests a tendency toward fixity in growth. The socializing force is directed towards the assimilation of radical deviancy into the normal practices of society by means of social intelligence—by an appeal to clarity and stability, and hence security. We might wonder if criteria such as Dewey describes will eventually mold the life of children into social conventions. Further, Dewey does not seem to be speaking from the perspective of the child. Cavell and Emerson suggest to Dewey that some invisible, unstable (and perhaps threatening), yet undeniable inner life of the recalcitrant child, and the sense of the infinite, the imperfect, and the unknowable that an adult might experience in the face of the child, disappear in these situations; and that the child and an adult are deprived of a chance of mutual perfection, to open themselves to the surprise that may be bequeathed by life.

To look at the issue from another perspective, Dewey creates a distance between *what he says* and *how he says* it. It is here that we are brought back to Cavell's criticism of Dewey's language as one that creates a distance from EMP. Anderson defends the idiosyncrasy of Dewey's language: "However inadequate his literary means . . . Dewey's philosophical means are neither inadequate nor sub-Emersonian."[22] Is it true, however, that a philosopher's *literary* means are separate from his *philosophical* means? Dewey would have said no to the question. For Dewey, language is "the tool of tools," which is "a natural bridge that joins the gap between existence and essence." Language is a medium for man's interaction in the world; "mind emerges" through linguistic activities, which enable humans to be engaged in "potential acts and deeds" (*EN*, 133–34). In his theory of habit reconstruction, Dewey attempts to overcome the "separation of habit and thought, action and soul," which he says requires the medium of language and communication (*HNC*, 52, 57). In Dewey's pragmatism and naturalism, language cannot afford to be a mere abstract representation in the head. Rather, it must serve an indispensable role in mediating thinking and action in particular situations; linguistic activities must embody the concrete process of *how* we live.

Despite what he says about language, however, Dewey's own use of language or "literary means" contains inconsistencies with his "philosophical means." First and foremost, the sense of distance that Dewey's readers feel from his text—what they express as being "impersonal," or "reticent," or "dry"[23]—suggests that his language creates a barrier between himself and readers—and perhaps between him as the adult and the children whom he speaks about: that it does not give a concrete indication about how we should live. This is also a betrayal of his own *philosophical*—and Emersonian—claim for "face-to-face" dialogue in reconstructing a democratic community from within.

Second, Dewey's idiosyncratic use of language is the indicator of a potential flaw in his pragmatic project: to overcome dualism for a unified life. In his theory of interaction, Dewey aims to return philosophy to everyday life, beyond diverse forms of dualism: theory and action, reason and emotion, inner mind and outward behavior, means (processes) and ends (goals), facts and values, particularity and universality, the self and the world; and beyond realism and idealism, and foundationalism and antifoundationalism. Since he speaks in the "middle term" (*HNC*, 51), however, Dewey's expression often confuses his readers and creates an impression that he merely juxtaposes traditionally divided categories.[24] Contemporary Deweyan philosophers such as John J. Stuhr and Jim Garrison defend Dewey, however, by pointing out that Dewey's Darwinian naturalism and scientific methods of thinking are fundamentally different from naive behaviorism or positivist scientism.[25] As Raymond D. Boisvert and Steven C. Rockefeller say, Dewey tries to present a new metaphysical theory.[26] Yet, Dewey's language allows room for the old categories and concepts of philosophy to sneak into his innovative philosophy. It is one thing to claim that the self is a social being; it is another to show specifically how such a self grows to be a communal being by overcoming diverse dualisms and conflicts. It is one thing to propose that education is one with growth and growth is an ongoing activity of growing; it is another to persuade people that one can keep growing without relying on fixed ends, to truly save them from a persistent temptation to old dualisms. It is the responsibility of the philosopher fully to resist the foe he fights against; it is the responsibility of the how-philosopher successfully to translate theory into practice.

These are the observations implied in Cavell's criticism of Dewey's use of language and the sense of distance that he perceives between Dewey and Emerson. His criticism can be reinterpreted as a voice of concern for the underestimation of language and a reminder of its significance for meaningful action. When Emerson makes the quasi-pragmatist statement that "I simply experiment, an endless seeker, with no Past at my back" ("Circles," 173), Cavell may hear Dewey's voice in Emerson. He is, however, skeptical of *how* Dewey says what he says; and *how* what Dewey says can possibly effect change in the world (as well as in the self). In Dewey's language, Cavell cannot find out where Dewey places himself in the world, or to whom he speaks. He invites Dewey to speak *in* his own voice, rather than *about* the child, growth, and for that matter, life as a whole.

Indeed, Cavell's criticism of Dewey's "scientific" methods is implicitly tied up with his criticism of Dewey's language. To Cavell, who is concerned that "we take too much for granted about what the learning and the sharing of language implies" (*Claim*, 173), and who cares about "shades of sense, intimations of meaning, which allow certain kinds of subtlety or delicacy of communication" (189), the way Dewey uses his language represents his scientific tendency to rush into generalization and clarification—a totalizing tendency to blind us to the sense of the unknowable and particular struggles entailed in the path of human perfection and to demystify the wonder of life. This, I believe, is what Cavell implies when he says that the distance between Dewey and Emerson represents "a certain air of conflict in philosophy between the appeal to science and the appeal to ordinary language" ("Calling Emerson," 74–75). The Emersonian child presented by Cavell suggests that the moment of perfecting cannot simply be the object of definite measurement through our scientific eyes. It symbolizes a call for infinity, a destabilizing and unsettling force of life that challenges the totalizing force of inclusion and assimilation. Pragmatists and Deweyan scholars who defend Dewey's richer concept of "science" may be right; and it may be true that Cavell's criticism of Dewey's view of "science" by definition is narrow and limited. However, it is worthwhile to lend a careful ear to Cavell's caution for the sake of helping Dewey realize his own vision of EMP.

Cavell, who asks us to see how close and how far Dewey and Emerson are, can now be reconsidered as a strong conversational partner for Dewey—an Emersonian friend who confronts Dewey with the distance that he himself unwittingly creates between what he says and how he says it, between the horizons of EMP and those scientific horizons of his naturalistic philosophy of growth. As much as we can learn from their closeness and precisely because Dewey shares a certain common ground with Emerson, we must also acknowledge the distance between the two. The paradox of closeness and distance now can be reconsidered as an internal tension within Dewey's philosophy of growth—and, one hopes, a rich source for its reconstruction. Dewey's naturalistic philosophy of growth is positioned precariously on the border between the philosophy of totality characterized by power and progress, and the Emersonian philosophy that treasures infinity and myth.

SEVEN

THE GLEAM OF LIGHT
Reconstruction toward Holistic Growth

A man should learn to detect and watch that gleam of light which flashes across his mind from within, more than the lustre of the firmament of bards and sages. Yet he dismisses without notice his thought, because it is his. In every work of genius we recognize our own rejected thoughts. (Emerson, "Self-Reliance")[1]

Dewey's naturalistic philosophy of growth has been found as one bordering on EMP, but with another internal force resisting to its full development. Dewey's voice is dissonant from Emerson's and Cavell's, most significantly in their divergent responses to the recalcitrant child. In order to elaborate more fully the potential of his idea of growth as perfection and to reclaim his muted Emersonian voice, we must rescue Dewey from a totalizing tendency that he reveals in his commitments to social intelligence. It requires that task of reconstruction in philosophy.

A promising clue to reconstruction is latent within the structure of Dewey's naturalistic philosophy of growth: his concept of *impulse* in habit reconstruction. If we read Dewey's text carefully, we hear most acutely his Emersonian voice when he discusses the significance of impulse. In *Democracy and Education*, he praises Emerson's respect for the immaturity of a child for his "naturel."[2] In *Human Nature and Conduct*, when he proposes the liberation of the novel impulse of the young in aid of the reconstruction of culture, Dewey's Emersonian perfectionist spirit of anticonformity stands out. Most strikingly, in *Construction and Criticism*, Dewey presents the Emersonian claim of the self-reliant individual who would be courageously engaged in criticism for the reconstruction of democracy. There he discusses the significance of the child's impulse that brings "something fresh into the world" as "one's own true nature" or "some deeper and more primitive reaction of emotion."[3] He then tries to associate it with Emerson's idea of the "gleam of light"—the aesthetic and spiritual dimension of EMP. A link between Dewey's idea of impulse and Emerson's idea of the gleam of light seems to offer a promising clue to reconstructing his idea of growth in the light of EMP. Let us first examine Emerson's original idea of the gleam of light.

Emerson's Idea of the Gleam of Light

Emerson's essay, "Self-Reliance," begins with a poem by Beaumont and Fletcher:

> Man is his own star and the soul that can
> Render an honest and a perfect man,
> Commands all light, all influence, all fate;
> Nothing to him falls early or too late. . . .
>
> (*Epilogue to Beaumont and Fletcher's Honest Man's Fortune*)
> ("SR," 131)

As the poem presages, "Self-Reliance" is an essay on the perfection of human life, symbolized by the gleam of light. The following is a quotation from Emerson that Dewey cites in *Construction and Criticism*:

> A man should learn to detect and watch that gleam of light which flashes across his mind from within. . . . Great works of art have no more affecting lesson for us than this. They teach us to abide by our spontaneous impression with good-humored inflexibility then most when the whole cry of voices is on the other side. Else to-morrow a stranger will say with masterly good sense precisely what we have thought and felt all the time, and we shall be forced

to take with shame our own opinion from another. ("SR," 131–32 in *CC*, 139)

Emerson calls the gleam of light "Intuition," or "Instinct." It symbolizes one's inner soul, the sense of one's being, of who "I am" ("SR," 141), or "the integrity of mind" (133). The gleam of light originates in an undivided, holistic condition of life as the "fountain of action and of thought" (140). It is the mark of one's particular inclination, and serves as the origin of thinking or "tuitions" (139).

The gleam of light represents Emerson's transcendentalism and his perfectionism as a hybrid of the spiritual and natural, or what he calls "the transcendentalism of common life."[4] Light is of archetypal significance in human experience. In the course of Western philosophy, the metaphor of light connects especially with the spiritual perfection of the human soul but also with broader senses of enlightenment. Most famously, in Plato it is the light entering the mouth of the Cave, toward which benighted souls must turn. This is the image of the perfection of soul in its journey upward.[5] Plato's mysticism of light was expanded by Plotinus and neo-Platonism. In America, Emerson's gleam of light might be called a secular restatement of Jonathan Edwards's "divine and supernatural light."[6] It is the basis of spiritual conversion. In certain respects, Emerson's gleam of light inherits this spiritual tradition. But that is not all. He creates anew his own meaning of the *spiritual* and the *transcendent* in the American grain.

Emerson's transcendentalism is creative, but elusive in its many facets. Russell B. Goodman claims that Emerson is at once an "empiricist," a "transcendental idealist," and an "experimenter." Being the inheritor of the romantic tradition of Kant's transcendental idealism, Emerson validates empirical observations by "invoking some structure in us," that is, a transcendental scheme for the categorization of experience.[7] Emerson's transcendentalism also embraces the influence of Eastern thought. Arthur Versluis points out that Emerson's self-transcendence is based upon the concept of "the primordial One" in the traditions of Hinduism and Platonism. Versluis interprets Emerson's thought as an "assimilationism" of "a German mystical, a Vedantic, or even a Platonic origin." Emerson creates a unique "literary religion" that is "neither Eastern or Western." Indeed the significant role that "light" plays in Indian philosophy needs to be noted. Versluis discusses the relationship of light and soul that Emerson describes in connection with the ideas of the *karma yoga* (or the "path of works") and *jnana yoga* (or "direct illumination") in the *Bhagavad Gita*.[8] Buell also discusses at length Asian influence on American transcendentalism, and says: "Transcendentalism became the first intellectual movement in the United States to take Asian religious thought seriously." He claims that the "antidualistic spirituality" of Asian religion attracted Emerson and helped him "fortify his theory of spiritual impersonality." Buell also highlights Emerson's interests in the *Bhagavad Gita* in connection with the idea of acting with "integrity" in a "spirit of nonattachment to the fruits of one's action." Buell, like Versluis, however, claims that Emerson's interest was "eclectic and synthetic" and that he had "no intention of converting to Hinduism."[9]

In this characteristic brand of transcendentalism, Emerson's gleam of light is both spiritual and pragmatic. On the one hand, he claims that a transcendentalist is an idealist in the sense that he not only relies on the sensuous fact, but also sees it as "a spiritual fact."[10] He says: "Time and space are but physiological colors which the eye makes, but the soul is light; where it is, is day; where it was, is night" ("SR," 141). On the other hand, the gleam of light is pragmatic and earthbound. Dewey says that the transcendental and spiritual value claimed by Emerson does not exist in some remote "Reality" but in the "common experience of the everyday man," in the "pressing and so the passing Now."[11] Emerson emphasizes the changeable and unpredictable nature of the gleam of light. In Emerson's view, the original meaning of one's gleam of light needs to be continually (re)discovered in action:

> Your genuine action will explain itself, and will explain your other genuine actions. Your conformity explains nothing. Act singly, and what you have already done singly will justify you now. Greatness appeals to the future. If I can be firm enough to-day to

do right, and scorn eyes, I must have done so much right before as to defend me now. Be it how it will, do right now. ("SR," 137)

In this regard, Emerson is a proto-pragmatist who says: "I simply experiment as an endless seeker" ("Circles," 173). To be true to nature's laws for the "motions of the soul" and to treasure the unexpected power to reveal the gleam of light, a "foolish consistency" needs to be shunned as "the hobgoblin of little minds" ("SR," 136–37).

In association with the gleam of light, Emerson also evokes the scandalous notion of "Whim." This he associates with "Spontaneity or Instinct."

> I shun father and mother and wife and brother, when my genius calls me. I would write on the lintels of the door-post, *Whim*. I hope it is somewhat better than whim at last, but we cannot spend the day in explanation. Expect me not to show cause why I seek or why I exclude company. (134)

This is the moment when Genius calls us from within, when "our spontaneous impression" visits us (131). With the sense of greatness, we transcend existing relationships with others as well as our old selves. The word on the lintels, however, is not "Independence," "Authority," "Nonconformity," or "Disobedience." It is—surprisingly, provocatively, discouragingly—"Whim," a word whose ordinary and light simplicity promises nothing grand. In a conventional usage, the word "whim," or "whimsical" has a slightly negative connotation of triviality of impulse. Emerson throws the reader with this word, especially with its rather bizarre inscription. Yet Emerson places his faith in whim as leading to something more.

As Cavell reminds us, whim is natural—so is the sense of shame—as it is an impulse from below.[12] It is anything but spiritual in the sense of something that comes "from above" (ibid.). Paradoxically, we transcend ourselves from below. We experience transcendence *within* nature, in our common lives.[13] In this regard, Emerson's spiritual light as whim is radically different from Plato's or Augustine's who considers the spiritual light as belonging to the higher realm beyond nature. Whim is naturalistic as it is experienced in a dimension that extends into, or derives from, the physiological, to borrow Cavell's words, something "wrestling us for our blessing" (*Senses*, 137). Approaching Emerson's transcendentalism from the viewpoint of whim creates an image of Emerson that distances him both from the oneness of Asian thought and from the American philosophy and theology of Jonathan Edwards. Cavell's interpretation of Emersonian light as whim is also different from the one presented by Buell. Referring to Emerson's idea that the light must be better than whim at last, Buell suggests that what is "merely 'personal'" is not truly inspired, and that the "'I' of the passage [quoted above] is not the mundanely autobiographical 'I' who would gladly unfold a natural history of the intellect." As "[t]he inner light or authority was not idiosyncratic," he concludes, "[d]epersonalization was indispensable to a truly privatized spirituality."[14] In contrast, Cavellian-Emersonian whim is thoroughly personal and partial and is more process-oriented. There is no guarantee that authenticates the universality of the gleam of light until it is tested on the way. Despite Cavell's resistance to Emerson's being labeled a pragmatist, his Emerson is more pragmatic than Buell's.

In this fashion, Emerson's gleam of light is an inventive combination of the spiritual and the natural, the transcendental and the pragmatic. Although the gleam of light symbolizes the inner soul and being, Emerson's gleam of light as Instinct is not a static, causal determinant; rather, it is growing as "the soul becomes" ("SR," 142). In this respect, Emerson's gleam of light is remote from the Scottish intuitionism of which the young Dewey was critical.[15] Not unlike William James's "stream of consciousness," the gleam of light is a stream moved by its consequences as well as by its origin. As Steve Odin points out, in James's idea of pure experience, the self is always "in-the-making" and the stream of consciousness is related by "felt transitions."[16] Sharing the same structure as James's, the Emersonian gleam of light is a stream of light. It can be considered to serve as an intermediary in the cycle of experience between being and becoming, soul and action, "[c]ause and effect" ("Circles," 172). It symbolizes Emerson's holistic view of perfection.[17]

Dewey from Impulse to the Gleam of Light

It is this perspective of Emerson's gleam of light that can revitalize Dewey's idea of impulse, and by so doing can open a new passage for reconstructing his naturalistic philosophy of growth in the light of EMP. In *Human Nature and Conduct*, Dewey calls the association between impulse and intelligence a "twin" relationship.[18] Together they create the reconstructive growth of an organism in interaction with the environment, and the renewal of social habits and culture as a whole. Though Dewey claims an inseparable, as well as equal, function for the two, his description of habit reconstruction is weighted relatively in favor of intelligence. As the scientific procedure of observation, hypothesis, and experimentation, the function of intelligence is to control and direct impulse. In *The Quest of Certainty* Dewey calls intelligence "an art of control," the method of regulating natural change through experimentation.[19] He also associates intelligence with *active* behavior (*HNC*, 45, 52, 133), with the emphasis on the *consequences* of action (143–45). In this context, where intelligence seems to be given the central role, we are left with the impression that impulse is secondary (though it is primary in terms of temporal order).

In such works as *Experience and Nature* and *Art as Experience*, however, impulse is given greater emphasis. As a temporal event, an experience consists of a rhythm between the perceptual and reflective phases. In this regard, Dewey is influenced by William James's idea of "double-barrelled" experience. Experience contains "in its primary integrity no division between act and material, subject and object, but is constituted by them both in an unanalyzed totality."[20] This is the perceptual, "precognitive" phase.[21] Out of this primary experience, a discriminative phase of reflection is cultivated. Impulse plays the leading role in this original, perceptual phase. It initiates the rhythm and cycles of experience:

> Every experience, of slight or tremendous import, begins with an impulsion, rather *as* an impulsion. . . . 'Impulsion' designates a movement outward and forward of the whole organism to which special impulses are auxiliary.[22]

The movement is "an adventure in a world" initiated by a living creature in its interaction with the world (*AE*, 65). Discussing the "biosocial concept of personhood" developed by G. H. Mead in American pragmatism and his notion of the social self as "I-Me" interaction, Odin claims that the "biological" aspect of the "I" pole, in contrast to the "social" aspect of the "Me" pole, is the "source of creativity, novelty, and freedom in the evolutionary process."[23] The "I" here corresponds to the original, spontaneous impulse symbolized by the gleam of light.

The beginning of an experience initiated by impulse is crucial. Through impulse we are immediately connected with life. An organism experiences a thoroughgoing "participation" or immediate inhabitation in the world in a state of "surrender in perception" (*AE*, 25), and in complete "saturation" with objects (280). Dewey describes this state with the metaphor of *home*: "Through habits formed in intercourse with the world, we also in-habit the world. It becomes a home and the home is part of our every experience" (109). This original sense of being at home, a memory of inner harmony "persists as the substratum" and "haunts life like the sense of being founded on a rock" (23), or remains in "the depths of the subconsciousness" (155), even after we have begun the process of making distinctions and having reflections (196). There is a sense in these words of the inner that modifies and deepens his former behavioral description of impulse.

Indeed, Dewey's naturalistic idea of impulse is not merely a biological or reductionist concept. In *Construction and Criticism*, Dewey associates impulse with something that is "stirring within us" (*CC*, 139) or "the power that comes from command of ourselves" (136). It shares some common ground with the spiritual aspect of Emerson's gleam of light—something like what Dewey calls "a mind and soul, an integrated personality."[24] Dewey's impulse is also congruent with Emerson's gleam of light as whim. In acknowledging the significance of the original impression, Dewey says:

> There is about such occasions something of the quality of the wind that bloweth where it listeth. Sometimes it comes and some-

times it does not, even in the presence of the same object. It cannot be forced, and when it does not arrive, it is not wise to seek to recover by direct action the first fine rapture. *(AE, 150)*

The image of the original impression here is similar to Emerson's whim with respect to its unexpected, capricious arrival. Like Emerson's whim, Dewey's impulse originates from below, from the human body, and can be associated with "a commotion demanding utterance" (81). Yet, whim is only the beginning. Its meaning is gradually found only through experiments and action.

Although Dewey does not abrogate his allegiance to the scientific method of intelligence, the way he describes the relationship between impulse and intelligence in his later writings becomes progressively more rhythmic. He provides himself with a key to broaden the narrow definition of intelligence. Intelligence is the process of "nourishing" this original impression to be transformed into the capacity of critical discrimination. Dewey reminds us not to forget that the "direct and unreasoned impression comes first" (150).

It is a common misreading of Dewey to suppose that he subscribes to the Lockean empirical sense of impulse. This is not supported by a close reading of his text. Dewey shares with Emerson an idea that impulsive force is the primary source of self-reliant thinking. Cavell, who claims that Emerson is not only a philosopher of Intuition, but also of Tuition, interprets Emerson as saying that Tuition is the process of articulating Intuition, that "Tuition is to find its Intuition," and therefore, that thinking must realize and transfigure "indestructible instinct" as "something else."[25] Similarly, in Dewey's view, Emerson is a thinker who redefines philosophy as logic as the "procession or proportionate unfolding of the intuition" ("Emerson," 184). Dewey here refers to the following passage of Emerson in "Intellect":

> All our progress is an unfolding, like the vegetable bud. You have first the instinct, then an opinion, then knowledge, as the plant has root, bud, and fruit. . . . By trusting the [instinct] to the end, it shall ripen into truth, and you shall know why you believe.[26]

This is a horticultural metaphor. If Emerson's language of growth sometimes takes this botanical turn, this is not to be construed as in any way reductive. Any sense of reductive naturalism is totally dispelled by the spiritual force of the imagery of light. And Dewey shares with Emerson this direction. As an indestructible, original sense of one's individuality and as a source of perfection, the gleam of light is ever present in the course of experience. It is, however, only a beginning impulse; it must be watched, nurtured, and guided along the path of its growth.

In the concluding passage of *The Public and Its Problems*, Dewey writes: "We lie, as Emerson said, in the lap of an immense intelligence."[27] From the perspective of the gleam of light, the scientific concept of intelligence, which Dewey typically describes as the function of controlling impulse, can be reconstructed in broader terms. To be true to the original nature of the gleam of light, intelligence must be *receptive* as much as active. Thinking makes us receive the sense of our being, as Emerson says: "Our thinking is a pious reception. . . . We do not determine what we will think. We only open our senses, clear away, as we can, all obstruction from the fact, and suffer the intellect to see" ("Intellect," 177). Intellect connects us with the wholeness of nature: "The circle of the green earth he must measure with his shoes" (182–183).

Cavell interprets the receptive nature of Emerson's thinking by saying: "Emerson's most explicit reversal of Kant lies in his picturing the intellectual hemisphere of knowledge as passive or receptive and the intuitive or instinctual hemisphere as active or spontaneous" (*Senses*, 129). Emerson presents the concept of "intellectual intuition" (ibid.) or receptive thinking (*Conditions*, 39). Cavell connects this with Heidegger's concept of "thinking as thanking"—giving thanks for "the gift of thinking" (*Senses*, 132). Emerson's thinking is composed of the rhythm between "stopping to think" (*Conditions*, 21), suffering, thanking for the sense of being, and leaving and moving onward in "ever-widening circles" (*Senses*, 128). Cavell can be interpreted as saying that receptivity sows the seed for an ongoing growth. Based upon his interpretation of Emerson's thinking, Cavell criticizes Dewey's scientific concept of intelligence as active problem-solving for its inability to receive and give thanks for life. Instead, it severs us, Cavell claims, from a holistic condition of life (*Conditions,* 21, 42–43).

Dewey, however, in recognizing the significance of Emerson's gleam of light, would support Emerson's comprehensive notion of intelligence. Particularly in his writings in the late 1920s and thereafter, Dewey emphasizes the idea of reception as a crucial aspect of human experience. For example, in *Construction and Criticism* where he discusses Emerson's gleam of light, Dewey says: "Receptivity and assimilation are as much forms of vital action as are the overt actions that are visible." Here he recognizes the significance of the mode of "permit[ting] selected impressions to sink in until they have become truly our own capital to work with" in order to acquire "the courage to give out with assertive energy" (*CC*, 140). Also in the 1933 version of *How We Think*, Dewey says:

> Meditation, withdrawal or abstraction from clamorous assailants of the senses and from demands for overt action, is as necessary at the reasoning stage as are observation and experiment at other periods. The metaphors of digestion and assimilation, which so readily occur to mind in connection with rational elaboration are highly instructive.[28]

Dewey here implies that thinking necessitates a receptive phase. What he means by receptivity, however, is not merely "passivity" *(AE,* 58). He describes the difference as follows:

> The esthetic or undergoing phase of experience is receptive. It involves surrender. But adequate yielding of the self is possible only through a controlled activity that may well be intense. . . . Perception is an act of the going-out of energy in order to receive, not a withholding of energy. (59–60)

We need a certain type of energy to absorb, receive, and thereby, go out and act. An experience is made up of a cyclic rhythm involving a receptive mode of perception (in which impulse or the gleam of light plays a central role) and an active mode of inquiry (the narrow sense of intelligence that Dewey defines as a function of habit reconstruction)—"the alternative flights and perchings of a bird" (Dewey here using James's phrase [62]).

Thus, the gleam of light makes possible a broad sense of intelligence in which Dewey's concept of growth becomes all the more holistic.[29] The later Dewey expresses metaphorically the sense of the whole we experience in a pre-reflective phase: "At twilight, dusk is a delightful quality of the whole world" (*AE*, 198). With the gleam of light being added to this picture of the whole, we are able to reconfigure Dewey's view of the universe as expanding circles propelled by a central force of the light.[30]

> Every movement of experience in completing itself recurs to its beginning, since it is a satisfaction of the prompting initial need. But the recurrence is with a difference; it is charged with all the differences the journey out and away from the beginning has made. (*AE*, 173)

Dewey's idea of "recurrence" in experience is not one of repetitive circulation, but of expansion originating from the initial need or impulse. Further, when conjuring up an image of the qualitative whole of experience in the form of an arc penetrated by the light, Dewey cites the following poem of Tennyson:

> Experience is an arch wherethro'
> Gleams that untravell'd world, whose margin fades
> Forever and forever when I move.
>
> (Tennyson, quoted in AE, 197)

Dewey offers this interpretation of these lines:

> Whether the scope of vision be vast or minute, we experience it as a part of a larger whole and inclusive whole, a part that now focuses our experience. . . . But however broad the field, it is still felt as not the whole; the margins shade into the indefinite expanse beyond which imagination calls the universe. (*AE*, 198)

This passage conveys the image of an ever-expanding whole whose meaning is experienced only now in the ongoing movement of light—in "an actual focusing of the world at one point in a focus of immediate shining apparency"[31]—and whose margin is yet beyond our grasp. With the metaphor of light, Dewey here suggests a certain sense of infinity, that of the unknowable.

Perfecting the Gleam of Light in the Here and Now

Dewey states: "Perfection means perfecting, fulfillment, fulfilling, and the good is now or never" (*HNC*, 200). The perspective of the gleam of light also shows why the meaning of perfection lies in the moment of perfecting in the here and now.

Emerson says, "We do not guess to-day the mood, the pleasure, the power of to-morrow, when we are building up our being" ("Circles," 174). His metaphor of the rose conveys to us the depth and intensity of such a moment:

> Those roses under my window make no reference to former roses or to better ones; they are for what they are; they exist with God to-day. There is no time to them. There is simply the rose; it is perfect in every moment of its existence. . . . but man postpones or remembers; he does not live in the present, but with reverted eye laments the past, or, heedless of the riches that surround him, stands on tiptoe to foresee the future. He cannot be happy and strong until he too lives with nature in the present, above time. ("SR," 141)[32]

Cavell characterizes this Emersonian sense of the perfectibility of each moment by saying that "*each* state of the self is final" (*Conditions*, 12).

Dewey shares the Emersonian sense of the crucial moment of perfecting, a kind of time that is being fully lived and experienced only in the here and now. Dewey's expression of the consummatory moment sounds like the Emersonian transcendental moment:

> [Happiness and delight] come to be through a fulfillment that reaches to the depths of our being—one that is an adjustment of our whole being with the conditions of existence. . . . The time of consummation is also one of beginning anew. (*AE*, 23)

In such a moment, Dewey says, man is in "active and alert commerce with the world" with all senses being "on the *qui vive*" in "heightened vitality." Impulse plays a central role here as "sentinels of immediate thought and outposts of action" (24–25).

In EMP, the moment of perfecting is one in which the self has attained itself and, therefore, starts to unfound and unravel itself to the next state of unattainable self. This Cavell calls the time when the attained but attainable self is "knotted" (*Conditions*, 10). He further suggests that this is the moment of "discontinuity," as Emerson's expanding circles are characterized by "an ambiguity between the picturing of new circles as forming continuously or discontinuously" (*Senses*, 135). He raises the question of what it is that brings the very moment of the "leap" "from one circumference to another" when a new circle is drawn. He answers that "power seems to be the result of rising" (136). The gleam of light plays a crucial role in producing a critical juncture in the expanding passage of growth.[33] The radical moment of transcendence in perfection is the time when we leap from one sphere to another by trusting our whim. It is, as Emerson says, when one separates himself from his old state, leaving his father, mother, wife, and brother in response to the invitation of whim:

> The new position of the advancing man has all the powers of the old, yet has them all new. It carries in its bosom all the energies of the past, yet is itself an exhalation of the morning. I cast away in this new moment all my once hoarded knowledge, as vacant and vain. Now, for the first time, seem I to know any thing rightly. ("Circles," 174–175)

In this new moment, the trajectories created in the past find possible openings in the future; a new circle is drawn, but without negating the past trajectory. Emersonian gleam of light or whim is *prophetic* in producing such critical juncture in time (*Senses*, 156). In unpacking Emerson's statement that "I hope that it is somewhat better than whim at last" ("SR," 134), Cavell emphasizes that Emerson's whim is the indispensable beginning, but merely the beginning in the sense that its significance needs to be "proven only on the way" (*Senses*, 137), and seen "by its fruits" (154). It does not rely on any absolute ground of the good, but on its trust in the better that is yet to come;

it is *projective*. Whether it is good or bad, we cannot tell in advance. All we can do now is to trust "the instinct of the animal to find his road," hoping that new passages are opened.[34] The arrival of whim marks such moment of venturing into the unknown, the moment of a radical departure. Emerson's gleam of light has a pragmatic facet:

> Lest I should mislead any when I have my own head and obey my whims, let me remind the reader that I am only an experimenter. Do not see the least value on what I do, or the least discredit on what I do not, as if I pretended to settle any thing as true or false. I unsettle all things. ("Circles," 173)

It is whim that initiates and leads this onward moving.

This forward movement in Emerson's whim, however, is anything but an expression of a rosy optimism toward the future. Rather, it is accompanied by a certain rigor and stern willingness to commit oneself to the unknown out of a trodden path. Cavell reminds us that whim is only the manifestation of a *hope* that is born out of *despair*:

> [Emerson's] perception of the moment is taken in hope, as something to be proven only on the way, by the way. This departure, such setting out, is, in our poverty, what hope consists in, all there is to hope for; it is the abandoning of despair, which is otherwise our condition . . . Our fatality, the determination of our fate, of whether we may hope, goes by our making the path of whim. (*Senses*, 137)

Emerson's expression of whim manifests the courage to leave, to abandon, "power and courage to make a new road to new and better goals" ("Circles," 175).

While being under the influence of a Darwinian progressive and evolutionary concept of time, Dewey, in his appropriation of the Emersonian gleam of light, suggests its vital role in producing the new moment in the here and now. He insinuates Emersonian and Cavellian themes of the proximity of attainability and unattainability in perfecting. His pragmatic view of the universe in chance reinforces this trait. Scheffler discusses Peirce's notion of *tychism*, the idea that "[a]n element of absolute chance must rather be acknowledged in nature, along with the element of regularity."[35] Dewey, qua pragmatist, is opposed to the fixed view of universe, "the kingdom of the unchanging, of the complete, the perfect," and presents the idea of a temporal, changeable view of the universe with "genuine indetermination"—the universe of chance, contingency, and unpredictability in "temporal seriality."[36]

Dewey's idea of development in temporal continuity, however, is not merely a linear progression, repetitions, or "redistributions, rearrangements" of what existed before. Rather, like Emersonian and Cavellian concepts of time in EMP, it entails the moment of *discontinuity*. He introduces the idea of "genuine qualitative changes," or "genuine transformations," when "unpredictable novelties" break into a stream of time. This he calls "genuine time" as "breaches" or "breaks" in continuity, or the moments of "critical junctures." Based upon this concept of time, Dewey introduces the notion of genuine individuality—"individuality pregnant with new developments." The quality of change to produce genuine time hinges on unpredictable novelties that "individuals as individuals" can produce ("TI," 108–09, 111–12). This is the moment of individuation. Dewey acknowledges James's idea of the indispensable role played by the individual factor in the creation of an open universe as a fortress against determinism (101).[37] Here it is impulse that creates "the forward thrust of life" (ibid.). Impulse is "the living source of a new and better future" (114). Dewey shares Emerson's idea of the prophetic whim that produces the new moment. This certainly requires the self to exercise the courage to leave its established path.

In the temporal structure of selfhood of both the Japanese philosophy of Nishida and the American pragmatism of Mead and Whitehead, Odin identifies a "culminative nature of temporal becoming." The temporal flux in that structure, Odin says, is asymmetrical, and there is always an emergent "creative advance" in the "arrow of time." This he calls, with Nishida, Mead, and Whitehead, the temporal structure of "discontinuous continuity." As a result, the "sum total of events increases with each passing moment." In Mead's idea, it is the "flexible and open concept of impulses" that makes possible the moment of this leap.[38] Dewey's discussion of the discontinuous moment as the production of novel individuality and the role of impulse fits into this temporal structure running through Mead and Whitehead.

The perspective of the gleam of light would better satisfy Dewey's wish in later years, a wish to have done more justice to the individual perspective in his social and situational theory. In his account of aesthetic experience, he stresses the indispensable role of "a bias, a predilection," or "the instinctive preference," which he says is "bound up with the very existence of individuality" (*AE*, 327). Elsewhere he says, "we touch the world through some particular tentacle" (199). Later in "I Believe," faced with the need to defend democracy from the threat of totalitarianism in the late 1930s, Dewey acknowledges that "individuals will always be the centre and the consummation of experience," and continues: "I should now wish to emphasize more than I formerly did that individuals are the finally decisive factors of the nature and movement of associated life." Dewey expresses his sense of the indispensable role of an individual not as "a center without a field," but as one *within* a field, as one defined by the marking, or inscription, of that field.[39] This is a slight revision, but a significant deepening of his theory of situation and interaction, the concepts whose vagueness had tended to blur the account in his earlier work of the central life of the individual.

Directive Criteria: The Imaginative Role of Prophetic Light in EMP

From the standpoint of the prophetic light, the notion of criteria in Deweyan growth can be redefined. Like Emerson's gleam of light, Dewey's idea of impulse plays the role of projecting ahead a vision of the better. He tells us that the beginning of the course of forming aims is with "a wish, an emotional reaction against the present state of things and a hope for something different" (*HNC*, 161). The initial emotional wish projects a vague sense of the better—what Dewey calls "prophetic vision" ("TI," 113). By this, Dewey means the revelation of "potentialities hitherto unrealized" (114), or goods that are "relatively embryonic."[40] The good is anything but guaranteed in advance; it is to be created ahead, as "consequences" in the future, or as Cavell says, proven only on the way. Potentiality is not "a category of existence" that is being unfolded. Instead, "potentialities cannot be *known* till *after* the interactions have occurred" in terms of "consequences" (109).

In projecting a better vision ahead, the prophetic light is closely related to its aesthetic function of imagination. Emerson calls imagination "a higher sort of seeing, which does not come by study, but by intellect being where and what it sees." The imagination of a poet has an "intoxicating" power that brings force a "sublime vision" ("Poet," 207–09). Similarly, Dewey refers to the aesthetic role of imagination.

> The new vision does not arise out of nothing, but emerges through seeing, in terms of possibilities, that is, of imagination, old things in new relations serving a new end which the new end aids in creating. (*CF*, 34)

Imaginative projection is "the chief instrument of the good" (*AE*, 350). It functions as "the precursor of changes" (348). In imagination, we re-see the world in a new light. This is the moral function and implication of aesthetic imagination.

Dewey suggests that the emotional nature of impulse here plays a crucial role:

> An emotion is more effective than any deliberate challenging sentinel could be. It reaches out tentacles for that which is cognate, for things which feed it and carry it to completion. (73)

What Jim Garrison, along with Thomas Alexander, calls "the human eros"—a passionate desire to "become good"[41]—thrusts us toward the better, or in Dewey's words, "stirs human endeavor to its depths" ("TI," 114).[42] We experience "emotional stir by possibilities as yet unrealized" and then, we aim to realize them in action (*CF*, 39). Citing Santayana's idea of imagination, Dewey claims that the forces of impulse constitute "the starting-point for a creative movement of the imagination" (13). The function of imagination is typically manifested in aesthetic experience: "The first stirrings of dissatisfaction and the first intimations of a better future are always found in works of art" (*AE*, 348). Dewey describes such an original impression as "a peculiar musical mood" (195) that grasps a total vision—"some end dimly and imprecisely prefigured" as "an aura" (80).

The articulation and realization of this initial vision requires ongoing action in the here and now. We have to "enhance and steady" our original vision till it is "wrought into the texture of our lives" (*HNC*, 180). Like Emerson and Cavell, Dewey implies that the vision is embodied only in our ways of life. Alexander helps us understand this sense: "The imaginative appropriation of the world—which is also the imaginative appropriation of the self—demands a progressive (and critical) articulation of the ideal."[43] Alexander here communicates to us Dewey's Emersonian sense that the realization of a better vision is anything but guaranteed in advance. It needs to be articulated *progressively*. Emphasizing the unguaranteed nature of Emerson's idea of an ideal, Cavell says:

> Kant found an essential place for perfection in his view of it at the end, as it were, of his theory, as an unreachable ideal relation to be striven for to the moral law; in Emerson this place of the ideal occurs at the beginning of moral thinking, as a condition, let us say, of moral imagination, as preparation or sign of moral life. (*Conditions*, 62)

The creation of the future hinges on ongoing efforts, action, and thinking in the here and now, and its meaning signifies the unknowable. It is tested by the act of leaving rather than by arriving at a destination. These are the moral implications of Emersonian *moral perfectionism*.

It is in connection with the imaginative power of a prophetic light that Dewey's idea of "criteria" can be given a positive redefinition. In the following, he presents the idea of "directive criteria":

> The community of causes and consequences in which we, together with those not born, are enmeshed is the widest and deep-

est symbol of the mysterious totality of being the imagination calls the universe. It is the embodiment for sense and thought of that encompassing scope of existence the intellect cannot grasp. It is the matrix within which our ideal aspirations are born and bred. It is the source of the values that the moral imagination projects as directive criteria and as shaping purposes. (*CF*, 56)

Dewey here says that the source of the values is the totality of our existence, our holistic condition of life. Being enmeshed there, our imaginative power is exercised to project the sense of the good. Criteria are not fixed measures that identify the definite good. Dewey says that goods originated in nature are too "evanescent and unique" to be molded into principles and rules. "Standardizations, formulae, generalizations, principles, universals, have their place, but the place is that of being instrumental to better approximation to what is unique and unrepeatable" (*EN*, 97). Criteria are rather like purposes that are being progressively shaped with the sense of "coherency" (*AE*, 57). Criteria function to *direct* humans toward the better. Thus, to the question, "How do we know the moment of perfection?" Dewey, along with Emerson and Cavell, would answer: in the perfecting of our lives, we only approximate, neither knowing nor identifying.

Directive criteria maintain the evolving nature of good that is the essence of Dewey's pragmatism, but now with a sharper focus on the aesthetic and spiritual nature of the gleam of light, being more sensitive to the senses of myth and the infinite, and the wonder of life. In comparison to Dewey's typically pragmatic concept of criteria, which is heavily weighted with social intelligence, action, and situations, directive criteria, in so far as they incorporate the contribution of the imaginative power of impulse, do more justice to the inner soul of one who is struggling to articulate its invisible but undeniable urge toward the better. Dewey characterizes such a mode of living as the "religious"—a spirituality that originates in "natural goods" on earth (*CF*, 47).

Directive criteria embody the moment of perfecting, "critical junctures" of discontinuity in the continuity of time. They represent the nexus of the attained and unattained self—what Dewey calls the closure of "awakening" (*AE*, 174), what Emerson calls the "metamorphosis."[44] The production of directive criteria is the act of perfecting with the proximate sense of finitude and infinitude when the individual "raise[s] himself above himself, to work a pitch above his last height" ("Circles," 168). Criteria mark the moment of the leap when a new horizon expands beyond an existing circle and when the self seems to leave, to move on.

Though we have to admit that Dewey is not as explicit as Emerson and Cavell about the sense of shame and despair in the path of perfection (which I shall discuss in the next chapter), his concept of directive criteria has the potential to reconstruct Deweyan growth in the light of EMP. With the standpoint of the gleam of light, Dewey's idea of the social reconstruction of criteria can be now reconsidered as a more holistic process, involving interaction between the impulsive force of the young and the social intelligence of the adult, and as the process in which our inner sense of the better is thrown into the outer world to be tested. The gleam of light would allow Dewey to do more justice to the inner light of the recalcitrant child, whom he inadvertently sought to suppress. Directive criteria have a capacity, like Cavell's concept of criteria, to be a matter of mutual attunement.[45]

EIGHT

THE GLEAM OF LIGHT LOST

*Transcending the Tragic with
Dewey after Emerson*

"WHERE do we find ourselves? . . . Sleep lingers all our lifetime about our eyes, as night hovers all day in the boughs of the fir-tree." (Emerson, "Experience")[1]

But it is not easy to detect and watch the gleams of light that flash from within. Education and social surroundings are in a conspiracy to dim these flashes and to attract our watching to other things. . . . The beginning of all development of individuality with adults usually comes when one learns to throw off an outer slavery to second-hand and ready-made opinions and begins to detect, watch, and trust one's own intuitions, that is, one's own spontaneous, unforced reactions. (Dewey, *Construction and Criticism*)[2]

Dewey sheds an Emersonian light on the degenerate state of American democracy in his times—a state of darkness in which the gleam of light, the sense of being and becoming, are dimmed and even lost. This is, in his expression, the "tragedy of the 'lost' individual." In order to reevaluate the significance of Deweyan growth after Emerson, this chapter attempts to respond to these questions centering on the theme of the tragic sense in contemporary democracy and education. Can Dewey's progressive growth still be viable in times when flexible transaction is constantly dissipated? How can a Deweyan discourse of amelioration and progress protect us from the sense of isolation, separation, and loss that are at the heart of the contemporary crisis of democracy?

One of the criticisms consistently directed at Deweyan growth is that it lacks a sense of the tragic. In response to the criticism I shall argue that Deweyan pragmatism, if reconsidered and reconstructed in the light of EMP, can illuminate the tragic nature of contemporary democracy and education by allowing us to remember the loss that we are suffering. This will be to move in the direction of *Emersonian antifoundationalism*—toward a third way, beyond the alternatives of relativism and absolutism.

"Pragmatism and the Tragic Sense"

Pragmatism, especially Dewey's, tends to the stigma that it lacks a tragic sense of life. Criticisms have been made from diverse perspectives. It was Sidney Hook who first took up the issue with the following response:

> As I understand the pragmatic perspective on life, it is an attempt, to make it possible for men to live in a world of inescapable tragedy—a tragedy that flows from the conflict of moral ideals—without lamentation, defiance or make-believe. According to this perspective, even in the best of human worlds there will be tragedy—tragedy perhaps without bloodshed, but certainly not without tears.[3]

In Hook's definition, what is "tragic" in the human condition is not limited to the presence of evil, or even a matter of the necessity of death itself. Rather, the tragic, he claims, is a "moral phenomenon" where one good conflicts with another in the moment of moral choice. In other words, the tragic is a part of human life, this life we have to live in the here and now. Rather than mourning over the tragic conflict of goods, instead of yielding to despair, let us go forward in action and experiment to find a way to negotiate and resolve, or, at least, to reduce conflicts. In Hook's view, this is the heart of what Dewey means by the power of intelligent control. Pragmatism is heroic; it is the philosophy of courage.

A shared concern continues, however, over the image of powerful and progressive growth that colors Dewey's pragmatism and its concomitant notion of intelligent control, especially in these postmodern times. It is Cornel West who offers one of the most powerful criticisms concerning Dewey's lack of tragic sensibility. Despite his appreciation of "prophetic pragmatism," West is especially critical of Dewey's pragmatism for its inadequate realization of a tragic vision—a lack that West claims Dewey inherits from Emerson. Referring to Emerson's phrase, "the only sin is limitation," one that epitomizes his optimistic theodicy of extolling human power, West argues that a "deep sense of tragedy and irony" is alien to both Emerson and Dewey.[4] In his later writing he reiterates the theme:

> The point here is not so much that Emerson himself had no sense of the tragic, but rather that the way he formulated the relation of human powers and fate, human agency and circumstances, human will and constraints made it difficult for him and for subsequent pragmatists to maintain a delicate balance between excessive optimism and exorbitant pessimism regarding human capacities.[5]

In contemporary democracy, the sense of possibility toward the future narrows, and there is still a need to struggle with the "death and disease, that cut-off the joys of democratic citizenship," where the "ultimate facts of the human predicament" need to be recognized more than ever.[6] The context of modern tragedy, in contrast to Greek tragedy, West argues, is a state in which "ordinary individuals struggle against meaninglessness and nothingness," a feature of "a fragmented society with collapsing metaphysical meanings."[7] In these circumstances, Dewey's future-oriented pragmatism and his emphasis on the primacy of human will and action lack something crucial: a failure to define the relationship between a democratic way of life and a "profound sense of evil."[8]

West instead supports Josiah Royce's deeper idealism, which combines with a pessimism heavily influenced by Schopenhauer to produce his "absolute" version of pragmatism—one that is supported by the "concrete and practical notions of an absolute."[9] For Royce, far more than for Dewey, irrevocable deeds are the source of the tragic. West, like Royce, expresses the need for a thorough recognition of the tragic sense, a deep sense of defeat caused by brute chance. Real progress is impossible without the recognition of this sense of finitude and the appeal to this absolute reality.

More recently, Raymond D. Boisvert has presented similar criticism of Dewey's lack of the tragic sense, but with a tighter focus on his scientific concept of intelligence than West. In Boisvert's view, Dewey's pragmatism equates scientific advancement with moral progress, in a manner typical of nineteenth-century modernity. Dewey's faith in progress through scientific advancement led him to believe that in the power of intelligence, courage and effort there was the possibility of "the indefinite perfectibility of mankind on earth." His progressive view of the universe lacks a sensitivity to the tragic— what Boisvert calls a limitation inherent in the nature of things, "the Nemesis of Necessity." The problems afflicting human beings— murder, incest, adultery, jealousy, unfettered ambition, and the traumas of family relationships—are natural limitations put on us by necessity, limitations that will never be eliminated by the efforts of a "planned community."[10] Nor will a commitment to scientific progress guarantee moral progress. Dewey is mistaken when he believes that the human mind can eventually dominate necessity. In this sense, Boisvert finds Hook's defense inadequate. Hook commits the same mistake as Dewey when he fails to recognize necessity, a failure seen in Hook's optimism about the power of intelligence to resolve the problems of humanity once and for all.[11] For a philosophy more adequate to the tragic in human experience, Boisvert himself appeals to the ontology of Anaximander, a philosophy of the "all-mixed-together,"[12] and to the writings of Nathaniel Hawthorne, an author with a deep sense of the tragic—of "the constraints over which we have not control, to burdens for which we did not ask, to the inseparable mixture of good and evil in every reformist program, to the flaws in our condition and limitations in the nature of things which make our improvements temporary and fragmented."[13] As we become aware of the ever-increasing, global complexity of our times, with its attendant material affluence, technological development, and political sophistication, on the one hand, and the vicious cycle of retaliation through violence and the inflated rhetoric of good and evil, on the other, the calls made by West and Boisvert for the recognition of "evil" and "necessity" confront us in terms too real to be ignored—and indeed, in their own way they are seductive. In light of their criticism, Dewey's progressive notion of growth can seem naive, or even oppressively optimistic.

West's and Boisvert's criticisms are all the more persuasive in the postmodern context of tragedy. Megan Boler sees the postmodern sense of the tragic in terms of "groundlessness"—a sense that "the ground is torn from beneath one's feet" for there is no shared value, common ground or objective norm that one can rely on. "[T]ragedies of dissensus" arise in the face of "fundamental philosophical and strategic differences."[14] As a philosophy that seeks equilibrium, pragmatism cannot do justice, she suggests, to the postmodern tragic sense of dissonance and disequilibrium. Boisvert's alternative proposal of the tragic metaphysics of Necessity and West's call for the recognition of absolute evil sound plausible responses to Boler's postmodern sense of groundlessness. There is something in postmodern culture, however, that reinforces the mood of mourning, depriving us as a result of the energy for commitment, and lulling us into resignation: worse, it aggravates the prevalent tendency toward nihilism. Indeed, it is the concept of "hope" that those who claim the absolutism of tragedy shun. In line with Jacques Derrida's embracement of disappointment, Boler claims: "If a 'fundamental groundlessness' must be accepted, perhaps giving up hope is a fruitful directive."[15]

Choice, in this postmodern picture, becomes either a relativistic acquiescence to the condition of groundlessness, or a reactionary appeal to the absolute ground. Like West and Boisvert, René Arcilla takes the latter position. Arcilla resists Nicholas Burbules's apparent affirmation of Rorty's antifoundationalist position[16] Arcilla opposes pragmatism on the grounds that the acknowledgment of the tragic, which he defines in terms of irrecoverable loss, leads us to act "beyond the reach of pragmatist forms of justification," pragmatism's optimism being invested in its faith in outcomes and some kind of "observable success."[17] As an alternative, he proposes *tragic absolutism*—the acceptance of "absolute loss and vulnerability, absolute mortality," and an appeal to "an absolute faith in our personal sense of integrity," as the means of "absolute redemption."[18] Pragmatism, however, should not give in completely to such criticism. It is against the danger of this avenue of criticism, I believe, that its significance must be appreciated anew. To be more precise, it is this *tragedy* of the absolutism of tragedy, the fixation of the state of groundlessness, and its concomitant abrogation of hope that pragmatism resists; and it is in contradistinction to this that it demonstrates the promise of its philosophy of hope. It is precisely for the sake of enhancing its potential that the reconstruction of Dewey's pragmatism is urgently needed. This must be reconstructed in order to show that a philosophy of hope is distinguished from oppressive optimism; that its "tragic metaphysics" is not one that is based upon "necessity" or "evil" but upon *possibilities*, with the acknowledgment of the transitional nature of human being, including its precarious nature.

A signpost for such a reexamination can be found in Dewey's own writings from the late 1920s onward, especially in his aesthetic and religious works.[19] It is in these that his earlier idea of progressive growth, as seen in his educational writings, came to be underscored by his resistance to the "tragedy of the 'lost individual.'" In his criticism of an American individualism driven by capitalist economy and mass culture, Dewey laments the tragic state of American society—a state in which people drift "without sure anchorage" and suffer from the loss of any "sense of wholeness."[20] Conformity and standardization create a sense of "an inner void" and "vacuum" *(ION,* 83). Fear, dread, and anxiety "eat into self-respect" (68). The innovative impulses of, and independence in, the young mind are choked and stifled as they become part of the "chain-belt system of mass manufacture" (*CC*, 132). His concern is with the state of "moral subjection" in which a human being, in chains, loses the "mental freedom which is a condition of creation" (133, 136). The condition of imprisonment indicates the danger of an individual's being unable to be any longer a responsible generator of "genuine time," the moment of novelty and qualitative transformation. We are molded by the mechanical, linear, and flat repetition of time.[21]

Dewey's tragic sense over the loss that individuals suffer permeates his social and cultural criticism. This can be reread as Emersonian perfectionism—his pronouncement of a battle against those forces that conspire to hinder the passage of the gleam of light. He tells us that modernity and capitalism encroach upon our hearts and minds, and consistently threaten to benumb, suppress, and extinguish our gleam of light. He is prophetic about spiritual degeneration in postmodern democracy. In *Individualism Old and New*, Dewey cites Emerson's remark from "Self-Reliance": "Society everywhere is in conspiracy against its members" (*ION*, 122)[22]. People cannot say authentically, without fear of pretence, "I think" and "I am." One is no longer sure that it is this "I" that contributes to and participates in the reconstruction of "my" society. This, as Emerson says, brings forth a "tragic consequence."[23] The gleam of light lost does not manifest only the spiritual crisis of each individual: it is also the crisis of culture as a whole as it loses its prophetic power for regeneration.

There is a danger, however, that the reinterpretation of Dewey's tragedy of the lost individual in connection with the loss of the gleam of light can turn into the projection of our lament over conformity, into a nostalgic sense of loss over the irrecoverable, into mourning over separation, and even into a ranting over its suppression—in other words, into a certain form of the absolutism of tragedy. As an educational consequence, it can encourage a romanticization of childhood and a desire for a return to communion, as has so often been seen in diverse forms of progressive education in and after Dewey's times. In our times, the romanticization of tragedy can be tied up with the culture of personal narrative—a state in which the introspective self can become overly self-conscious, engaged in retrospective lamentation over irrecoverable loss or in narcissistic exercises in autobiography. Boler's pastiche subject—one with "the relentless gaze of self-reflective paralogy"—evokes the image of the guilt-stricken self who is engaged in a "confession of ignorance."[24]

Dewey's concerns here, however, are with something deeper and more subtle than a nostalgic mourning over loss. He suggests the second sense of the tragic: in our *obliviousness* to the gleam of light, we cannot even remember its loss. We cannot even imagine what it might mean. We subside in apathy and indifference or in a feel-good regime of desire-satisfaction that is ultimately nihilistic in kind. As Dewey says: "We do not know what we really want and we make no great effort to find out" (*CC*, 133). It is a state in which our tranquilized nature is desensitized to its most insidious effects.

In Dewey's idea of habit reconstruction, the gleam of light suggests a spiritual dimension of impulse as a cultivating ground of human intelligence. Without the prophetic vision that is constantly illuminated by our own light, progressive growth is impossible. And such progress is something we have to be constantly fighting for in a humble recognition of the imperfect state of democracy. To commit oneself to the kind of continuous growth that Dewey has in mind comes to imply the acknowledgment of the double sense of the tragic as inherent in the human condition, and an endless tension between the attainment and unattainment of democracy. Hence, Dewey says: "Since things do not attain such fulfillment but are in acutuality distracted and interfered with, democracy in this sense is not a fact and never will be." For him, democracy is both an ideal state that is never fully "perfected" and a state that is achieved in the "actual phases of associated life as they are freed from restrictive and disturbing elements, and are contemplated as having attained their limit of development."[25] It is this double nature in Dewey's conception of democracy as both attained and unattained, his aching sense of imperfection, that warns us of our obliviousness to the lack of the tragic. And this state of obliviousness itself is the symptom of nihilism in democracy and education.

*Nihilism in Democracy and Education:
The Double Sense of the Tragic*

Dewey, after Emerson and Cavell, can help us re-see and recount the tragic state of democracy and education in postindustrial democratic societies. In such countries as Japan, the United Kingdom, and the United States, there is a widespread sense of crisis in education. One of its most serious factors is the erosion of the public realm and a consequent distortion of the relationship between the private and the public. This is not, however, an easy task, for in certain respects education is itself complicit with these problems. The practice of education is heavily dominated by neoliberal ideology and by the language of performativity; it has become dominated by procedures of standardization and quantification, in the name of efficiency and effectiveness. Facile notions of the ethical emerge in what is heralded as "values education" or in a new moralistic commitment to moral education, with a concomitant suppression of the possibility of any real engagement with the complexity of the ethical demands that run throughout education and life. In an attempt to make all aspects of practice transparent and efficient and subject to systematic accounting, there may well be lack of imaginative sensitivity to the invisible and the silent, to something in the human condition that cannot be readily expressed or presented in an articulated, either-or form; this is something to which myth has sometimes answered. The relative absence of a serious ethical language amongst adults, which has become typical of our age, means that young people do not encounter the kind of discourse that would enable them to think differently about these matters. Lives are lived out in dislocation and in a muted but surreptitious despondency.

Whether it comes as an appeal to raise standards, to increase school effectiveness, to teach right and wrong in moral education, or to increase the understanding of other cultures, education today—especially in such postindustrial countries as the United States, the United Kingdom, and Japan—is so often driven by assumptions of gaining and raising. A drive to achieve "excellence" measured by a definite set of goals never wanes. Contemporary policy and practice have generally been based on the assumption that appropriate planning means the clear identification of ends and the systematic creation of means to their realization. As Richard Rorty cynically puts this: "Unless the youth is raised to believe in moral absolutes, and in objective truth, civilization is doomed."[26] Concomitant to the drive toward raising, fixing, and articulating is a rhetoric of freedom that permeates the language of educational reforms in the globalized economy.

This is true even, ironically, of certain aspects of moral education or citizenship education. For example, Paul Standish discusses the idea of citizenship education proposed by the Crick Report in 1998, which led to legislation for citizenship education for all children up to the age of sixteen in England. Its focus is on: (1) the acquisition of "knowledge" about the political institutions that shape and govern society; (2) the development of "skills" appropriate to participating in the political life of their society; and (3) the development of "dispositions" appropriate to participating in modern democracy, including toleration and the inclination to listen to the other's point of view. With good intent, no doubt, citizenship education is here characterized by the language of articulation in goals and skills to achieve it. While acknowledging the value of such endeavors, Standish criticizes the idea that "citizenship education" per se might be introduced as a separate subject, or even a separate strand running through the curriculum, and turned into a sort of accessory to the main business of education.[27] In order to realize the "inextricably interwoven" relationship between the good of the individual and the good of the larger society—following Plato and Rousseau, and for that matter, Dewey—and especially to respond to the contemporary nihilistic tendency of "withdrawal" among young people, an attempt to join the private and the public in citizenship education requires something more than words celebratory of democracy.[28] It also needs an approach to the moral life other than the political or quasi-contractual approach—one that addresses the "spiritual excess that is dissipated or dulled."[29]

Similarly in Japan a series of educational reforms has been conducted. On the one hand, there are policies of decentralization and privatization. The direction of education here demonstrates that Japanese society, as a critical case of postindustrial democratic societies, is now in search of the education of a new type of individual, fit for the age of "globalization." The concepts emphasized here are: individuality (*Kosei*), internationalization (*Kokusai-ka*), the power to live (*Ikiru chikara*), and freedom for leisure and creative activities (*yutori*). The number of days of attendance per year has been cut down.

The minimum levels of achievement in terms of the knowledge required of learners have been reduced.[30] Freedom in the choice of curriculum and schools has increased. In these respects, education seems to have become more liberalized. There is a danger here, however, that the concept of freedom is quantified as if it were merely a matter of either increasing or reducing. Japanese scholars such as Manabu Sato and Hidenori Fujita criticize the trend toward liberalization as one based upon the ideology of neoliberalism associated with free competition and free choice in the global—liberalism that in reality increases inequality and leads to a more stratified society.[31]

On the other hand, a new emphasis is being put on the reinforcement of moral education in a conservative direction. In view of the alleged moral decline of young people, in 1997 the Ministry of Education[32] initiated a program called "Education of the Heart" (*Kokoro no Kyoiku*). Its main features are the provision of advice and guidance for the young and the reinforcement of more rigorous disciplining of children, not only in schools but also at home.[33] In 2002 the government started to distribute a booklet entitled *Kokoro-no-Note* (*The Notebook for the Heart*—a guidebook for moral education for teachers, students, and parents) to all elementary and secondary schools in Japan. Its basic direction, however, is conservative, looking inward into the culture with an emphasis on cultural identity and traditional values, even with a tendency toward nationalism. "Love for Japan" can be used as a mask for defensive and inward-looking exclusion of the foreign and the deviant—despite calls for internationalization. A move to change the Fundamental Law of Education—which was originally implemented after the Second World War and based on the American model of democracy—has recently gained momentum. Intellectuals on the left are wary of a return to the totalitarianism and militarism of pre-war Japan.[34]

Seen through the eyes of Deweyan growth after Emersonian perfectionism, however, such policy and practice—notwithstanding its good intent to rebuild and join the impoverished state of the private and the public—is troubled neither by the aching sense of imperfection nor by the sharp sense of shame over the degenerate condition of democracy—over what might be called the spiritual enfeebling of the culture. As Emerson's radical words put this: "Public and private avarice make the air we breathe thick and fat. The scholar is decent, indolent, complaisant. See already the tragic consequence. The mind of this country, taught to aim at low objects, eats upon itself" ("AMS," 52). And worse, in their language of transparency and efficiency, and in the constrained choice between a neoliberal concept of freedom and a conservative moral absolutism, the dominant policies and practices of education today expel from the space of education what is beyond the grasp of calculation and exchange—something in the human condition that cannot be readily expressed or presented in an articulated, fixed form, the unknowable, or what is yet to come, which can be grasped only in this moment of transition, in the process of the ongoing middle. It seems to be getting more and more difficult to enjoy the sense of what Dewey calls "the *qui vive*"—the sense of one's whole being "fully alive" in "heightened vitality."[35]

In these contexts, school for many young students today is not necessarily a place to experience the joy of learning, to reconfirm their sense of existence. "WHERE do we find ourselves? . . . Sleep lingers all our lifetime about our eyes, as night hovers all day in the boughs of the fir-tree" ("Experience," 216). The question Emerson once raised concerning the loss of the self is still relevant for young people today. What prevents people from bridging this gap is well captured by Sato in what he calls the phenomenon of children's "escape from learning." According to his research, many Japanese children cannot find any hope in what they learn; they feel that nothing makes a difference in their lives. The social background of this phenomenon is, in Sato's analysis, the compressed and accelerated form of modernization East Asian style. Since its peak in Japan in the 1980s, young people cannot find meaning in learning any more.[36] The phenomenon of nihilism, as Sato analyzes this, illustrates that neither young people nor adults can experience the joy of liberation through learning, even if the freedom increases quantitatively. Behind the language of moral absolutes and the measured criteria of achievement, the sense of the loss of orientation, the lack of confidence, and the feeling of isolation are left untouched.

The invisible but undeniable sense of loss behind the drive toward gaining, as Dewey, with Emerson, reminds us, is one of the most tragic conditions of contemporary education and democracy. In a second sense, it is tragic that educational reform today has lost its sensitivity to this duplicitous condition. In the light of the double condition of the tragic, a void or lack created in the state of oblivion is the crisis of nihilism in democracy and education. In the limited sense of freedom, the impulsive energy of the young is directed toward the immediate satisfaction of pleasures and desires; it cannot find an alternative channel through which it can be liberated and through which it might revitalize culture. As Emerson remarks: "The state of society is one in which the members have suffered amputation from the trunk, and strut about so many walking monsters—a good finger, a neck, a stomach, an elbow, but never a man" ("AMS," 38). This image of dissemblance symbolizes the impoverished state of the private and the public in contemporary democracy. We have seen that Dewey, with Emerson, suggests the second sense of the tragic: in our obliviousness to the gleam of light, we cannot even remember its loss. In the face of the current situation in democracy and education, Dewey, after Emerson and Cavell, would argue that what is missing from contemporary democracy and education is the hope that each of us can become the creator of our own culture, as ours, and the bearer of history by producing "critical junctures" in time; and that what is missing from the dominant discourse of education—but what devoted teachers and parents in fact need—is the trust in what is yet to come, the force of prophetic impulse. This is the courage to open oneself to the potential in the evolving circles of growth, and the courage to receive the otherness of the world that endlessly transcends one's existing knowledge.

Transcending the Tragic with Dewey after Emerson: Emersonian Antifoundationalism

What then is the Emersonian perfectionist way of going through the double condition of the tragic? It is more than retrospective mourning over loss; it is not constrained by an absolute sense of mortality. The keen recognition of a reality in which distance and proximity are forever "knotted" is internal to EMP.[37] Suppose we see our age as impoverished in the first sense of the tragic, the sense of irrecoverable loss, our response is one of grief. Grief, however, was not Emerson's response to his own tragic experience—the loss of his young son, Waldo. A day after Waldo's death at the age of five, Emerson wrote a letter to his close friend, Margaret Fuller : "Shall I ever dare to love any thing again. Farewell and Farewell, O my Boy!"[38] An entry in his journal written some two months later demonstrates Emerson's continuing grief:

> A new day, a new harvest, new duties, new men, new fields of thought, new powers call you, and an eye fastened on the past unsuns nature, bereaves me of hope, and ruins me with a squalid indigence which nothing but death can adequately symbolize.[39]

Two years later, however, his tone changes:

> In the death of my son, now more than two years ago, I seem to have lost a beautiful estate—no more . . . So is it with this calamity; it does not touch me: some thing which I fancied was a part of me, which could not be torn away without tearing me, nor enlarged without enriching me, falls off from me, and leaves no scar. It was caducous. I grieve that grief can teach me nothing, nor carry me one step into real nature. ("Experience," 218)

His sense of the tragic has been metamorphosed, toward a quiet resolve.

Emerson's provocative statement that "grief can teach me nothing" has generated a range of discussions on Emerson's sense of the tragic. For example, George Santayana asserts that the Emersonian law of compensation teaches "the lesson of indifference to circumstances." As he explains, "[Emerson] merely points out how the good and evil of our lives grow out of each other; he shows them to be inseparable. Far from making the evil disappear, he teaches that it is the foundation of the good . . . [and] . . . unless we admit that suffering and wrong are a necessary and desirable part of the scheme of things, our optimism does not deserve the name."[40] More recently, in response to the conventional view that Emerson has no sense of tragedy, Buell acknowledges the sense of limits and struggles in Emerson's thought.[41]

In this context, Cavell's interpretation sheds new light on Emerson's tragic sense as a crucial component of his perfectionism—one that is related to the idea of "finding as founding."[42] Emerson's response to the tragic sense of groundlessness when we lose our way is not grief, but the awareness of the futility of grieving. Cavell elaborates on this as follows. To make sense of the life of his lost son, Emerson has to declare himself as a philosopher, to be a founder. Philosophy begins in loss, with the experience of "the world falling away" (*America*, 109). Emerson's philosophical task, however, is not the building of the unified foundation of philosophy as a kind of the ground we reach once and for all. "Foundation reaches no farther than each issue of finding" (114).[43] Paradoxically, it is the process of the establishing of "founding without a founder" (117). Cavell claims that Emerson's effort of finding himself again in this world symbolizes "finding a new America in the West while being, or because, lost"(90–91). This is a process of finding one's location as a newcomer, to be "the first philosopher of this new region" (106). Philosophical writing, then, involves the task of "founding a nation" (93). In contrast to Derrida, whose task is to deconstruct the "finished edifice of philosophy," Cavell claims that Emerson's is "to avert foundation, in advance" in "founding, or deconfounding, American thinking."[44] This might be called Emerson's antifoundationalism, his middle way of living beyond the restrictive, fixed choice between no ground and absolute ground.

In response to "cynicism and disillusion" as politically devastating passions in a democracy (*America*, 113) and the imminent sense of groundlessness in our times, Emerson and Cavell encourage us to follow the path of finding as founding—in recognition of the impoverished state of the existing self with the sense of shame. The flying Perfect always leaves the possibility of its own transcendence through imperfection: it consistently drives us to depart again. Its focus is on an endless *searching* for the common with the sense of defeat and pain as much as the hope for advancement; and with the acknowledgment that unity is always beyond our full grasp. The life of Emersonian perfection is tested, and indeed, starts in the very moment when we are mired in loss and face—whether it involves the impossibility of the full understanding of different values, or the imperfectability of democratic ideals. Directive criteria to *measure* Deweyan growth operates in the moment of leaving the existing limitations, that of "disjunction"—when we start to make the effort of searching something different from within the state of loss and groundlessness. A hope for unity is regenerated from within the conditions of dissonance, disequilibrium, and imperfection. As Cavell says: "[Emerson's] perception of the moment is taken in hope, as something to be proven only on the way, by the way."[45]

Dewey, who praises Emerson as "the Philosopher of Democracy," would endorse Emersonian antifoundationalism, and Cavell's interpretation of Emerson's "finding as founding" opens a window through which Dewey's double sense of the tragic can be descried. Being in tune with the "metaphysics" of Dewey in *Experience and Nature* and *Art as Experience*, Emersonian antifoundationalism directs Deweyan growth in a way different from Rorty's relativist antifoundationalism. Unlike Rorty's Dewey, whose thought is characterized by power and progress, Dewey in these writings presents the transitory view of the world. The sense of the attained and unattained perfection that Dewey shares with Emerson suggests loss, limitation, or failure as a part of the human condition.[46]

In this regard, Odin's discussion of the "sense of the tragedy" ingrained in both Mead's and Whitehead's worldviews and the Zen philosophy of Nishida helps to underscore the nature of the tragic dimension peculiar to American philosophy. Referring to Whitehead's idea of the existential experience of "perpetual perishing," Odin highlights the point that the sense of the tragic is a structural component of the transitory worldview of American philosophy. In contrast to Heidegger's notion of the authentic selfhood that is realized by the anticipation of "oncoming death," the selfhood developed by Mead and Whitehead as well as by Nishida, Odin claims, undergoes death in the here and now in immediate experience, through "living by dying."[47] This matches the Emersonian perfectionist view of finding as founding, the perpetual deconfounding of the ground.

A contribution of EMP as a means of reconstruction in Dewey's pragmatism is to help it maintain its merit as a philosophy of hope, while defending it from the charge of Rorty's antifoundationalism or West's appeal to absolute pragmatism. In comparison to West's Emerson, Cavell's Emerson is more in tune with the tragic sense of loss and groundlessness in our times. While resisting the absolutism of tragedy like Rorty and sharing with Rorty Nietzsche's morality beyond good and evil, Cavell's Emerson offers a different way of transcending the tragic without falling into Rortian moral relativism. Going beyond debates between relativism and absolutism, Deweyan growth, if reconsidered as a form of Emersonian perfectionism, can open a way to finding as founding.

The Emersonian antifoundationalist way of transcending the tragic can still appeal to the voice of the "recalcitrant" child—a child whose life cannot be accommodated in the limited space of education that is defined in the neoliberal discourse of freedom or in the absolutist language of moral education. The voice of a fourteen-year-old Japanese boy reminds us of the need for such space in education:

> The present society does not easily accept my existence. Therefore, I throw my poetry to the society which rejects me. Looking around me, there is no place for me to be accepted. There is no one around me with whom I can talk about the philosophical question, "Why do we live?".... The minds of friends at school are occupied with entrance exams into high schools and they cannot afford to talk about the concerns of the heart. In contemporary education, the emphasis is put more on clearing the goal of the entrance exam than discussing the issues of human dignity. They do not understand how important it is to think and discuss the problems of life. This is why a person like me becomes isolated.[48]

While being a thoroughly personal and private voice, this betokens the suppressed gleam of light—the blocked entrance into the culture, a negative manifestation of prophetic whim trapped in an icy cave. It is the voice of a young person who wants to grow, but who, in the current system of goal-oriented education, does not know how. Simultaneously, however, this is a voice of social criticism issued from within private suffering. The boy is isolated in frustration and loses his way, perhaps experiencing the sense of void, groundlessness. Still, however, he yearns for connection and therefore expresses his poetic words to unknown others. Increased freedom alone will not resolve his agony. Nor can he rely on a therapeutic healing through recounting and mourning over the past. He will resist even the language of social inclusion and the principle of equality based upon exchange in which his inarticulate sense of the unknown is flattened, fixated, and worse, assimilated. By the very act of addressing the question, "Why do we live?" he manifests a need for a philosophical dialogue with others. He tells us that generalized moral concepts alone will not save him from suffering. He knows that it is this "I" who can concretize and has even created moral language and moral ideals—no one else. Unless one utters one's words here and now, nothing will start. The boy's words resonate with and invigorate Dewey's: "Perfection means perfecting, fulfillment, fulfilling, and the good is now or never."[49] He lets us know that it is in a prophetic move, not by grieving or revenging, but through exercising the power of poetic creation, that he may be able to create ahead the foundation of life from within the loss of foundation, to liberate us from chains of the void. He is in need of Emerson's middle way of living: finding as founding. He suggests to us that the criteria of the good life are not pre-given but are only directive criteria that each of us must keep finding as our own foundation. He needs other(s)—teachers, friends, or parents—who can imaginatively capture this crucial moment of leaping.

In its negative, dark tone, this boy's words remind us of the voice of Emerson's son, Waldo: grieving and ranting do not save us. The words also echo the hopeful voice of Emerson: "The heart refuses to be imprisoned; in its first and narrowest pulses, it already tends outward with a vast force, and to immense and innumerable expansions"[50]; and the encouraging voice of Cavell: you can have the courage to leave poverty only by trusting the prophetic whim. In his despair and hope, the boy reminds us that there should be a way of education that can guide him to remember the gleam of light lost—a space of Emersonian perfectionist education that can respond to the spiritual crisis of the young, and that can awaken their prophetic whim and creative force for the revitalization of culture from within. This is Emerson's call for the education of the American Scholar—"He is one, who raises himself from private consideration, and breathes and lives on public and illustrious thoughts" ("AMS," 46)—and Nietzszche's Emersonian call for the education of Genius: when he writes that "the fact of our existing at all in this here-and-now must be the strongest incentive to us to live according to our own laws and standards," and that "*A new degree of culture would instantly revolutionize the entire system of human pursuits.*"[51] The boy, however, tells us that a single gleam of light cannot grow alone, but needs others—an interpersonal philosophical conversation that can inwardly empower the young to battle outwardly against forces of dulling convention.

In dialogue with the Emersonian child, Dewey's muted voice, with its sense of the tragic, can be revived—the voice of criticism in resistance to cynicism and nihilism, the voice against the internal foe of democracy that threatens to suppress the poet in each of us, and the voice that seeks to revive it. This is a voice of hope for education.[52]

NINE

THE REKINDLING OF THE GLEAM OF LIGHT
Toward Perfectionist Education

The account with democratic ideals is still far from being settled. But if it turns out in the end a failure, it will not be because it is too low a doctrine but because it is too high morality for human nature, at least as that human nature is now educated. It is a strenuous doctrine that demands courage of thought and belief for realization. (Dewey, *Construction and Criticism*)[1]

The soul's advances are not made by gradation, such as can be represented by motion in a straight line; but rather by ascension of state, such as can be represented by metamorphosis—from the egg to the worm, from worm to the fly. The growths of genius are of a certain *total* character. (Emerson, "The Over-Soul")[2]

Dewey says: "MANKIND likes to think in terms of extreme opposites. It is given to formulating its beliefs in terms of Eithers-Ors, between which it recognizes no intermediate possibilities."[3] We are, are we not, still bound by this fatal drive toward dichotomous choice. Yet there are times today when it seems that there is only one alternative—when other possibilities are made to seem beyond the pale or absurd or just unrealistic. The clamor of urgency about the raising of standards and levels of achievement has expressed itself in part in a new obsession with assessment. Whatever cannot be measured (and that is to say, quantified) does not exist. This has arisen in a context where the purpose of education is largely taken for granted in the vocabulary of the new competitive "knowledge economy." The concept of liberty has become confined in the too-narrow space of neoliberalism. The busy, apparently forward-looking tone of this way of thinking couples ironically with a conservative call for a return to moral discipline. Moreover, behind the enlightened call for social inclusion, there may then be a lack of imaginative sensitivity to the invisible and the silent, to what cannot be readily expressed or presented. Signs of unrest and disturbance among the young are viewed with fear, and even covered over, and in various quarters the solution is seen in a reactionary turn to clear—perhaps absolute—standards of right and wrong; or even to the fervor of religious fundamentalism. There is a fear of the amorphous, the uncertain, and the unknown, that lurks behind this absolutism in education. On the global scene, conflicts and tensions among different values and beliefs aggravate our sense of living in a state of groundlessness, where the hope of finding common ground becomes more and more dim. Talk of globalization simply exacerbates this trend, while "multiculturalism" either is resisted because of its apparent endorsement of relativism (a relativism that is, it is assumed, the road to moral confusion), or is accepted in terms of a toleration reduced to the token recognition of difference, or—worse—is exploited by advertisers who, in effect, assimilate difference into sameness. Such solutions impoverish private and public lives and widen the gap between them, alienating us from the sense of the whole.

Under these circumstances Dewey's pragmatism and conception of growth, along with the related tradition of progressive education (typically characterized as "child-centered education"), become the target of conservative attack—allegedly the very cause of the decline in standards of knowledge and morality among young people. Pragmatism and progressive education continue to be stigmatized as naively optimistic. It is true that we cannot live today with a simple faith in progress. Deweyan growth, however, reconstructed in the light of EMP—the idea of perfection without final perfectibility, and of democracy never finally to be achieved—reminds us today that the solutions these limited choices seem to offer simply cover up the sense of loss and groundlessness from which we suffer: the potential of the inarticulate yet prophetic impulse for the assiduous reconstruction of culture is numbed and obliterated. Dewey, after Emerson and Cavell, would argue today that the prophetic light, which can never be grasped through fixation, is to be watched in its transition, in the "intermediate possibilities," that it offers. It requires another space, another language, and another vision of education—a turning of our ways of seeing education. Dewey follows Emerson in naming this the space for the "education of the human soul." This is no return to any rosy picture of child-centeredness; it is rather a strenuous call, in these nihilistic times, for endless human perfection and for the revitalization of the culture from within. This necessitates the practical and ethical task, as Dewey says in *Democracy and Education*, of philosophy as education.[4] Now reconsidered in dialogue with Emerson, the notion of philosophy as education can be reinterpreted as the critical reexamination and transformation of the spiritual, aesthetic and moral basis of our living. It can be captured only as a matter of ongoing process, as the process of becoming; and as the process of *searching* for the common, the universal, or the whole—for what is beyond the existing boundary of the self. Dewey, with Emerson, reminds us that the regaining of this spiritual aspiration is the task of creative democracy—democracy as a personal way of living.[5]

In this concluding chapter, I would like to discuss *how* Deweyan growth, after Emersonian perfectionism, can point us to a form of education sufficient to rebuild a route from the private to the public. Dewey can guide us to another possibility of social or political education, one that permeates and integrates diverse areas of education. It is the aesthetic turn in Dewey's pragmatism that makes this possible.

The Intensity of the Gleam of Light: Dewey's Aesthetic Turn

For both Dewey and Emerson, as well as for Cavell, the task of creative democracy is the rebuilding of the public, starting from within the private. Dewey says that "democracy must begin at home."[6] With the metaphor of "home" Dewey means not only the local community and neighborhood; he means also one's being oneself. Later in "Creative Democracy: The Task Before Us," he continues this theme in a sharper tone:

> To denounce Naziism for intolerance, cruelty and stimulation of hatred amounts to fostering insincerity if, on our personal relations to other persons, if, in our daily walk and conversation we are moved by racial, color or other class prejudice. ("CD," 226)

The task of connecting the private and the public, he suggests, must start at this level by somehow transforming one's personal way of being in the world. This is why in his later period Dewey renews his faith in the idea that "individuals who are democratic in thought and action are the sole final warrant for the existence and endurance of democratic institutions."[7]

This passage from the private to the public, indeed, is none other than what is urged in Emerson's (and Cavell's) call for the education of "Man Thinking"[8]:

> [T]he deeper he dives into his privatest, secretest presentiment, to his wonder he finds, this is the most acceptable, most public, and universally true. The people delight in it; the better part of every man feels, This is my music; this is myself. ("AMS," 49)

Education of such an individual, Emerson suggests, is the sole way of shedding a new light again on the world—the world in darkness in which man "has almost lost the light" (48)—to bring forth the moment of its "conversion" (52). This is neither selfish individualism nor the hubris of the chosen elite. This is Emerson's expression of "hope" for the genius in each of us, for the part of us that does not yet see (48, 52). It is a hope that "the inmost in due time becomes the outmost."[9] Following such a path, he says, requires "patience" ("AMS," 52): education is the patient process of the conversion of the human spirit.

Similarly, Dewey, especially in his later writings, presents the Emersonian route from the inmost to the outmost. He argues that "self-criticism" functions as social criticism as the condition of construction and revitalization in democracy. By citing Emerson's idea of the gleam of light as a symbol of self-reliance, Dewey tells us to "detect, watch, and trust [our] own intuitions" and "speak with authority" (*CC*, 136). He suggests that trusting one's own light and expressing it is the "moral" condition of criticism; it is prior to intellectual criticism. To be moral here means to exercise the "courage first to think and then to think out loud" (135–36). Dewey reminds us that this is not the province of an aggressive, argumentative self; rather, it is a kind of self-reliance that is made possible by finding one's own language. To borrow Cavell's phrase in EMP, it is "authorship" of "my constitution."[10]

To further this line of thinking, Dewey in *Art as Experience* says that the "reeducation" of aesthetic perception and imagination is a key to recovering drained energy and the creative drive to live forward, to experience again the "wonder and splendor of this world.[11] Education that serves human perfection is re-envisioned now as an endeavour to release our impulses through expression and action. It is found in a critical rhythm whose receptive, passive phases give way not to aggressive self-assertion but to a recovery of voice; this enables us to transcend the current boundaries of our experience.

Something of what is at stake in aesthetic experience—one that creates the moment of conversion in the ordinary—is suggested for Dewey by comments of the artist W. H. Hudson, whose remarks he links with Emerson:

> As to absorption of the esthetic in nature, I cite a case duplicated in some measure in thousands of persons, but notable because expressed by an artist of the first order, W. H. Hudson. "I feel when I am out of sight of living, growing grass, and out of the sound of birds' voices and all rural sounds, that I am not properly alive." He goes on to say, ". . . when I hear people say that they have not found the world and life so agreeable and interesting as to be in love with it, or that they look with equanimity to its end, I am apt to think that they have never been properly alive, nor seen with clear vision the world they think so meanly of or anything in it—not even a blade of grass." The mystic aspect of acute esthetic, that renders it so akin as an experience to what religionists term ecstatic communion, is recalled by Hudson from his boyhood life. He is speaking of the effect the sight of acacia trees had upon him. "The loose feathery foliage on moonlight nights had a peculiar hoary aspect that made this tree seem more in-

tensely alive than others, more conscious of me and of my presence . . . Similar to a feeling a person would have if visited by a supernatural being if he was perfectly convinced that it was there in his presence, albeit silent and unseen, intently regarding him and divining every thought in his mind." Emerson as an adult said, quite in the spirit of the passage quoted from Hudson: "Crossing a bare common, in snow puddles, at twilight, under a clouded sky, without having in my thought any occurrence of special good fortune, I have enjoyed a perfect exhilaration. I am glad to the brink of fear." (*AE*, 35)

If there is some intimation of a Wordsworthian pantheism here, not least in the adjacency of exhilaration and fear, at times there is also in this text the suggestion of "emotion recollected in tranquillity"(75). Dewey makes clear that the immediacy of experience initially suggested by Hudson's words is something recalled from "boyhood life." Art is the province not of an exuberant, animal absorption in the world but of its recollection, and that recollection is necessary— perhaps is made possible—because of an intermediate loss. We lose our early vitality when we live in the mode of abandoning the present to the past and future in apprehensions (24–25). We subside in apathy, torpor, and indifference, and then the shell is built around us and within us: we have mouths, but cannot express; we have eyes, but cannot see; we have ears, but cannot hear (109–110). It is blindness to or forgetfulness of these unhandsome conditions that we must keep resisting. The enemies of a union of form and matter spring from our own limitations, which acquiesce too easily in the extinguishing of the gleam of light: "They spring from apathy, conceit, self-pity, tepidity, fear, convention, routine, from the factors that obstruct, deflect and prevent vital interaction of the live creature with the environment in which he exists" (138). This learned apathy, the blindness in which we persist, then (wrongly) seeks from art either transient excitement or "medicinal solace." In contrast, the clarification and concentration effected through art is an intensification that constitutes new experience. As Dewey puts this, "Art celebrates with particular intensity the moments in which the past reinforces the present and in which the future is a quickening of what now is" (24).

This is an intensification that involves sometimes a newfound sense of the ordinary and sometimes rare adventure. But whatever direction the art work pursues, its intensification revivifies the sense of being fully alive in the here and now, "the power to experience the common world in its fullness" (138). The burden that the past can inflict on us in regret, and the weight of the future felt in apprehension, can then be transformed into a "storehouse of resources by which to move confidently forward." Thus, "[e]very living experience owes its richness to what Santayana called 'hushed reverberations'" (23). In a footnote to these words, Dewey cites a passage from George Eliot's *The Mill on the Floss*:

> These familiar flowers, these well-remembered bird-notes, this sky with its fitful brightness, these furrowed and grassy fields, each with a sort of personality given to it by the capricious hedge, such things as these are the mother-tongue of our imagination, the language that is laden with all the subtle inextricable associations the fleeting hours of our childhood left behind them. Our delight in the sunshine on the deep-bladed grass to-day might be no more than the faint perception of wearied souls, if it were not for the sunshine and grass of far-off years, which still live in us and transform our perception into love. (23–24)

The hushed reverberations that sound through this passage justify the emphasised prefix that has marked the language of this essay: Dewey calls for a continuing *re*-education in the name of a *re*-awakening of the intensity of impulse that we have lost, a *re*membering of the light that is always under threat of being extinguished. Growth as perfection and democracy to be attained require the cultivation of this poignant sense of imperfection. Furthermore, this is the re-education not only—perhaps not primarily—of the young but of adults in order that they should transcend their existing circles, in order that they should, as McDermott says with Dewey, "experience the world in all of its potential intensity."[12] Experience and perception have always, on Dewey's account, been characterised by their temporal structure, but here this acquires a deeper and somewhat darker, indeed tragic, resonance: they are transformed in an intensity attained and still to be attained. Dewey says that peace and courage are obtained only "in the midst of effort," only "in action not after."[13]

In the project of reconstructing Dewey's pragmatism in the light of EMP, his aesthetic turn points to reconsidering the meaning of intelligence—the allegedly narrow concept of intelligence associated with its scientific method of problem-solving—in the broader terms of "creative intelligence" (*AE*, 351). It is a kind of intelligence that integrates the spiritual and aesthetic dimensions of human nature, symbolized by the gleam of light, as prophetic energy for continual perfecting. In other words, creative intelligence is the "arts of living" (339): intelligence through which we live in affirmative energy *despite* the tragic human condition. This resonates with Emerson's "onward thinking," as Cavell calls it.[14] From another perspective, the notion of creative intelligence is the culmination of Dewey's project of joining art and science that he presents in *Experience and Nature*.[15]

The aesthetic experience that Dewey describes here might be called the process of internal transformation—what Emerson calls the "total character" of the "metamorphosis" involved in the "growths of genius" ("OS," 155–56). This represents Emerson's notion of self-transcendence. It is not mysticism, otherworldly spiritualism, or selfish individualism but rather a strong ethic of self-reliance as a *social* morality, a morality that resists the tragic loss of the gleam of light. The foremost task of Emersonian education is to awaken the lost gleam of light, to become a "hero who is immovably centered."[16] Yet this centeredness is not a form of hedonism; instead, it aims for a thorough confrontation with one's self in order to reclaim one's natural proclivity, symbolized by the gleam of light. As Cavell says, in EMP individuation and socialization are inseparable: before "the process of individuation," he writes, "there are no individuals, hence no humanity, hence, no society" (*Conditions*, 11). Individuation requires the concrete other in the here and now—the other, as Emerson says, who returns to us "our own rejected thoughts" and the other who reminds us of our lost light ("SR," 131). This revisits Emerson's idea of friendship. As Cavell says, "we need not, we should not, take

[Emerson] to imagine himself as achieving a further state of humanity in himself alone" (*Conditions*, 11).

In a process of thorough individuation, the self, in encountering its own limitations with the other, learns to transcend the existing boundary, and acquires, so to speak, the standpoint of otherness within and without the self. Emerson's transcendental perspective of the gleam of light enables us envision our "I" from the "third" standpoint, the "Over-Soul, within which every man's particular being is contained and made one with all other." In "the soul of the whole, we transcend private interests ("OS," 153). This is the condition of human perfection and fullest happiness. In its quest for "impersonality" (157)—what is beyond the self—Emerson's transcendentalism is universalist in its ethical standpoint; at the same time it does not diffuse personality. As Cavell interprets this, unlike Kant's notion of a noumenal self in connection with the idea of "selflessness," in EMP "partiality" never disappears (*Conditions*, xxxiv). In this dual structure, one central aim of education for the gleam of light is to overcome the apparently contradictory elements of human nature—an inclination toward strong self-centeredness and the aspiration toward the whole, beyond a narrow egocentrism. Emerson fully acknowledges this dilemma as "fate"—the natural law that "[w]e can only obey our own polarity."[17] His "Over-Soul" is anything but a pre-existing metaphysical or immortal realm that guarantees peaceful harmony from the beginning; rather, it is the common, universal state that humans continuously struggle to build from within their fated partiality. In Emerson's and Dewey's process-oriented perfectionism, conversion takes place not once and for all, but here and now, again and again.

Self-transcendence, Emerson suggests, is made possible with the art of detachment. This implies a manner of living in which: "I desire and look up and put myself in the attitude of reception, but from some alien energy the visions come" ("OS," 210). In *The Senses of Walden*, Cavell finds, as implied by the imagery of circles, a key to converting the loss of one's way to "onward thinking" in "abandonment" and "leaving," power is derived from "crossing, or rather leaping." This is both fate and freedom—a hope that is found in our possibility and capacity to leave the state of loss and poverty (*Senses*, 136–37). Referring to Thoreau's celebrated expression of this in *Walden*, Cavell says that leaving is "the transfiguration of mourning as grief into morning as dawn." In Emerson and Thoreau, this experience of ecstasy does not resolve mourning all at once but continues to be "part of the *work* of mourning."[18] It is through this work of mourning that one's prophetic voice is cultivated. The possibility that we can always depart again from within loss, by "bearing pain," is the ground of Emerson's hope. In EMP freedom is found in this critical moment of leaving, leaving made possible by the power of prophesy and creation. Dewey also suggests that such a manner of living is learned from aesthetic experience: "'Detachment' is a negative name for something extremely positive. There is no severance of self, no holding of it aloof, but fullness of participation" (*AE*, 262). Art enables us to transcend our habitual framework of thinking and ways of seeing, to "forget ourselves by finding ourselves in the delight of experiencing the world about us in its varied qualities and forms" (11).[19]

The courage to detach oneself from one's previous state and existing framework of thinking—oftentimes in the sorrowful state of the gleam of light being lost—is a key to creating a new path in expanding circles without negating the past trajectories of life. Dewey suggests the image in the expression "recurrence with difference" (173). The way of living in detachment also implies the courage to open oneself to the potential in the evolving universe, the courage to receive the otherness of the world that endlessly transcends one's existing knowledge. Then, as Nietzsche says with Emerson, the moment visits us with "bright sparks of the fire of love in whose light we cease to understand the word, 'I,' as something beyond our being."[20] Emerson's transcendentalism offers a standpoint that encourages us to overcome the fatal entanglement of individualization and socialization that is ever present on the path of human perfection. From the detached standpoint of life, care for one's self and others will become inseparable. Emersonian perfectionist education may sound like a political approach, but it presents a way toward political life through, as it were, the internal route—a route through which the personal and the public are progressively joined. The ethical, the aesthetic, and the spiritual are preconditions of the political.

Toward Emersonian Perfectionist Education

But how can Deweyan growth after Emerson and Cavell offer the language and theory of perfectionist education in service to the gleam of light? How can educators incorporate this other invisible, but essential route of spiritual and aesthetic education into the existing practice and discourse of democracy and education? How can we defend it from the expected charge of selfish individualism, from an apolitical, amoral, or narcissistic theory of self-creation, or from the romanticization of childhood? And most challengingly, how can Emersonian perfectionist education show, in sensible language, that the life of perfection without final perfectibility is needed today precisely because we live in the age without any grand telos?

Deweyan and Emersonian perfectionist education can contribute to the reconsideration and recreation of the language of education, hence, our ways of seeing the world. The language of education is at present dominated by a debased jargon of economics ("the bottom line" and "competitiveness") and technology ("teaching as a technology"), with the emphasis on performance targets, efficiency, and effectiveness. Such discourse is most typically found in the language of *excellence* and *standards* in connection with academic performance and achievement. Contemporary attempts to raise standards tend to take reductive, positivistic forms based upon a firm belief in definite criteria. Such a belief is illustrated by language used in educational policy—framed, as these are, by behavioristic objectives and clearly itemized achievement goals, conjoined incongruously with the language of higher moral ideals. Such a language of education is a thin and misleading abstraction from the real experience of teachers and students.

Dewey's aesthetic idea of directive criteria can point us away from such a fixed conceptualiztion of criteria, and by so doing realize an alternative understanding of excellence and standards. In his pragmatist concept of the good as the better, Dewey shows us that a *search* for excellence and standards is at the heart of human perfection. Criteria for excellence are not merely handed down from the past or uncritically derived from the prevailing culture; neither can they be imparted from above. Instead measurement in itself must be grounded in an endeavor of raising excellence and standards in the ongoing interaction among teachers, students, parents, and policy makers, involving their live voices in engagement with their daily struggles. It is a cooperative project of mutual perfection, involving the creation and revision of criteria. Since growth as perfection is an endless, ongoing process, a careful attention to the visible and invisible processes of this particular growth, especially to the crucial moment of the rebirth of prophetic light, is required for a teacher in interacting with her students. Such teaching requires an eye to spiritual transformation, to a "movement of the soul" impossible to measure by "impartial" or "objective" test scores. Growth can be "measured" only by the step that the student now takes, by her voice that now speaks, and by the power of her words. The intensity of the light is not metered. It is the total weight and quality of the life as a whole; we can perceive and communicate it only in approximation.

The classroom must then become a place to cultivate the art of patient listening and imaginative seeing in resistance to the incessant threat of blindness to, and suppression of, internal light. It is only then that students and teachers come to acquire the sense of responsibility to their own words and to learn what it means to join the "city of words" (*Conditions*, 8). Dewey, with Emerson, would argue that hope for education is justifiable not by any fixed, absolute ground, but by the way—on the way—of living. Here the "ground" of justification is achieved through the creation of words in dialogue. Following Emersonian perfectionist education, the classroom must in some sense become the forum for a mutual finding of inner light, through awakening and remembrance. The classroom is a place, to borrow Cavell's phrase, for "autobiographical exercises."[21] But finding one's light is something more than a merely verbal formula, or than the assertion of one's position in the name of social justice. Unlike the typical orientation of narrative education, inclined toward nostalgia and sometimes a kind of *ressentiment*, and often ending up with a romanticizing of one's tragic sense, the focus of Emerson's and Dewey's perfectionist education is on the drawing out of creative energy by transcending the tragic. As a patient acquiring of the sense of trust in one's own voice, it ranges over and permeates such diverse aspects of the curriculum as history or literature, multicultural education, education for global understanding, and citizenship education, as well as the daily interactions of teachers and students.

Dewey's idea of the art of communication is a good starting point in considering how to create an environment for mutual perfection. In *Democracy and Education* he presents the view that communication is the condition of growth. He says that "communication insures participation in a common understanding" (*DE*, 7) and that "[c]onsensus demands communication" (8). In his later writing during the 1920s and 1930s he develops the idea that communication is not simply a matter of skill or means, but rather an *art* for creating a democratic community (*PP*, 350). Along these lines, in "Creative Democracy: The Task Before Us" (1938), he introduces the idea of "friendship" as a condition of creative democracy :

> [D]emocracy as a way of life is controlled by personal faith in personal day-by-day working together with others. Democracy is the belief that even when needs and ends or consequences are different for each individual, the habit of amicable cooperation—which may include, as in sport, rivalry and competition—is itself a priceless addition to life. To take as far as possible every conflict which arises—and they are bound to arise—out of the atmosphere and medium of force, of violence as a means of settlement into that of discussion and of intelligence is to treat those who disagree—even profoundly—with us as those from whom we may learn, and in so far, as friends . . . To cooperate by giving differences a chance to show themselves because of the belief that the expression of difference is not only a right of the other persons but is a means of enriching one's own life-experience, is inherent in the democratic personal way of life. ("CD," 228)

Here he makes it clear that the notion of "friends" touches upon a dimension of our moral life that precedes the political concept of "right." It is also tied to the process of mutual education. In *Art as Experience* (1934), he makes it clearer that friendship and conversation are "arts of living":

> Friendship and intimate affection are not the result of information about another person even though knowledge may further their formation. But it does so only as it becomes an integral part of sympathy through the imagination. It is when the desires and aims, the interests and modes of response of another become an expansion of our own being that we understand him. We learn to see with his eyes, hear with his ears, and their results give true instruction, for they are built into our own structure. (*AE*, 339)

Conversation among friends involves more than the understanding of the other as the object of knowledge, or framing the other in one's own perspective. Rather it is the matter of mutual learning by being attentive to the different other. Openness to the difference of others means the reception of the other's life as a part of one's own structure of thought.[22] It provides a momentum to release oneself toward what is beyond the self.

While the Deweyan art of communication and conversation among friends can provide teachers and students with a key to achieving education for global understanding from within the classroom, a challenge still remains. Garrison cites a passage from *Democracy and Education,* in which Dewey identifies the need for "breaking down barriers of class, race, and national territory which kept men from perceiving the full import of their activity."[23] A challenge to education in these nihilistic times is how to make possible the transformative experience of breaking down the rigidities of one's framework of thinking through the opening of one's eyes and ears to the faces and voices of different others. In response to this challenge, I would like to make an Emersonian move and extend the Deweyan notion of the art of communication into *the art of translation*— translation as a specific mode of communication that at once highlights the gap between languages and is driven by the hope of creating a common ground of conversation.

The art of translation is crucially related to the idea of *poiesis*. In his aesthetic turn Dewey suggests that the education of the poet is a condition of democracy—where poetry is not the activity of an exclusive group of talented individuals, but is the possibility in each of us of our finding our own language as founders of democracy. This is a return to a vision he presented as early as in 1903 when he praised Emerson as the poet-philosopher of democracy.[24] Dewey says, with Matthew Arnold, that "poetry is criticism of life." Poets are "moral prophets" who, in their prophetic lights, and in their imaginative power, let us envision the world anew (*AE*, 350). With Keats, he claims that, not by disputing or asserting but by "whispering," poetry exercises its power of transformation through disclosure (349). Poetry is critical and moral because its function is to "remove prejudice, do away with the scales that keep the eye from seeing, tear away the veils due to want and custom, perfect the power to perceive" (328). The prophetic and projective power exercised by the poet initiates a break. Dewey suggests that the education of the poet in each of us is a condition for perfecting democracy from within. Dewey places Emersonian perfectionist education at the intersection of the political, the aesthetic, and the moral, even the "religious."[25]

Emerson elaborates on *poiesis* as the art of word- and world-making (and re-making), an initiation of the transformation of the self and its relationship to the world. In his words, it is a "metre-making": "it is not metres, but a metre-making argument that makes a poem—a thought so passionate and alive that like the spirit of a plant or an animal it has an architecture of its own, and adorns nature with a new thing."[26] The poet, he says, witnesses a "metamorphosis" ("Poet," 205). Taking one step further, Emerson shows us that the prophetic and transforming power of the poet is related to the art of translation: "The experience of poetic creativeness [is] not found in staying at home, nor yet in traveling, but in transitions from one to the other."[27] This communicates to us the sense of transition and traveling involved in the activity of metre-making. In this patient act, poetry exercises its power of resistance—to conformity and to comfortable complacency. He describes poets as "liberating gods" who help men find "within their world, another world, or nest of worlds" ("Poet," 209). They are translators of nature into thought (211) who "re-attach things to nature and the Whole" (204). By doing so, they help us transcend our habitual ways of seeing the world, emancipate us from the "prison" of our thoughts, and make possible a "metamorphosis" (209). Serving as a translator and interpreter between men and the world, the poet produces "the best success in conversation, the magic of liberty" (210). The poet starts at home, but does not stay there. He perseveres *in the in-between*, in transition from one place to another. Unlike Dewey, Emerson brings us deeper into the nature of poetic language in his own poetic voice. The key to poetry's liberation and metamorphosis lies in its power of *trans*ition, *trans*lation, and *trans*cendence, what Emerson describes as the *trans*itory nature of language. The boundaries of the poet's language are always being reformulated and expanded—breaking the ground for founding. In Emerson's discursive circles, Poirier says, "at every moment there is movement with no place to rest."[28] Harold Bloom calls Emerson the "American Gnosis," the writer who discontinuously breaks into the aboriginal absence, the Abyss, and thus, who continuously creates a new voice[29] Bloom asserts that for Emerson "[p]ower is an affair of crossings, of thresholds or transitional moments" and that "[p]ower is in the traversing of the black holes of rhetoric." In each act of breaking and throwing oneself "forward" into the realm of the absence, one finds his voice in the "Newness."[30] Emerson tells us that the poet cannot stay within the existing categories of language and states of mind, but constantly has to move outward ("Poet," 205).

Emersonian perfectionist education requires translation in a broader sense than the experience of self-transcendence. As a mediator between two parties whose worlds are mutually alien at the outset, the translator needs to travel from one place to another and then travel back again. In search of the shared areas of language and culture, she struggles to redefine the still indefinite boundary of one language in the light of another. Like the Emersonian poet, a translator must have the courage to persevere in the face of uncertainty, searching gradually for a common focus through which both parties to the dialogue can perceive the world again and, with luck, can transform their mutual identities. This often involves the poet's suffering from a sense of her own anonymity. But she knows that it is not by disputes, aggressive persuasion, problem-solving, or moral impeachment, but through the mode of mutual learning that the common may be found within diversity. In this process she must accept the impossibility of a perfect translation in order to find some common focus and to narrow the initial difference. Different voices invite us to start again from the lack of common ground by reminding us of the impossibility of full articulation, understanding, and translation. Those who have the experience of studying and living abroad undergo this sense of imperfect translation between two cultures—of crossing distances and sometimes of falling into an abyss. Dewey states that "democracy must begin at home" (*PP*, 368). The experience of a translator points us beyond this remark: we must unsettle ourselves and leave home to find home again.

Thus, if Dewey's idea of the art of communication is developed into translation, diverse educational implications can be seen. For example, something of the experience of leaving home can be created in the foreign language classroom, without going abroad. Cultivating the awareness of difference and distance is a precondition for the teaching of foreign language as the art of translation. If students are encouraged to study a foreign language with a sense of the impossibility both of full translation and of perfect understanding, the very experience of difficulty may cultivate in them a drive for further perfection in their understanding of unknowable others, at the same time as a recognition of its impossibility. This approach unsettles the naive assumption that a foreign language is simply a different code for saying the same thing, realizing at the same time a kind of humility in relation to others.

Similarly, education for global understanding can benefit from the wisdom of Emersonian perfectionist education. When we face a gap as we encounter the other, we encounter Dewey's words anew; there is no occasion for mutual learning if we leave the gap untouched and stay safely within our separate homes or appeal to our "genuine" ideal in an attitude of self-righteousness and complacency. We cannot simply resort to a utopian vision of a global community as if the distance created by difference were merely a temporal source of insecurity, uncertainty, or even an evil to be got rid of. Both modes of life entail the danger of obliviousness, and even violence, to the lives of different others. Instead, if we follow the path of Deweyan democracy, we will start in the midst of ambiguity and groundlessness (which can become the source of further inquiry); we will gain distance in our thinking and gradually narrow the existing gap to work toward common ground. For Deweyan democracy reconstructed in the light of EMP, what is common is not pregiven but something to be realized in the process of searching; it is always on the way, in the process of becoming, but never finally perfected.

In a world into which the tragic continually and inevitably enters, perfectionist education offers another way of living with the tragic beyond the absolute distinction between good and evil, or right and wrong. Emerson, Dewey, and Cavell together suggest a way of education that can enable us to overcome the tragic that is not mired in the negativity of revenge or retaliation. The lesson of perfectionist education is indeed the art of transcendence, the pragmatic search for the better through patient dialogue as the most practical, intelligent means to live with suffering and to convert it to hope. By preparing a ground for dialogue among conflicting values and religions, the transcendental standpoint of mutual perfection serves the conversation of mankind.

Citizenship education also can be reconsidered in terms of the art of translation. In resistance to our fated drive toward totality—assimilation of the unfamiliar into the familiar and toward disclosure, and articulation of the unknown in the name of public participation and social inclusion—Deweyan democracy, combined with Emersonian perfectionist education, offers an alternative understanding of citizenship education: education with a tragic sense. Here the experience of translation is crucial to creating a breathing space for the ineffable and anonymous part of a human being. The presence of the anonymous can be a disturbing factor within a culture, and the acknowledgment of the unknown calls for the courage to reach out and welcome it. This is an education that encourages the gleam of light of the dissident and that starts with the sense of homelessness. The resuscitation of culture awaits the prophetic light of the alien. Here the art of translation is a precondition for the epistemological and cognitive understanding of different others, and an integral element of our moral life. It prepares a form of citizenship where an ethical obligation precedes equality and the politics of mutual recognition.[31] The perspective of the gleam of light has shown that "understanding" of the other and "mutual recognition" require as their precondition the aesthetic perception into the quality of the human life as a whole: they require seeing the unseen and the unknown.

Furthermore, education for the gleam of light in Emersonian *moral* perfectionism reconceptualizes morality itself. It presents an alternative, far-reaching ethic of education beyond existing limitations, especially those limitations that are posed by teleological conceptions of moral or religious education. The standpoint of mutual perfection extends the reach of Dewey's theory of the social self not only toward the ethic of care and otherness but also toward the ethics of self-reliance and self-transcendence. This is an ethics that is built not on the perspective of the "I" of the self isolated from the world, or on that of the "I" of the autonomous, rational self, but on the "I" of what Dewey envisions in "I Believe" as the individual self that is *a center in the field* ("IB," 91). This is light that illuminates the whole.[32]

With its emphasis on an encounter with one's singularity through the "pain of individuation" as much as with the joy of communion, Emersonian perfectionist education encourages the cultivation of *self-knowledge* among teachers and students, but only in the way of acquiring the standpoint of otherness within and without one's self—in order to undergo the "incessant want of knowledge" (*Tears*, 22). This requires an openness to unforeseen possibilities and the aspiration toward further perfections of the self, but this is not to be understood, still less to be realized, in any self-conscious self-aggrandizement, still less in any narcissism. Rather it is realized in self-transcendence through an immersion in those challenges that confrontation with the other presents—confrontations with the demands of other people but also with those difficulties in (the otherness of) what is taught. In the encounter with one's limitations, the energy for the affirmation of life is released through mutual illumination and intensification.

The perspective of mutual perfection transcends conventional boundaries in the moral concepts of egoism and altruism, of autonomy and heteronomy, and in debates between virtue ethics of care and universalistic moral reasoning. The mediation of these divisions through perfectionist education is not achieved without courage, to be sure: "the courage to be what you are" is an idea that Cavell finds running through Emerson to Nietzsche (*Pitch*, 35), and that Dewey appropriates from Emerson in *Construction and Criticism*. Such courage, from the perspective of mutual perfection, implies the self's courage to receive and respond to the unknowability of the other, and the courage to open oneself to the potential of the evolving universe, the courage to receive the otherness of the world endlessly transcending one's existing knowledge. In education for mutual perfection, such courage cannot be taught as a moral imperative, an isolated item of virtue, or a trait of character, as the telos on which moral education is grounded and toward which it should be directed. There are many occasions when moral imperatives, such as the call for courage, open-mindedness, or sympathy, lose their purchase on our lives, as if the grounds of morality that those concepts have seemed to secure are shaken, as if they falter and abandon us. It is then that we face the limitation of moral concepts as the object of knowledge, and that we become aware of the need to come face to face with ourselves and with the other in the here and now.

The Rekindling of the Gleam of Light

Starting, in "Experience," with the skeptical question, "WHERE do we find ourselves?" Emerson concludes his essay with a scene of awakening:

I am at first apprised of my vicinity to a new and excellent region of life. By persisting to read or to think, this region gives further sign of itself, as it were in flashes of light, in sudden discoveries of its profound beauty and repose.³³

This is the moment of the rebirth. This internal transformation is crucially related, Emerson claims, to the consummatory and ecstatic moment of aesthetic experience—the moment of conversion when, in the flash of light, one re-encounters the intensity and depth of life. It is the moment of turning away from the darkness to the light, of seeing oneself and the world in a new light.

The imagery that has been elaborated in this book has served to evoke the vision of a Deweyan-Emersonian perfectionist education. We have seen that the gleam of light is the symbol of aesthetic and spiritual impulses, of being and becoming; it implies the inventive combination of the spiritual and the natural, the transcendental and the pragmatic; and it is crucially related to the experience of internal transformation. It enables a new appreciation of the role of impulse (its prophetic and imaginative power now evident) as the spur and driving force of creative intelligence. Yet this light is plainly not the forceful, unremitting illumination of the sun: it defies any easy optimism. We have been moved beyond the conventional framework of "Dewey between Hegel and Darwin." At the same time, in the three-sided dialogue between Emerson, Dewey, and Cavell, Emerson's thought has been reclaimed as social and democratic philosophy.

To assert the spiritual and aesthetic turn in Deweyan growth is in no way to deny its social philosophy. As Dewey later restates, it is a shifting of attention in order to shed a new light on the role of an individual, say, a private, dimension of democracy; rebuilding the public by beginning at home. The individual redeemed by the gleam of light is a manifestation of the new individualism Dewey envisions. Yet the spiritual and aesthetic turn in no way points us to the secluded or isolated individual: this is not the self in contemplation. In Deweyan-Emersonian perfectionist education, the rekindling of the gleam of light requires an encounter with the other(s). The experience of morning suggested by Emerson in the above passage is our re-turn to the otherness of the world, turning away from our captivity in the cave, whether or not we are alone there. Aesthetic and spiritual experience also lays the way for the criticism of the self and society as a precondition of the political. As Dewey says, "criticism, self-criticism, is the road to [the] release of [creative activity]" (*CC*, 143). Self-transcendence through self-criticism takes place in the common world, in the ordinary, and it does this not once, but again and again. This is the philosophy of continuous departure—a philosophy that acknowledges a space for the infinite and the unknown, and that resists our fated drive toward assimilation into totality.

At the heart of Deweyan-Emersonian perfectionist education must be the rekindling of the gleam of light, but it must do this starting from a state of loss. The specific loss we suffer today is the state of nihilism in democracy and education, the state in which the sense of what is beyond, the sense of otherness, and the sense of the whole, have been obliterated. Dewey and Emerson, however, give us hope that we shall be able to experience the moment of conversion in self-transcendence. Conscientious and devoted educators, as well as many young people who have lost their way, await such flashes of illumination—irradiating from a source that they have perhaps not yet seen but that they wish, or can be led to wish, or in any case need to see.

At the start of the twenty-first century we cannot merely rely on progress. We cannot simply start with the presumption of light. As Dewey once said, "Progress [is] not necessarily an advance and, practically never an advance in all respects" (*AE*, 216). Neither should we think of progress as in simple contrast to the reactionary turn to the past. Such dichotomous thinking will obscure the subtle light that dawns on the horizon. Hence we need to transcend any conventional boundary between, for example, "Traditional vs. Progressive Education" (*EE*, 17), as Dewey put this in 1938, or between moral absolutism and relativism, say, or for that matter between political liberalism and communitarianism. Instead we will do better to reconsider *liberal learning*: learning as a patient process of liberating human impulse from within, through our engagement with culture, tradition, and texts. In other words, EMP works as an intermediary and interdisciplinary force that permeates all dimensions of education—whether it involves human relationships between teachers and students in the classroom, or diverse realms of the curriculum.

With these implications for contemporary democracy and education, Deweyan growth can reemerge as holistic growth—growth toward a whole, with the irruption of departure and loss. Growth is the infinite process of self-overcoming in expanding circles. It is precisely because we cannot simply rely on progress any more that we need Dewey's Emersonian prophetic pragmatism, the philosophy of endless growth in our attained and unattained perfection. This alerts us to the prevailing instrumentalism with its emphasis on skills and its reduction of knowledge to information—a form of assimilation into totality that incessantly deprives us of the intensity of the gleam of light. Moreover, Deweyan progressivism, reconstructed as Emersonian perfectionist education, is not for childhood alone: it is a lifelong process of perfection. Perfectionist education for the liberation of human potential makes possible a democracy attained yet unattained, our best hope. This involves transcendence from within: only by pursuing a passage from the innermost to the outmost can the light one lives by be hoped eventually to illuminate the public world.[34]

Notes

CHAPTER ONE
IN SEARCH OF LIGHT IN DEMOCRACY AND EDUCATION
Deweyan Growth in an Age of Nihilism

1. Ralph Waldo Emerson, "American Scholar," in *Ralph Waldo Emerson*, ed. Richard Poirier (Oxford: Oxford University Press, 1990), 41.

2. John Dewey, *The Public and Its Problems* in *The Later Works of John Dewey*, vol. 2, ed. Jo Ann Boydston (Carbondale: Southern Illinois University Press, 1984), 311–12.

3. John Dewey, *Construction and Criticism*, in *The Later Works of John Dewey*, vol. 5, ed. Jo Ann Boydston (Carbondale: Southern Illinois University Press, 1984), 133.

4. John Dewey, *Individualism Old and New*, in *The Later Works of John Dewey*, vol. 5, ed. Jo Ann Boydston (Carbondale: Southern Illinois University Press, 1984), 81 (hereafter cited as *ION*).

5. John Dewey, "Creative Democracy—The Task Before Us," in *The Later Works of John Dewey*, vol. 14, ed. Jo Ann Boydston (Carbondale: Southern Illinois University Press, 1988).

6. Tadashi Nishihira and René Vincent Arcilla, "Nihilism and Education" (symposium held at the University of Tokyo, 21 July 1999); Nigel Blake, Paul Smeyers, Richard Smith, and Paul Standish, *Education in an Age of Nihilism* (London: Routledge-Falmer, 2000).

7. John Dewey, *Democracy and Education*, in *The Middle Works of John Dewey*, vol. 9, ed. Jo Ann Boydston (Carbondale: Southern Illinois University Press, 1980), 338 (hereafter cited as *DE*).

8. Stanley Cavell, *Conditions Handsome and Unhandsome: The Constitution of Emersonian Perfectionism* (La Salle, IL: Open Court, 1990).

9. Ralph Waldo Emerson, "Self-Reliance," in *Ralph Waldo Emerson*, ed. Richard Poirier (Oxford: Oxford University Press, 1990), 131.

10. John Dewey, *Experience and Education* (New York: Macmillan, 1938), 35.

11. Boyd H. Bode, *Progressive Education at the Crossroads* (New York: Newson, 1938), 82–85.

12. I. L. Kandel, *The Cult of Uncertainty* (New York: Macmillan, 1943), 6–7, 30–31.

13. Randolph Bourne, "Twilight of Idols," in *The Radical Will: Selected Writings 1911–1918*, ed. Olaf Hansen (Berkeley: University of California, 1977), 343–44.

14. Allan Bloom, *The Closing of the American Mind* (New York: A Touch Stone Book, 1987), 29–30, 56.

15. John Patrick Diggins, *The Promise of Pragmatism: Modernism and the Crisis of Knowledge and Authority* (Chicago: University of Chicago Press, 1994), 305–21.

16. For example, Japanese moral education has recently taken a conservative turn. In this context Yutaka Okihara criticizes liberal, progressive education for creating an "excessively tolerant society" and the moral decline of youth both in Japan and America (Yutaka Okihara, *Shin Kokoro no Kyoiku* [*New Education of the Heart*], Tokyo: Gakuyo-Shobo, 1997).

17. George Santayana's critique of the "genteel tradition" of American philosophy criticizes optimism and progressivism in American thought (*The Genteel Tradition: Nine Essays by George Santayana*, ed. Douglas L. Wilson [Lincoln: University of Nebraska Press, 1967]).

18. Bourne, "Twilight of Idols," 338–39, 341–43.

19. Richard Hofstadter, *Anti-Intellectualism in American Life* (New York: Alfred A. Knopf, 1963), 386–88.

20. Steven C. Rockefeller, *John Dewey: Religious Faith and Democratic Humanism* (New York: Columbia University Press, 1991), 486–87

21. Cornel West, *The American Evasion of Philosophy: A Genealogy of Pragmatism* (Madison: University of Wisconsin Press, 1989), 101.

22. Raymond D. Boisvert, "The Nemesis of Necessity: Tragedy's Challenge to Deweyan Pragmatism," in *Dewey Reconfigured*, ed. Casey Haskins and David I. Seiple (Albany: State University of New York Press, 1999), 157-63.

23. Richard Rorty, *Philosophy and the Mirror of Nature* (Princeton: Princeton University Press, 1979); *Truth and Progress: Philosophical Papers*, (Cambridge: Cambridge University Press, 1998).

24. The contrast between philosophies of totality and philosophies of infinity is drawn most powerfully by Emmanuel Levinas. For a succinct expression of this, see especially: Emmanuel Levinas, *Collected Philosophical*

Papers, trans. A. Lingis (Pittsburgh: Duquesne University Press, 1998), 48–49. A more elaborate account is, of course, worked out in his *Totality and Infinity: An Essay on Exteriority*, trans. A. Lingis (Pittsburgh: Duquesne University Press, 1969). I am grateful to Paul Standish for helping me to appreciate this way of understanding this limitation in Rorty's reading.

25. R. S. Peters, *John Dewey Reconsidered* (London: Routledge and Kegan Paul, 1977); Anthony O'Hear, *Father of Child-Centredness: John Dewey and the Ideology of Modern Education* (London: Centre for Policy Studies, 1991).

26. John Dewey, "Emerson—The Philosopher of Democracy," in *The Middle Works of John Dewey*, vol. 3, ed. Jo Ann Boydston (Carbondale: Southern Illinois University Press, 1977).

27. Hilary Putnam with Ruth Anna Putnam, "Education for Democracy," in *Words and Life*, ed. James Conant (Cambridge, MA: Harvard University Press, 1994), 223.

28. Stanley Cavell, *The Claim of Reason: Wittgenstein, Skepticism, Morality, and Tragedy* (Oxford: Oxford University Press, 1979), 125.

CHAPTER TWO
DEWEY BETWEEN HEGEL AND DARWIN

1. Richard Rorty, *Philosophy and the Mirror of Nature* (Princeton: Princeton University Press, 1979), 10, in Richard J. Bernstein, "The Resurgence of Pragmatism," *Social Research*, 59 (Winter 1992), 817.

2. John Dewey, *Democracy and Education*, in *The Middle Works of John Dewey*, vol. 9, ed. Jo Ann Boydston (Carbondale: Southern Illinois University Press, 1980), 4 (hereafter cited as *DE*).

3. Israel Scheffler, *Four Pragmatists: A Critical Introduction to Peirce, James, Mead and Dewey* (London: Routledge and Kegan Paul, 1974), 5, 118–19.

4. Steven C. Rockefeller, *John Dewey: Religious Faith and Democratic Humanism* (New York: Columbia University Press, 1991), 165.

5. John Dewey, *Psychology*, in *The Early Works of John Dewey*, vol. 2, ed. Jo Ann Boydston (Carbondale: Southern Illinois University Press, 1967), 358, cited in Robert B. Westbrook, *John Dewey and American Democracy* (Ithaca: Cornell University Press, 1991), 45.

6. John Dewey, *Reconstruction in Philosophy* (Boston: Beacon Press, 1920), 177 (hereafter cited as *RP*).

7. John Dewey, *Human Nature and Conduct*, in *The Middle Works of John Dewey*, vol. 14, ed. Jo Ann Boydston (Carbondale: Southern Illinois University Press, 1983) (hereafter cited as *HNC*).

8. John Dewey, *A Common Faith*, in *The Later Works of John Dewey*, vol. 9, ed. Jo Ann Boydston (Carbondale: Southern Illinois University Press, 1986), 38 (hereafter cited as *CF*).

9. John Dewey, *Experience and Education* (New York: Macmillan, 1938), 36 (hereafter cited as *EE*).

10. Sidney Hook, "John Dewey: Philosopher of Growth," *The Journal of Philosophy*, 56 (Dec. 1959): 1010–18.

11. John Dewey, *Ethics* (1932), in *The Later Works of John Dewey*, vol. 7, ed. Jo Ann Boydston (Carbondale: Southern Illinois University Press, 1985), 192.

12. John Dewey, *The Quest for Certainty*, in *The Later Works of John Dewey*, vol. 4, ed. Jo Ann Boydston (Carbondale: Southern Illinois University Press, 1984), 212.

13. John Dewey, *Experience and Nature*, in *The Later Works of John Dewey*, vol. 1, ed. Jo Ann Boydston (Carbondale: Southern Illinois University Press, 1981), 11.

14. John Dewey, "Anti-Naturalism in Extremis," in *The Later Works of John Dewey*, vol. 15, ed. Jo Ann Boydston (Carbondale: Southern Illinois University Press, 1989), 47–48 (hereafter cited as "Anti-Naturalism").

15. John Dewey, *Art as Experience*, in *The Later Works of John Dewey*, vol. 10, ed. Jo Ann Boydston (Carbondale: Southern Illinois University Press, 1987), 156.

16. Sidney Hook discusses an inseparable relationship between Dewey's naturalism and democracy (Sidney Hook, "Naturalism and Democracy," in *Naturalism and the Human Spirit*, ed. Yervant H. Krikorian [New York: Columbia University Press, 1944]).

17. John Dewey, "From Absolutism to Experimentalism," in *The Later Works of John Dewey*, vol. 5, ed. Jo Ann Boydston (Carbondale: Southern Illinois University Press, 1984), 154.

18. Scheffler, *Four Pragmatists*, 195.

19. Richard J. Bernstein, *John Dewey* (New York: Washington Square Press, 1966), 15.

20. Rockefeller, *John Dewey*, 217.

21. Alan Ryan, *John Dewey and the High Tide of American Liberalism* (New York: W. W. Norton, 1995), 93.

22. Russell B. Goodman, *American Philosophy and the Romantic Tradition* (Cambridge: Cambridge University Press, 1990), 96.

23. John Dewey, *Outlines of a Critical Theory of Ethics*, in *The Early Works of John Dewey*, vol. 3, ed. Jo Ann Boydston (Carbondale: Southern Illinois University Press, 1969), cited by Hilary Putnam in his lecture, "Pragmatism

and Neo-Pragmatism" (lecture given at Harvard University, Cambridge, MA., 17 Apr. 2000), tape recording; also in Westbrook, *John Dewey and American Democracy*, 62.

24. John Dewey, *Ethics* (1908), in *The Middle Works of John Dewey*, vol. 5, ed. Jo Ann Boydston (Carbondale: Southern Illinois University Press, 1978), 286 (hereafter cited as *E1908*).

25. John Dewey, *The Public and Its Problems*, in *The Later Works of John Dewey*, vol. 2, ed. Jo Ann Boydston (Carbondale: Southern Illinois University Press, 1984), 328.

26. G. E. Moore, *Principia Ethica*, in *Ethics*, ed. Peter Singer (Oxford: Oxford University Press, 1994), 218–19.

27. W. K. Frankena, "The Naturalistic Fallacy," *Mind*, 48 (Oct. 1939): 464–77.

28. Charles Taylor, *Sources of the Self: The Making of the Modern Identity* (Cambridge, MA: Harvard University Press, 1989), 19–20, 48.

29. Bernard Williams, *Ethics and the Limits of Philosophy* (Cambridge, MA: Harvard University Press, 1985).

30. Morton White, "Is Ethics an Empirical Science?" in *Social Thought in America: The Revolt against Formalism* (New York: Viking Press, 1952), 212–19.

31. Walter Feinberg, "Dewey and Democracy: At the Dawn of the Twenty-First Century," *Educational Theory*, 43.2, 1993), 204.

32. Ryan, *John Dewey and the High Tide of American Liberalism*, 130. Ryan is especially doubtful of Dewey's "packing [of] human wishes and moral values into the 'environment,'" which Ryan associates with the struggle of survival (132).

33. Nel Noddings, "Thoughts on John Dewey's 'Ethical Principles Underlying Education,'" *The Elementary School Journal* 98 (May 1998): 485–87. In conversation, Noddings mentions that she is convinced that on non-moral matters, we can establish criteria by use of Dewey's method of intelligence, by testing and predicting consequences. She emphasizes, however, that she does not see how we can do this with all moral matters since "the question often is pressing whether we should seek certain outcomes." Therefore, she clarifies her position that her objection is not to missing criteria for growth, but to "missing a criterion for moral judgment" (my conversation with Noddings [Oct. 26, 1999]).

34. Rorty, *Philosophy and the Mirror of Nature*, 362.

35. Ibid., 292.

36. Richard Rorty, "Pragmatism as Romantic Polytheism," in *The Revival of Pragmatism: New Essays on Social Thought, Law, and Culture*, ed. Morris Dickstein (Durham, NC: Duke University Press, 1998), 31.

37. John Dewey, "Maeterlinck's Philosophy of Life," in *The Middle Works of John Dewey*, vol. 6, ed. Jo Ann Boydston (Carbondale: Southern Illinois University Press, 1978), cited in Rorty, "Romantic Polytheism," 32.

38. Rorty, "Romantic Polytheism," 32–34.

39. Richard Rorty, "Dewey between Hegel and Darwin," in *Truth and Progress: Philosophical Papers*, 3 (Cambridge: Cambridge University Press, 1998), 292.

40. Ibid., 305.

41. Ibid., 304.

42. John Dewey, cited in Rorty, "Dewey between Hegel and Darwin," 305.

43. Rorty, "Dewey between Hegel and Darwin," 297–98.

44. Cornel West, *The American Evasion of Philosophy: A Genealogy of Pragmatism* (Madison: University of Wisconsin Press, 1989), 96.

45. Richard Rorty, "Dewey's Metaphysics," in *Consequences of Pragmatism* (Minneapolis: University of Minnesota Press, 1982).

46. Ibid., 83–84.

47. Rorty, *Philosophy and the Mirror of Nature*, 379.

48. Ibid., 387.

49. I thank Hilary Putnam for helping me interpret the implication of this passage of Rorty's.

50. James Gouinlock, "What Is the Legacy of Instrumentalism? Rorty's Interpretation of Dewey," in *Rorty and Pragmatism: The Philosopher Responds to His Critics*, ed. Herman J. Saatkamp, Jr. (Nashville: Vanderbilt University Press, 1995), 87.

51. Ralph W. Sleeper, *The Necessity of Pragmatism: John Dewey's Conception of Philosophy* (New Haven: Yale University Press, 1986), 119.

52. Gouinlock, "What Is the Legacy of Instrumentalism?" 82–83, 86–87.

53. West, *The American Evasion of Philosophy*, 96.

54. Westbrook, *John Dewey and American Democracy*, 540–42. In response to Westbrook's criticism that Rorty dissipates "the general 'ground maps' that philosophers could provide," Rorty insists that Dewey's attempt to provide ground maps to human experience is futile (Rorty, "Dewey between Hegel and Darwin," 295).

55. Rorty, "Response to Thelma Lavine," in *Rorty and Pragmatism*, 53.

56. Gouinlock, "What Is the Legacy of Instrumentalism?", 88.

57. Ibid., 89.

58. Larry Hickman, "Pragmatism, Technology, and Scientism," in *Pragmatism: From Progressivism to Postmodernism*, ed. Robert Hollinger and David Depew (Westport, CT: Praeger, 1995).

59. Andrew Feenberg, "Pragmatism and Critical Theory of Technology: Reply to Hickman" (paper presented at a meeting of the Society for Philosophy and Technology, Aberdeen, Scotland, 10 July 2001. Its longer version is published in: Andrew Feenberg, "Pragmatism and Critical Theory of Technology," *The Proceedings for the UTCP International Symposium on Pragmatism and the Philosophy of Technology in the 21st Century*, 2 (Tokyo: The University of Tokyo, Center for Philosophy, 2003), 115–25.

60. Feenberg discusses this issue in detail in connection with Marcuse's philosophy, in *Heidegger and Marcuse: The Catastrophe and Redemption of History* (New York: Routledge, 2005).

61. Hilary Putnam, "Are Moral and Legal Values Made or Discovered?" *Legal Theory*, 1 (1995), 9–12. The article was revised and published more recently in: Hilary Putnam, *The Collapse of the Fact/Value Dichotomy and Other Essays* (Cambridge, MA: Harvard University Press, 2002).

62. Hilary Putnam and Ruth Anna Putnam claim that "Dewey's picture of human nature is Darwinian and naturalistic, but not reductionist" (Hilary Putnam with Ruth Anna Putnam, "Education for Democracy," in Hilary Putnam, *Words and Life*, ed. James Conant [Cambridge, MA: Harvard University Press, 1994], 229).

63. Hilary Putnam, *The Threefold Cord: Mind, Body, and World* (New York: Columbia University Press, 1999), 5.

64. Hilary Putnam, *Realism with Human Face* (Cambridge, MA: Harvard University Press, 1990), 165.

65. Hilary Putnam with Ruth Anna Putnam, "Dewey's Logic: Epistemology as Hypothesis," in Hilary Putnam, *Words and Life*, 217–18. Putnam and Putnam point out that John Makie and Bernard Williams hold a dichotomous view on fact and value.

66. Hilary Putnam, "Pragmatism and Moral Objectivity," in Putnam, *Words and Life*, 168.

67. In his recent book, *The Collapse of the Fact / Value Dichotomy and Other Essays*, Putnam reiterates the point that the position he defends concerning the relationship between facts and values is commensurate with Dewey's, namely, the attack on "fact/value 'dualism.'" In this book Putnam tries to expand upon "the ways in which factual description and valuation can and must be entangled" (Putnam, *The Collapse of the Fact/Value Dichotomy and Other Essays*, 9, 27).

68. Putnam, "Pragmatism and Moral Objectivity," 172–73. Putnam asserts that it is the social and cooperative dimension of inquiry in Dewey's scientific method that distinguishes itself from the scientific inquiry of logi-

cal positivism that is featured by "a single isolated spectator" (Hilary Putnam, *Pragmatism: An Open Question* [Oxford: Blackwell, 1995], 70–71).

69. Putnam, "Pragmatism and Moral Objectivity," 176; Hilary Putnam with Ruth Anna Putnam, "Dewey's Logic," 214–15, 217–18. In an introduction to *Realism with Human Face*, James Conant discusses Putnam's "Kantian quest for a coherent conception of what is 'objective humanly speaking'"—a third position between relativism and metaphysical absolutism (James Conant, Introduction to *Realism with a Human Face* by Hilary Putnam, xix).

70. John Dewey, *Logic: The Theory of Inquiry*, in *The Later Works of John Dewey*, vol. 12, ed. Jo Ann Boydston (Carbondale: Southern Illinois University Press, 1986), 16–17.

71. Conant, Introduction to *Realism with a Human Face* by Hilary Putnam, xxxi.

72. Hilary Putnam with Ruth Anna Putnam, "Education for Democracy," 237–39.

73. Ibid., 229.

74. Hilary Putnam, "A Reconsideration of Deweyan Democracy," in *Renewing Philosophy* (Cambridge, MA: Harvard University Press, 1992), 196. Putnam points out that Dewey commits himself to a positivist position of "a bifurcation of goods," a division between social goods (the realm of social betterment through intelligence), on the one hand, and aesthetic goods (the realm of passive enjoyment of intrinsic goods).

75. Ibid., 190–91.

76. Putnam, *Pragmatism*, 75.

77. Earlier versions of parts of this chapter were published in *Gendai-Shiso* (*Contemporary Thoughts*) ("Owari Naki Seicho he no Chosen: Hegel to Darwin no Aida no Dewey" ["A Challenge to Growth without Ends: Dewey between Hegel and Darwin"]) 28, 5 [2000]: 167–89).

CHAPTER THREE
EMERSON'S VOICE
Dewey beyond Hegel and Darwin

1. Neil Coughlan, *Young John Dewey: An Essay in American Intellectual History* (Chicago: University of Chicago Press, 1973), 7–9; George Dykhuizen, *The Life and Mind of John Dewey* (Carbondale: Southern Illinois University Press, 1973), 10.

2. Dykhuizen, *Life and Mind of Dewey*, 16–17; Steven C. Rockefeller, *John Dewey: Religious Faith and Democratic Humanism* (New York: Columbia

University Press, 1991), 7–8, 54–55; John Dewey, "From Absolutism to Experimentalism," in *The Later Works of John Dewey*, vol. 5, ed. Jo Ann Boydston (Carbondale: Southern Illinois University Press, 1984), 148–149 (hereafter cited as "FATE").

3. Dykhuizen, *Life and Mind of Dewey*, 16.

4. Alan Ryan, *John Dewey and the High Tide of American Liberalism* (New York: W. W. Norton, 1995), 50.

5. Dykhuizen, *Life and Mind of Dewey*, 9; Rockefeller, *John Dewey*, 11–12; 51–65, 571–72; Ryan, *John Dewey and the High Tide of American Liberalism*, 49; Marjorie H. Nicholson, "James Marsh and the Vermont Transcendentalism," *Philosophical Review*, 34 (Jan. 1925): 28–50.

6. Nicholson, "James Marsh"; Rockefeller, *John Dewey*, 12; Ryan, *John Dewey and the High Tide of American Liberalism*, 49.

7. James Marsh, cited in Nicholson, "James Marsh," 39.

8. Nicholson,"James Marsh," 40

9. Rockefeller, *John Dewey*, 14.

10. Ibid., 83.

11. John Dewey, "James Marsh and American Philosophy," in *The Later Works of John Dewey*, vol. 5, ed. Jo Ann Boydston (Carbondale: Southern Illinois University Press, 1984). Rockefeller points out that there were also a number of dualisms that Dewey found in Coleridge and Marsh that he could not accept (Rockefeller, *John Dewey*, 64).

12. Rockefeller, *John Dewey*, 58–63. To support Dewey's trust in the power of the rational mind, Dykhuizen points out that Dewey, in opposition to intuitionism, "dimly felt that reason would confirm valid intuitions and that valid intuitions would function as hints or clues to reason as to where truth might lie" (Dykhuizen, *Life and Mind of Dewey*, 17). Dewey's appreciative regard for Marsh's and Coleridge's view of the active and rational power of mind based upon spiritual intuition and will suggests that he found hope in the particular view of "intuition" that they proposed.

13. Dewey as quoted by Herbert Schneider in Oral History Interview (29 June 1967), Special Collections, Morris Library, Southern Illinois University (Carbondale), cited in Rockefeller, *John Dewey*, 56–57.

14. Ryan, *John Dewey and the High Tide of American Liberalism*, 51.

15. John Dewey, "Emerson—The Philosopher of Democracy," in *The Middle Works of John Dewey*, vol. 3, ed. Jo Ann Boydston (Carbondale: Southern Illinois University Press, 1977) (hereafter cited as "Emerson").

16. Cornel West, *The American Evasion of Philosophy: A Genealogy of Pragmatism* (Madison: University of Wisconsin Press, 1989), 73, 212–13.

17. Ibid., 69.
18. Ibid., 103.
19. Ibid., 100.
20. Ibid., 21, 24.
21. Russell B. Goodman, *American Philosophy and the Romantic Tradition* (Cambridge: Cambridge University Press, 1990), 45–46, 91.
22. Ibid., 103, 112.
23. Ibid., 103.
24. Richard Poirier, *Poetry and Pragmatism* (Cambridge, MA: Harvard University Press, 1992), 11.
25. Ibid., 12–13, 22.
26. Lawrence Buell, *Emerson* (Cambridge, MA: Belknap Press of Harvard University Press, 2003), 158, 200, 210, 220.
27. Stanley Cavell, *Conditions Handsome and Unhandsome: The Constitution of Emersonian Perfectionism* (La Salle, IL: Open Court, 1990) (hereafter cited as *Conditions*).
28. Stanley Cavell, "What's the Use of Calling Emerson a Pragmatist?", in *The Revival of Pragmatism: New Essays on Social Thought, Law, and Culture*, ed. Morris Dickstein (Durham, NC: Duke University Press, 1998) (hereafter this essay by Cavell is abbreviated as "Calling Emerson").
29. Cavell's criticism of Dewey's concept of intelligence as the method of problem solving is also revealed in his comparison of Dewey's philosophy to Wittegenstein's. Cavell characterizes Dewey's problem of "human superstition, unintelligence, dogma, rigidity, expressed socially as well as intellectually" as his "monster" which rationality and science should combat. In contrast, Wittgenstein's monster is "despair and a false sense of human limitation, a false sense of human powers," to which science and intelligence do not answer. "We are confused beyond the place where reason can help us" (Stanley Cavell, "Nichijosei he no Kaiki: Watashi no Koe, Amerika no Koe" ["Return to the Ordinary: The Voice of Myself and the Voice of America"], interview and translation by Naoko Saito (11 Nov. 1997), *Gendai-Shiso* [*Contemporary Thoughts*], 26.1[1998]: 50–59).
30. Cavell, "Nichijosei he no Kaiki." Cavell goes on to say: "if we are at odds with others [in polemics] we are also at odds with ourselves and we have to somehow take the mind apart further in order to see what lies at the bottom of this distress."
31. This is one of the fundamental claims in *The Claim of Reason*, particularly in Part Three, where Cavell says that morality hinges on "what position you are taking responsibility for," and "the nature or quality of our relation-

ship to one another," not "the validity of morality as a whole" (Stanley Cavell, *The Claim of Reason: Wittgenstein, Skepticism, Morality, and Tragedy* [Oxford: Oxford University Press, 1979], 268). In the interview Cavell also says: "that sense that the human being expresses itself, and expresses itself in a voice, and must express itself or it falls ill, and drives itself mad, that was the release that I felt explicit in Austin and Wittgenstein" (Cavell, "Nichijosei he no Kaiki").

32. Cavell says that even if Dewey's essay on Emerson is "one of the best written about [Emerson], [Dewey] cannot let it be philosophy for him, not all of philosophy" (Cavell, "Nichijosei he no Kaiki").

33. Stanley Cavell, *Emerson's Transcendental Etudes* (Stanford: Stanford University Press, 2003), 7–9.

34. Douglas R. Anderson, "American Loss in Cavell's Emerson," *Transactions of the Charles S. Peirce Society*, 29.1 (1993): 72–74.

35. Ibid., 75.

36. Ibid., 76–77.

37. West, *American Evasion of Philosophy*, 74, cited in Anderson, "Cavell's Emerson," 76.

38. Anderson, "Cavell's Emerson," 77.

39. Ibid., 69, 82.

40. Ibid., 83.

41. Ibid., 85.

42. Ibid., 82.

43. Ibid., 73.

44. Ibid., 82.

45. Hilary Putnam, "Pragmatism and Neo-Pragmatism" (lecture given at Harvard University, Cambridge, MA, 17 April 2000), tape recording. The following summary of Putnam's position is based upon the recorded lecture with the permission of Putnam.

46. More recently, Putnam has advanced his position in terms of a "pragmatist enlightenment"—a third enlightenment beyond that of the "rationalist wing" and that of the "empiricist wing." In contrast to their presumption of "a priori," Putnam claims that Dewey' enlightenment is one that is "fallibilistic and antimetaphysical, but without lapsing into skepticism" and that is shaped by his concern to apply "scientifically disciplined intelligence to the problems of social reform." (Hilary Putnam, *Ethics without Ontology* [Cambridge, MA: Harvard University Press, 2004], 7, 98, 99, 110, 129)

47. In *Ethics without Ontology*, Putnam reinforces this point by saying that for Dewey social science is "in the service of ordinary people." In re-

sponse to Cavell's charge that Dewey was a "social activist" in his "What's the Use of Calling Emerson a Pragmatist?", Putnam states: "The most objectionable statement about Dewey, in an essay I find uncharacteristically insensitive for Cavell, is this one (on p. 79): 'But what Dewey calls for other disciplines can do as well, maybe better, than philosophy.'" (Putnam, *Ethics without Ontology*, 99, 133–34.)

48. Dewey's writings that Putnam cites for illustration include *Outlines of a Critical Theory of Ethics*, in *The Early Works of John Dewey*, vol. 3, ed. Jo Ann Boydston (Carbondale: Southern Illinois University Press, 1969); and *Ethics* (1908), in *The Middle Works of John Dewey*, vol. 5, ed. Jo Ann Boydston (Carbondale: Southern Illinois University Press, 1978).

49. Parts of this chapter were published in *Transactions of the Charles S. Peirce Society* ("Reconstructing Deweyan Pragmatism in Dialogue with Emerson and Cavell," 37.3 [2001]: 389–406).

CHAPTER FOUR
EMERSONIAN MORAL PERFECTIONISM
Gaining from the Closeness between Dewey and Emerson

1. Stanley Cavell, *Conditions Handsome and Unhandsome: The Constitution of Emersonian Perfectionism* (La Salle, IL: Open Court, 1990) (hereafter cited as *Conditions*). Russell B. Goodman discusses Cavell's idea of EMP, focusing on Cavell's question of how Emersonian (and Nietzschean) perfectionism is compatible with democracy (Russell B. Goodman, "Moral Perfectionism and Democracy: Emerson, Nietzsche, Cavell," in *ESQ: A Journal of the American Renaissance*, 43.1–4[1997]: 159–80. Stephen Mulhall also reviews Cavell's EMP, especially in its contrast to John Rawls's critical interpretation of Nietzsche's perfectionism in his theory of justice (Stephen Mulhall, *Stanley Cavell: Philosophy's Recounting of the Ordinary* [Oxford: Clarendon, 1994], 263–282).

2. Stanley Cavell, *A Pitch of Philosophy: Autobiographical Exercises* (Cambridge, MA: Harvard University Press, 1994), 142. (Hereafter cited as *Pitch*).

3. Aristotle, *Nicomachean Ethics*, in *Classic and Contemporary Readings in the Philosophy of Education*, ed. Steven M. Cahn (New York: McGraw-Hill 1997), 126. (Originally translated by David Ross, revised by J. L. Ackrill and J. D. Urmson [Oxford: Oxford University Press, 1980]).

4. Stanley Cavell, *Emerson's Transcendental Etudes* (Stanford: Stanford University Press, 2003), 190 (hereafter cited as *ETE*).

5. Matthew Arnold, *Culture and Anarchy*, ed. Samuel Lipman (New Haven: Yale University Press, 1994), 8.

6. Ibid., 6.

7. Cavell's Emersonian perfectionism contrasts sharply with the definition of Aristotelian perfectionism given by Thomas Hurka. Hurka's view of perfectionism presupposes the highest degree of the true self "apart from any pleasure of happiness they bring," which he calls "teleological" and "objective" (Thomas Hurka, "Perfectionism," in *Routledge Encyclopedia of Philosophy*, 7, ed. Edward Craig [London: Routledge, 1998], 299–302).

8. Ralph Waldo Emerson, "History," in *Ralph Waldo Emerson*, ed. Richard Poirier [Oxford: Oxford University Press, 1990], 115.

9. Goodman claims that there is a "perfectionistic telos" to these features of Emerson's idea (Goodman, "Moral Perfectionism and Democracy," 166). Lawrence Buell's reading of Emerson is teleological not in Cavell's perfectionist sense. Buell claims that Emerson's cosmopolitanism relies on the "spirit that potentially includes the whole world" and "faith in a common spirituality behind the veils of difference" (Lawrence Buell, *Emerson* [Cambridge, MA: Belknap Press of Harvard University Press, 2003], 188).

10. Ralph Waldo Emerson, "The American Scholar," in *Ralph Waldo Emerson*, 52 (hereafter cited as "AMS").

11. George Kateb, *Emerson and Self-Reliance* (Walnut Creek, CA: Altamira Press, 2000). In general Kateb's writing style, in contrast to Cavell's, is more restrained, a well-balanced analysis of the complexities of Emerson's idea.

12. Ralph Waldo Emerson, "Self Reliance," in *Ralph Waldo Emerson*, 133 (hereafter cited as "SR").

13. Buell emphasizes the "cosmopolitan" dimension of Emerson's thought—namely, its cross-cultural, even universal influence. In opposition to the connection of Emerson's thought merely with the American context, Buell claims that "a national ideology of personal or collective particularism suppresses Emerson's cosmic monism"(Buell, *Emerson*, 195). While Cavell praises Buell's attempt to situate Emerson in a broader context beyond American cultural life, he suggests that his own way of reading Emerson with regard to the American context is to show that the "power of [Emerson's] thinking" is not acknowledged adequately in his own country, America, and that Emerson shows "a doubt to America," to its "terrible arrogance" (*ETE*, 5–6). I would claim that Cavell's "American" interpretation is thoroughly contextual, and hence that it resists a universalization of Emerson's language and thought. They are embedded in America, articulating America's voice, echoing its peculiar needs and hopes, and its question of democracy. This does not make Emerson's thought parochial or exclusive, but rather, helps its American voice engage in dialogue with other cultural voices—facing and

acknowledging difference and separation, rather than relying on the anticipation of common ground from the beginning.

14. Hurka, "Perfectionism," 302.

15. Supporting Kateb's interpretation of Emerson, Goodman claims that Emersonian self-reliance has "an internal relation to democracy" as its presupposition. In Kateb's words, "[Emerson] is presenting and defending the aspirations of the mind of democratic culture." Goodman finds in Cavell's idea an Emersonian representative figure who functions as a provocative defender against cynicism, and who shows others the ideal standpoint of democracy. Mulhall also highlights "Emersonian representativeness" in Cavell's conception as the condition of democratic morality (Goodman, "Moral Perfectionism and Democracy, 172"; Kateb, *Emerson and Self-Reliance*, 6; Mulhall, *Stanley Cavell*, 282).

16. Stanley Cavell, *The Claim of Reason: Wittgenstein, Skepticism, Morality, and Tragedy* (Oxford: Oxford University Press, 1979), 27.

17. Goodman supports this position of Cavell by saying that in Emersonian perfectionism "the potential for original existence or insight is not confined to one or only a few selves" (Goodman, "Moral Perfectionism and Democracy," 169).

18. Goodman also pays attention to this participatory dimension of Cavell's thinking. EMP is democratic as it involves the issues of the "self's duties or responses to others" (ibid., 168).

19. In contrast, Cornel West emphasizes the aspect of individualism in Emerson's thought. He characterizes it as what promotes "separateness over against solidarity, detachment over against association, and individual intuition over against collective action" (Cornel West, *The American Evasion of Philosophy: A Genealogy of Pragmatism* [Madison: University of Wisconsin Press, 1989], 18). Buell divides Emerson into the "Pragmatist Emerson" (in association with public citizenship) and the "Nietzschean Emerson" (the "anti-social" and "anti-popular" thinker) (Buell, *Emerson*, 223). In Cavell's EMP, such a dualistic scheme as West's and Buell's is implausible. The private and the public, in Cavell and Emerson, are inseparable; they are always together in process, from the inmost to the outmost.

20. Goodman also pays attention to the idea of representativeness in EMP: "[I]n Emerson's democratic rendition of perfectionism, each person may be a representative" (Goodman, "Moral Perfectionism and Democracy," 174).

21. Stanley Cavell, *Philosophical Passages: Wittgenstein, Emerson, Austin, Derrida* (Oxford: Blackwell, 1995), 26–27 (hereafter cited as *Passages*).

22. Emerson suggests the idea of a relationship based upon representativeness in such writings as "The American Scholar," "Self-Reliance," and "Friendship" (in *Ralph Waldo Emerson*) Kateb discusses at length Emerson's idea of friendship as a crucial condition of self-reliance. He characterizes it as the paradoxical relationship between antagonism and complementation, separation and union, distance and closeness, and exclusiveness and openness. He also associates it with the notion of "sincerity" as a matter of "mutual intellectual nakedness" (Kateb, *Emerson and Self-Reliance*, 96–129). In opposition to Kateb's interpretation of Emerson's idea of friendship as a "small circle of friends," Cavell says that "there is, as I imagine it, no intuitive size of the figure enclosing us, since each of us keeps on encountering, here and there, and always with surprise, other Emersonian ears." Furthermore, in opposition to the typical interpretation of Emerson's distance to others, Cavell claims: "No reader of Emerson is a priori closer to him than a true reader." Cavell expresses this relationship in the imagery of Emerson's expanding circles: "[Emerson] makes a circle with each reader; and in a sense he and the reader make two circles, each around the other, depending on whose turn it is" (*ETE*, 188–89).

23. Kateb, *Emerson and Self-Reliance*, 103.

24. John Dewey, "Emerson—The Philosopher of Democracy," in *The Middle Works of John Dewey*, vol. 3, ed. Jo Ann Boydston (Carbondale: Southern Illinois University Press, 1977) (hereafter cited as "Emerson").

25. Vincent Colapietro also draws attention to the Emersonian voice and tone in Dewey's text in: "The Question of Voice and the Limits of Pragmatism: Emerson, Dewey, and Cavell," in *Metaphilosophy*, 35.1–2 (2004): 178–201.

26. Steven C. Rockefeller, *John Dewey: Religious Faith and Democratic Humanism* (New York: Columbia University Press, 1991), 353–54. Rockefeller attributes this style to Dewey's Vermont religious upbringing that made it difficult for him to express his emotions. He points out that Dewey tended to avoid "direct personal encounters" due to his shyness, and disliked introspection because of his childhood aversion to puritan moral thinking which demanded inner purity (ibid., 35, 38).

27. Alan Ryan, *John Dewey and the High Tide of American Liberalism* (New York: W. W. Norton, 1995), 37–39.

28. Ryan, *John Dewey and the High Tide of American Liberalism*, 20.

29. Raymond D. Boisvert, *Dewey's Metaphysics* (New York: Fordham University Press, 1988), 210–12.

30. Rockefeller, *John Dewey*, 22.

31. John Dewey, "From Absolutism to Experimentalism," in *The Later Works of John Dewey*, vol. 5, ed. Jo Ann Boydston (Carbondale: Southern Illinois University Press, 1984) (hereafter cited as "FATE").

32. Ralph Waldo Emerson, "Circles," in *Ralph Waldo Emerson*, 175.

33. John Dewey, *Democracy and Education*, in *The Middle Works of John Dewey*, vol. 9, ed. Jo Ann Boydston (Carbondale: Southern Illinois University Press, 1980), 61 (hereafter cited as *DE*).

34. John Dewey, *Human Nature and Conduct*, in *The Middle Works of John Dewey*, vol. 14, ed. Jo Ann Boydston (Carbondale: Southern Illinois University Press, 1983), 196 (hereafter cited as *HNC*).

35. John Dewey, *Reconstruction in Philosophy* (Boston: Beacon Press, 1920), vi (hereafter cited as *RP*).

36. John Dewey, *The Public and Its Problems*, in *The Later Works of John Dewey*, vol. 2, ed. Jo Ann Boydston (Carbondale: Southern Illinois University Press, 1984), 311–12 (hereafter cited as *PP*).

37. John Dewey, *Individualism Old and New*, in *The Later Works of John Dewey*, vol. 5, ed. Jo Ann Boydston (Carbondale: Southern Illinois University Press, 1984), 53 (hereafter cited as *ION*).

38. Ralph Waldo Emerson, "Experience," in *Ralph Waldo Emerson*, 217.

39. John Dewey, "Construction and Criticism," in *The Later Works of John Dewey*, vol. 5, ed. Jo Ann Boydston (Carbondale: Southern Illinois University Press, 1984), 139 (hereafter cited as *CC*).

40. John Dewey, "Creative Democracy—The Task Before Us," in *The Later Works of John Dewey*, vol. 14, ed. Jo Ann Boydston (Carbondale: Southern Illinois University Press, 1988) (hereafter cited as "CD").

41. Earlier versions of parts of this chapter were published in *Transactions of the Charles S. Peirce Society* ("Reconstructing Deweyan Pragmatism in Dialogue with Emerson and Cavell," 37.3[2001]:389–406).

CHAPTER FIVE
DEWEY'S EMERSONIAN VIEW OF ENDS

1. John Dewey, *Democracy and Education*, in *The Middle Works of John Dewey*, vol. 9, ed. Jo Ann Boydston (Carbondale: Southern Illinois University Press, 1980), 54 (hereafter cited as *DE*).

2. John Dewey, *Human Nature and Conduct*, in *The Middle Works of John Dewey*, vol. 14, ed. Jo Ann Boydston (Carbondale: Southern Illinois University Press, 1983), 88 (hereafter cited as *HNC*).

3. Steven C. Rockefeller, *John Dewey: Religious Faith and Democratic Humanism* (New York: Columbia University Press, 1991), 335; Robert B. West-

brook, *John Dewey and American Democracy* (Ithaca: Cornell University Press, 1991), 287, 291.

4. Alan Ryan, *John Dewey and the High Tide of American Liberalism* (New York: W. W. Norton, 1995), 46.

5. Thomas M. Alexander, *John Dewey's Theory of Art, Experience, and Nature: The Horizons of Feeling* (Albany: State University of New York Press, 1987), 62–68. Hans Joas also discusses the pragmatist idea of creativity that is "performed within situations" (Hans Joas, *The Creativity of Action* [Chicago: University of Chicago Press, 1996], 129).

6. Russell B. Goodman, *American Philosophy and the Romantic Tradition* (Cambridge, UK: Cambridge University Press, 1990), 103, 112.

7. John Dewey, *Art as Experience*, in *The Later Works of John Dewey*, vol. 10, ed. Jo Ann Boydston (Carbondale: Southern Illinois University Press, 1987), 336 (hereafter cited as *AE*).

8. Dewey's behaviorist tendency is controversial. Rockefeller recognizes Dewey's predilection toward Alexander's physiological unity of body and mind (Rockefeller, *John Dewey*, 333–34). In contrast, Ryan takes the view that "[Dewey] did not quite swallow whole the 'scheme of universal salvation' that Alexander offered" (Ryan, *John Dewey and the High Tide of American Liberalism*, 187). Westbrook argues that Dewey's stance towards behaviorism is "oblique" as he opposes it to instinct theories (Westbrook, *John Dewey and American Democracy*, 292).

9. Dewey says: "MANKIND likes to think in terms of extreme opposites. It is given to formulating its beliefs in terms of Either-Ors, between which it recognizes no intermediate possibilities" (John Dewey, *Experience and Education* [New York: Macmillan, 1938], 17) (hereafter cited as *EE*).

10. Israel Scheffler, *Four Pragmatists: A Critical Introduction to Peirce, James, Mead, and Dewey* (London: Routledge and Kegan Paul, 1974), 44.

11. John Dewey, *Experience and Nature*, in *The Later Works of John Dewey*, vol. 1, ed. Jo Ann Boydston (Carbondale: Southern Illinois University Press, 1981), 137, 149 (hereafter cited as *EN*).

12. I thank Hilary Putnam for suggesting this terminology.

13. Hilary Putnam and Ruth Anna Putnam discuss Peirce's and Dewey's ideas of a kind of inquiry that begins and is conducted in "an indeterminate situation," a situation that is "inherently doubtful" (Hilary Putnam with Ruth Anna Putnam, "Dewey's Logic: Epistemology as Hypothesis," in Hilary Putnam, *Words and Life*, ed. James Conant [Cambridge, MA: Harvard University Press, 1994], 201). Francisco Varela, et al. discuss the Buddhist's "middle way as a third way beyond Cartesian dualism and materialism."

Pragmatism, they argue, is a good first step, but not as insightful as Buddhism (Francisco Varela, Evan Thompson, and Eleanor Rosch, *The Embodied Mind: Cognitive Science and Human Experience* [Cambridge, MA: MIT Press, 1993], 234). Steve Odin also discusses the Mahayana Buddhist philosophy of the "Middle Way" and the "nondual worldview of Japanese Buddhism," with its concomitant notion of the "embodied self," in terms of their common ground with American pragmatism (Steve Odin, *The Social Self in Zen and American Pragmatism* [Albany: State University of New York Press, 1996], 302, 362–63).

14. J. J. Chambliss examines the common ground between Dewey and Aristotle in their theory of conduct. He claims that "Dewey's own experimental naturalism came about, in large part, as a reconstructing of the Aristotelian way in which 'nature does things'" (J. J. Chambliss, "Common Ground in Aristotle's and Dewey's Theories of Conduct," *Educational Theory*, 43.3. [1993]: 249–60).

15. In *The Quest for Certainty*, Dewey says that "nature, including humanity, with all its defects and imperfections, may evoke heartfelt piety as the source of ideals, of possibilities, of aspiration in their behalf, and as the eventual abode of all attained goods and excellencies" (John Dewey, *The Quest for Certainty*, in *The Later Works of John Dewey*, vol. 4, ed. Jo Ann Boydston [Carbondale: Southern Illinois University Press, 1984], 244).

16. In *Art as Experience*, Dewey also refers to the concept of means as the middle: "'Medium' signifies first of all an intermediary. The import of the word 'means' is the same. They are the middle, the intervening, things through which something now remote is brought to pass" (*AE*, 201).

17. John Dewey, *Reconstruction in Philosophy* (Boston: Beacon Press, 1920), 162, 174.

18. Addressing Dewey's concept of ends-in-view, Hilary Putnam says as follows: "Dewey, then, is not just talking about finding better means to preexisting ends-in-view (about what Habermas calls 'means-ends rationality'—*Zweckmittelrationalität*—or about what Kant called 'hypothetical imperatives'). Dewey is really talking about learning through experimentation and discussion how to increase the amount of *good* in our lives" (Hilary Putnam, "Are Moral and Legal Values Made or Discovered?", *Legal Theory*, 1 [1995], 9).

19. Stanley Cavell, *Conditions Handsome and Unhandsome: The Constitution of Emersonian Perfectionism* (La Salle, IL: Open Court, 1990), 12 (hereafter cited as *Conditions*).

20. Stanley Cavell, *The Senses of Walden* (Chicago: University of Chicago Press, 1992), 128 (hereafter cited as *Senses*), in Goodman, *American Philosophy and the Romantic Tradition*, 46.

21. Ralph Waldo Emerson, "Circles," in *Ralph Waldo Emerson*, ed. Richard Poirier (Oxford: Oxford University Press, 1990), 166 (hereafter cited as "Circles").

22. Though Emerson's idea of expanding circles is progressive and forward-looking, it is not a simple negation of the past as he says: "The new position of the advancing man has all the powers of the old, yet has them all new. It carries in its bosom all the energies of the past, yet is itself an exhalation of the morning" ("Circles," 174).

23. Cornel West cites Emerson's phrase, "the only sin is limitation," as a symbol of Emerson's optimistic theodicy of extolling human power and the rejection of "a tragic vision" (Cornel West, *The American Evasion of Philosophy: A Genealogy of Pragmatism* [Madison: University of Wisconsin Press, 1989], 17, 35).

24. Earlier versions of parts of this chapter were published in the *Journal of Philosophy of Education* ("Pragmatism and the Tragic Sense: Deweyan Growth in an Age of Nihilism," 36.2 [2002]: 247–63) and in *Philosophy of Education 2000* ("Perfecting Democracy through Holistic Education: Dewey's Naturalistic Philosophy of Growth Reconsidered" [2001]: 155–63.

CHAPTER SIX
GROWTH AND THE SOCIAL RECONSTRUCTION OF CRITERIA
Gaining from the Distance between Dewey and Emerson

1. Stanley Cavell, "What's the Use of Calling Emerson a Pragmatist?" in *The Revival of Pragmatism: New Essays on Social Thought, Law, and Culture*, ed. Morris Dickstein (Durham, NC: Duke University Press, 1998), 75 (hereafter cited as "Calling Emerson").

2. John Dewey, *Experience and Education* (New York: Macmillan, 1938), 36–37 (hereafter cited as *EE*).

3. John Dewey, *Human Nature and Conduct*, in *The Middle Works of John Dewey*, vol. 14, ed. Jo Ann Boydston (Carbondale: Southern Illinois University Press, 1983), 193 (hereafter cited as *HNC*).

4. John Dewey, *The Quest for Certainty*, in *The Later Works of John Dewey*, vol. 4, ed. Jo Ann Boydston (Carbondale: Southern Illinois University Press, 1984), 212.

5. John Dewey, *Experience and Nature*, in *The Later Works of John Dewey*, vol. 1, ed. Jo Ann Boydston (Carbondale: Southern Illinois University Press, 1981), 97 (hereafter cited as *EN*).

6. John Dewey, *Logic: The Theory of Inquiry*, in *The Later Works of John Dewey*, vol. 12, ed. Jo Ann Boydston (Carbondale: Southern Illinois University Press, 1986), 16–17.

7. Hilary Putnam, "Pragmatism and Moral Objectivity," in Putnam, *Words and Life*, ed. James Conant (Cambridge, MA: Harvard University Press, 1994), 172–73.

8. John Dewey, *Democracy and Education*, in *The Middle Works of John Dewey*, vol. 9, ed. Jo Ann Boydston (Carbondale: Southern Illinois University Press, 1980), 44–45 (hereafter cited as *DE*).

9. With respect to Dewey's view of a teacher, Robert B. Westbrook states that "a teacher had to be capable of seeing the world as both a child and an adult saw it" (Robert B. Westbrook, *John Dewey and American Democracy* [Ithaca: Cornell University Press, 1991], 101).

10. John Dewey, *The Child and the Curriculum*, in *The Middle Works of John Dewey*, vol. 2, ed. Jo Ann Boydston (Carbondale: Southern Illinois University Press, 1976), 280.

11. Israel Scheffler, *Four Pragmatists: A Critical Introduction to Peirce, James, Mead, and Dewey* (London: Routledge and Kegan Paul, 1974), 222.

12. Ibid., 222–26.

13. Westbrook, *John Dewey and American Democracy*, 289–90.

14. John Dewey, *Ethics* (1932), in *The Later Works of John Dewey*, vol. 7, ed. Jo Ann Boydston (Carbondale: Southern Illinois University Press, 1985), 230–31.

15. Ralph Waldo Emerson, "Self-Reliance," in *Ralph Waldo Emerson*, ed. Richard Poirier (Oxford: Oxford University Press, 1990), 135 (hereafter cited as "SR").

16. Alan Ryan, *John Dewey and the High Tide of American Liberalism* (New York: W. W. Norton, 1995), 148–49.

17. Stephen Mulhall points out that a dialogue between "the older and younger friends" is a common theme running in Cavell's various writings (Stephen Mulhall, *Stanley Cavell: Philosophy's Recounting of the Ordinary* [Oxford: Clarendon, 1994], 266).

18. Stanley Cavell, *The Claim of Reason: Wittgenstein, Skepticism, Morality, and Tragedy* (Oxford: Oxford University Press, 1979), 112 (hereafter cited as *Claim*).

19. Interpreting Wittgenstein's concept of criteria, Cavell says: "Criteria are 'criteria for something's being so,' not in the sense that they tell us of a thing's existence, but of something like its identity, not of its *being* so, but of its being *so*. Criteria do not determine the certainty of statements, but the application of the concepts employed in statements" (*Claim*, 45).

20. This position is inherited in Cavell's later idea of EMP when he says: "A moral advance on the journey may not be measurable from outside, so to speak, since a crisis may take the form of a refusal to yield to the acclaim

of a false, or falsifying step" (Stanley Cavell, *A Pitch of Philosophy: Autobiographical Exercises* [Cambridge, MA: Harvard University Press, 1994], 142).

21. This again reflects Cavell's view of skepticism, when he says: "Our relation to the world as a whole, or to others in general, is not one of knowing, where knowing construes itself as being certain" (*Claim*, 45).

22. Douglas R. Anderson, "American Loss in Cavell's Emerson," *Transactions of the Charles S. Peirce Society*, 29. 1 (1993), 73.

23. Ryan, *John Dewey and the High Tide of American Liberalism*, 37–39; Steven C. Rockefeller, *John Dewey: Religious Faith and Democratic Humanism* (New York: Columbia University Press, 1991), 353–54.

24. This is a part of the criticism that Richard Rorty directs against Dewey's "metaphysics" (Richard Rorty, "Dewey's Metaphysics," in *Consequences of Pragmatism* [Minneapolis: University of Minnesota Press, 1982]).

25. John J. Stuhr, *Genealogical Pragmatism: Philosophy, Experience, and Community* (Albany: State University of New York Press, 1997), 126–30; Jim Garrison, "Realism, Deweyan Pragmatism, and Educational Research," *Educational Researcher*, 23.1 (1994), 5–14.

26. Raymond D. Boisvert, *Dewey's Metaphysics* (New York: Fordham University Press, 1988). 210–12; Rockefeller, *John Dewey*, 22.

CHAPTER SEVEN
THE GLEAM OF LIGHT
Reconstruction toward Holistic Growth

1. Ralph Waldo Emerson, "Self-Reliance," in *Ralph Waldo Emerson*, ed. Richard Poirier (Oxford: Oxford University Press, 1990), 131 (hereafter cited as "SR").

2. Ralph Waldo Emerson, cited in John Dewey, *Democracy and Education*, in *The Middle Works of John Dewey*, vol. 9, ed. Jo Ann Boydston (Carbondale: Southern Illinois University Press, 1980), 56.

3. John Dewey, *Construction and Criticism*, in *The Later Works of John Dewey*, vol. 5, ed. Jo Ann Boydston (Carbondale: Southern Illinois University Press, 1984), 138–139 (hereafter cited as *CC*).

4. Ralph Waldo Emerson, "Circles," in *Ralph Waldo Emerson*, 172 (hereafter cited as "Circles").

5. Plato, *The Republic*, trans. G. M. A. Grube (Indianapolis: Hackett Publishing, 1992), 189–90.

6. Lawrence Buell, *Emerson* (Cambridge, MA: Belknap Press of Harvard University Press, 2003), 167.

7. Russell B. Goodman, *American Philosophy and the Romantic Tradition* (Cambridge, UK: Cambridge University Press, 1990), 44–45. As an example

of Emerson's unique revision of Kantian transcendental idealism, Goodman discusses Cavell's interpretation of Emerson's "epistemology of moods," a mood as a way of constructing the world beyond Kant's twelve categories.

8. Arthur Versluis, *American Transcendentalism and Asian Religions* (Oxford: Oxford University Press, 1993), 55, 66.

9. Buell, *Emerson*, 172–73, 179. Buell thus claims that Emerson's influence transcends America, and opens up "cosmopolitanism" with "a common spirituality behind the veils of difference" (ibid., 188).

10. Ralph Waldo Emerson, "The Transcendentalists," in *Ralph Waldo Emerson*, 97.

11. John Dewey, "Emerson—The Philosopher of Democracy," in *The Middle Works of John Dewey*, vol. 3, ed. Jo Ann Boydston (Carbondale: Southern Illinois University Press, 1977), 188–190 (hereafter cited as "Emerson").

12. Stanley Cavell, *The Senses of Walden* (Chicago: University of Chicago Press, 1992), 154 (hereafter cited as *Senses*).

13. Steve Odin suggests that in Kitaro Nishida's Japanese philosophy, this theme is developed as "immanent transcendence." This is an idea that "transcendence moves not in the direction of an other-worldly beyond, but in the direction of bottomless depths in the absolute present" (Steve Odin, *The Social Self in Zen and American Pragmatism* [Albany: State University of New York Press, 1996], 432).

14. Buell, *Emerson*, 169, 236.

15. Paul F. Boller, Jr., notes that Emerson and other transcendentalists discarded the idea in Scottish philosophy of an intuitive moral sense, popular in New England in Emerson's time. Instead, New England transcendentalism was influenced by Kant's transcendental idealism, though it stressed the intuitive rather than the rational elements in Kant's philosophy. The English romantic poet, Samuel Taylor Coleridge, is a significant influence. According to Boller, Coleridge, who studied Kant, makes an original distinction between Reason and Understanding. While understanding is a "faculty for dealing with material objects," reason is the one for "apprehending spiritual truths" through immediate intuition. Emerson's idea of intuition or the gleam of light is associated with the faculty of Reason in Coleridge's sense. Boller cites the following passage of Emerson: "Reason is the highest faculty of the soul, what we mean often by the soul itself: it never reasons, never proves; it simply perceives, it is vision" (Paul F. Boller, *American Transcendentalism, 1830–1860: An Intellectual Inquiry* [New York: G. P. Putnam's Sons, 1974], 42, 44–46, 50). Steven C. Rockefeller points out that

the young Dewey also was rebellious against New England intuitionism and identified with Coleridge, whose *Aids to Reflection* had influenced him (Steven C. Rockefeller, *John Dewey: Religious Faith and Democratic Humanism* [New York: Columbia University Press, 1991]: 51–65).

16. Odin, *The Social Self in Zen and American Pragmatism*, 157.

17. The approach to Emerson's idea of self-reliance from the perspective of the gleam of light, I believe, is more holistic than George Kateb's approach in a division between "mental self-reliance" and "active self-reliance" (George Kateb, *Emerson and Self-Reliance* [Walnut Creek, CA: AltaMira Press, 2000], 33).

18. John Dewey, *Human Nature and Conduct*, in *The Middle Works of John Dewey*, vol. 14, ed. Jo Ann Boydston (Carbondale: Southern Illinois University Press, 1983), 118 (hereafter cited as *HNC*).

19. John Dewey, *The Quest for Certainty*, in *The Later Works of John Dewey*, vol. 4, ed. Jo Ann Boydston (Carbondale: Southern Illinois University Press, 1984), 80.

20. John Dewey, *Experience and Nature*, in *The Later Works of John Dewey*, vol. 1, ed. Jo Ann Boydston (Carbondale: Southern Illinois University Press, 1981), 18–19 (hereafter cited as *EN*). Thomas M. Alexander claims that situations, as a basic unit in Dewey's theory of experience, are "primarily organized, active, lived experiences unified by a prelogical or preanalytical qualitative unity" (Thomas M. Alexander, *John Dewey's Theory of Art, Experience, and Nature: The Horizons of Feeling* [Albany: State University of New York Press, 1987], 105).

21. John Dewey, *Logic: The Theory of Inquiry*, cited in S. Morris Eames, "The Cognitive and the Non-Cognitive in Dewey's Theory of Valuation," *The Journal of Philosophy*, 58 (Mar. 1961), 183.

22. John Dewey, *Art as Experience*, in *The Later Works of John Dewey*, vol. 10, ed. Jo Ann Boydston (Carbondale: Southern Illinois University Press, 1987), 64 (hereafter cited as *AE*).

23. Odin, *The Social Self in Zen and American Pragmatism*, 279.

24. John Dewey, *Individualism Old and New*, in *The Later Works of John Dewey*, vol. 5, ed. Jo Ann *Boydston* (Carbondale: Southern Illinois University Press, 1984), 64 (hereafter cited as *ION*). With respect to the concept of the soul, Dewey emphasizes its non-occult nature, by citing Bernard Miall's statement in his *Mysteries of the Soul* (1929) that the soul is "the manifold living reciprocal reactions between the self and the universe" (ION, 51).

25. Stanley Cavell, *Conditions Handsome and Unhandsome: The Constitution of Emersonian Perfectionism* (La Salle, IL: Open Court, 1990), 36, 42 (hereafter cited as *Conditions*).

26. Ralph Waldo Emerson, "Intellect," in *Ralph Waldo Emerson*, 178. (hereafter cited as "Intellect").

27. John Dewey, *The Public and Its Problems*, in *The Later Works of John Dewey*, vol. 2, ed. Jo Ann Boydston (Carbondale: Southern Illinois University Press, 1984), 372.

28. John Dewey, *How We Think* (1933), in *The Later Works of John Dewey*, vol. 8, ed. Jo Ann Boydston (Carbondale: Southern Illinois University Press, 1986), 335.

29. Jim Garrison also discusses the "rhythm of growth" in Dewey's concept of experience (Jim Garrison, *Dewey and Eros: Wisdom and Desire in the Art of Teaching* [New York: Teachers College Press, 1997], 47–53).

30. In "Qualitative Thought," Dewey discusses the qualitative whole as the background of thinking, as "the directive clue in what we do expressly think of." In the qualitative background, he says, "intuition" is "inarticulate and yet penetrating" and it underlies "all the details of explicit reasoning." In this regard, he supports Bergson's view of intuition and claims: "Reflection and rational elaboration spring from and make explicit a prior intuition. . . . Thinking and theorizing about physical matters set out from an intuition, and reflection about affairs of life and mind consists in an ideational and conceptual transformation of what begins as an intuition." What Dewey says here about intuition can be reinterpreted as referring to the central and penetrating force of experience (John Dewey, "Qualitative Thought," in *The Later Works of John Dewey*, vol. 5, ed. Jo Ann Boydston [Carbondale: Southern Illinois University Press, 1984], 248–49).

31. John Dewey, *Essays in Experimental Logic* (New York: Dover, 1916), 7.

32. Versluis discusses the Emersonian concept of time in connection with Zen Buddhist wisdom of the affirmation of the present instant, the idea that "every day is the best day in the year" (Versluis, *American Transcendentalism and Asian Religions*, 67, 109).

33. Richard Poirier also discusses Emerson's circles as the movement of the soul, saying that "individuals have the freedom and power to break out of a circle," and that "the soul knows that it is creating only a new orbit or limit as it surges past and sweeps up the boundaries of an old one." Poirier interprets Emerson's idea of the soul not as "an entity" but as "a function." Poirier also says: "Soul repeatedly finds itself in a circle, a circle which is already one of its creations, one of its texts one of the governing principles that it has helped bring, or is in the act of bringing, to consciousness" (Richard Poirier, *Poetry and Pragmatism* [Cambridge, MA: Harvard University Press, 1992], 23–24).

34. Ralph Waldo Emerson, "The Poet," in *Ralph Waldo Emerson*, 208 (hereafter cited as "Poet").

35. Israel Scheffler, *Four Pragmatists: A Critical Introduction to Peirce, James, Mead, and Dewey* (London: Routledge and Kegan Paul, 1974), 29.

36. John Dewey, "Time and Individuality," in *The Later Works of John Dewey*, vol. 14, ed. Jo Ann Boydston (Carbondale: Southern Illinois University Press, 1988), 99, 101–02 (hereafter cited as "TI").

37. Supporting Darwin's view of individual variations in evolutionary development, William James claims the significance of the power of individual initiative exercised upon social environments. "The community stagnates without the impulse of the individual. The impulse dies away without the sympathy of the community" (William James, "Great Men and Their Environment," in *The Will to Believe: And Other Essays in Popular Philosophy* [New York: Dover, 1956], 232).

38. Odin, *The Social Self in Zen and American Pragmatism*, 338–49.

39. John Dewey, "I Believe," in *The Later Works of John Dewey*, vol. 14, ed. Jo Ann Boydston (Carbondale: Southern Illinois University Press, 1988), 91–92.

40. John Dewey, *A Common Faith*, in *The Later Works of John Dewey*, vol. 9, ed. Jo Ann Boydston (Carbondale: Southern Illinois University Press, 1986), 35 (hereafter cited as *CF*).

41. Jim Garrison, "Dewey and the Education of Eros" (paper presented at the International Conference on the Philosophy of John Dewey, Cosenza, Calabria, Italy, 10–13 Apr. 2000, photocopied). Garrison borrows from Alexander the notion of "the human eros": in Thomas M. Alexander, "The Human Eros," in *Philosophy and the Reconstruction of Culture*, ed. John J. Stuhr (Albany: State University of New York Press, 1993).

42. Garrison highlights the significance of "an affective, intuitive background and imagination" and the qualitative context in Dewey's concept of inquiry. Imagination, in his interpretation, is the function of exploring alternative possibilities for action with selective interests (Garrison, *Dewey and Eros*, 96).

43. Alexander, *John Dewey's Theory of Art, Experience, and Nature*, 263.

44. Ralph Waldo Emerson, "The Over-Soul," in *Ralph Waldo Emerson*, 155.

45. Earlier versions of parts of this chapter were published in *Philosophy of Education 2001* ("Education for the Gleam of Light: Emerson's Transcendentalism and Its Implications for Contemporary Moral Education" [2002]: 144–52).

CHAPTER EIGHT
THE GLEAM OF LIGHT LOST
Transcending the Tragic with Dewey after Emerson

1. Ralph Waldo Emerson, "Experience," in *Ralph Waldo Emerson*, ed. Richard Poirier (Oxford: Oxford University Press, 1990), 216 (hereafter cited as "Experience").

2. John Dewey, *Construction and Criticism*, in *The Later Works of John Dewey*, vol. 5, ed. Jo Ann Boydston (Carbondale: Southern Illinois University Press, 1984), 139 (hereafter cited as *CC*).

3. Sidney Hook, *Pragmatism and the Tragic Sense of Life* (New York: Basic Books, 1974), 22.

4. Cornel West, *The American Evasion of Philosophy: A Genealogy of Pragmatism* (Madison: University of Wisconsin Press, 1989), 17, 111.

5. West, *The Cornel West Reader* (New York: Basic Civitas Books, 1999), 164.

6. Ibid., 179.

7. Ibid., 165.

8. Ibid., 175. Steven C. Rockefeller, though a staunch defender of Dewey's spiritual vision of democracy, also argues that Dewey failed to develop a convincing explanation of human evil (Steven C. Rockefeller, *John Dewey: Religious Faith and Democratic Humanism* [New York: Columbia University Press, 1991], 486–87).

9. West, *The Cornel West Reader*, 180–81.

10. In fact, in his contributions to *The Educational Frontier* (1933), Dewey's preference is for the phrase, "a planning community" (in *The Later Works of John Dewey*, vol. 8, ed. Jo Ann Boydston [Carbondale: Southern Illinois University, 1986]), 70. I thank Jim Garrison for drawing this to my attention.

11. Raymond D. Boisvert, "The Nemesis of Necessity: Tragedy's Challenge to Deweyan Pragmatism," in *Dewey Reconfigured: Essays on Deweyan Pragmatism*, ed. Casey Haskins and David I. Seiple (Albany: State University of New York Press, 1999). In response to a paper by Donald Morse, Boisvert reiterates this position ("Updating Dewey: A Reply to Morse," *Transactions of the Charles S. Peirce Society*, 37.4, [2001], 573–83).

12. Raymond D. Boisvert, "Forget Emerson, Forget Growth, Embrace Anaximander: Pragmatism and the Tragic Sense," a response to Naoko Saito, "Pragmatism and the Tragic Sense: Deweyan Growth in an Age of Nihilism," (paper presented at Society for the Advancement of American Philosophy [8 Mar. 2002, Portland, ME]).

13. Raymond D. Boisvert, "Toward a Programmatic Pragmatism: A response to Naoko Saito," *Journal of Philosophy of Education*, 36.4 (2002), 621–28.

14. Megan Boler, "An Epoch of Difference: Hearing Voices in the Nineties," *Educational Theory*, 50.3 (2000), 359, 370, 375.

15. Ibid., 380.

16. René V. Arcilla, "Tragic Absolutism in Education," *Educational Theory*, 42.4 (1992): 473–81.

17. Ibid., 476–77.

18. Ibid., 478, 480.

19. Comparing Dewey's *Ethics* (1932) to *Ethics* (1908), Robert B. Westbrook asserts that while the fundamental principle of the growing self remained unchanged, a tragic view of experience had crept into the former, and that Dewey had started to recognize the rarity of consummatory experience and growth (Robert B. Westbrook, *John Dewey and American Democracy* [Ithaca: Cornel University Press, 1991], 416). Boisvert is opposed to this interpretation, claiming that the change was peripheral (Boisvert, "The Nemesis of Necessity," 154).

20. John Dewey, *Individualism Old and New*, in *The Later Works of John Dewey*, vol. 5, ed. Jo Ann Boydston (Carbondale: Southern Illinois University Press, 1984), 62, 67 (hereafter cited as *ION*).

21. John Dewey, "Time and Individuality," in *The Later Works of John Dewey*, vol. 14, ed. Jo Ann Boydston (Carbondale: Southern Illinois University Press, 1988), 113.

22. Ralph Waldo Emerson, "Self-Reliance," in *Ralph Waldo Emerson*, 133.

23. Ralph Waldo Emerson, "The American Scholar," in *Ralph Waldo Emerson*, ed. Richard Poirier (Oxford: Oxford University Press, 1990), 52 (hereafter cited as "AMS").

24. Boler, "An Epoch of Difference," 370, 379–80.

25. John Dewey, *The Public and Its Problems*, in *The Later Works of John Dewey*, vol. 2, ed. Jo Ann Boydston (Carbondale: Southern Illinois University Press, 1984), 328.

26. Richard Rorty, *Philosophy and Social Hope* (London: Penguin Books, 1999), xxviii.

27. Paul Standish, "From Moral Education to Citizenship: Principles and Problems in UK Policy," *International Christian University Publications 1-A, Educational Studies*, 44 (Mar. 2002): 243–62.

28. Paul Standish, "Democratic Participation and the Body Politic" (a paper to be published in *Educational Theory*).

29. Paul Standish, "Shimin-sei to Kyoiku no Mokuteki: Eikoku ni Okeru Seisaku to Jissen no Igi" ("Citizenship and the Aims of Education," trans. Naoko Saito, in *Shimin-sei no Kyoiku* (Education for Citizenship) (temporary

title), eds. Manabu Sato, Ryoko Tsuneyoshi, and Hidenori Fujita (Tokyo Daigaku Shuppan-kai) (to be published in 2005).

30. More recently, however, there have been reactionary measures in response to concern over declining levels of knowledge.

31. Manabu Sato, "Kodomotachi wa Naze 'Manabi' kara Toso Suru ka?: 'Gakuryoku-Teika' ni Miru Nihon-Shakai no Bunka-teki Kiki" ("Why Are Children Escaping from 'Learning'?: Cultural Crisis of Japanese Society Indicated by a 'Decline of Knowledge Level,'" *Sekai* (*The World*), 674 (2000): 77–85; Hidenori Fujita, "Shin-Jidai no Kyoiku o Do Koso Suruka: Kyoiku-Kaikaku Kokumin Kaigi no Nokoshita Kadai" ("How to Envision Education in New Era: Tasks Left by the National Commission on Educational Reform," *Iwanami Booklet*, 533 (Tokyo: Iwanami Shoten, 2001).

32. As of 6 Jan. 2001, its name was changed to the Ministry of Education, Culture, Sports, Science, and Technology.

33. Takashi Kosugi, *Ushinawareta "Kokoro no Kyoiku" o Motomete: Niju-Isseiki ni Okuru Kyoiku-Kaikaku* (*In Search of the Lost "Education of the Heart": Educational Reform for the 21st Century* (Tokyo: Diamond-Sha, 1997); Toshio Hiei, "Kokoro no Kyoiku' tte Nani?" ("What Is the 'Education of the Heart'?"), *The Yomiuri Newspaper* (5 Oct. 1997).

34. Tetsuya Takahashi and Akiko Miyake, "Kore wa 'Kokumin Seishin Kaizo Undo' da" ["This Is the 'Movement for Reconstructing the National Spirit'"], in *Sekai* (*The World*), 712 (2003): 33–47; Manabu Sato, "Gakuryoku o Toi-naosu: Manabi-no Curriculum he" ["Re-questioning Academic Achievement: Toward a Curriculum for Learning"], in *Iwanami Booklet*, 548 (Tokyo: Iwanami Shoten, 2001), 36.

35. John Dewey, *Art as Experience*, in *The Later Works of John Dewey*, vol. 10, ed. Jo Ann Boydston (Carbondale: Southern Illinois University Press, 1987), 24, 25.

36. Manabu Sato, "Kodomotachi wa Naze 'Manabi' kara Toso Suru ka?; Nishihira Tadashi also points to the phenomenon of nihilism among Japanese youth today from the perspective of the crisis of their soul. (Tadashi Nishihira and René Vincent Arcilla, "Nihilism and Education" [lecture given at the University of Tokyo, Tokyo, 21 July 1999]).

37. Stanley Cavell, *Conditions Handsome and Unhandsome: The Constitution of Emersonian Perfectionism* (La Salle, IL: Open Court, 1990), 12.

38. *The Selected Letters of Ralph Waldo Eme*rson, ed. Joel Myerson (New York: Columbia University Press, 1997), 263.

39. *The Heart of Emerson's Journals*, ed. Bliss Perry (New York: Dover., 1958), 178.

40. George Santayana, *George Santayana's America: Essays on Literature and Culture*, Collected and with an Introduction by James Ballowe (Urbana: University of Ilinois Press, 1967), 73, 80.

41. Lawrence Buell, *Emerson* (Cambridge MA: Belknap Press of Harvard University Press, 2003), 126.

42. Stanley Cavell, "Finding as Founding, Taking Steps in Emerson's 'Experience,'" in *This New Yet Unapproachable America: Lectures after Emerson after Wittgenstein* (Albuquerque, NM: Living Batch Press, 1989) (hereafter cited as *America*).

43. Santayana makes a similar point when he says "ground is lost as fast as it is gained" in Emerson's idea of the "ascending effort" of the universe. Santayana indicates that Emerson's worldview is characterized not so much as progress as "succession" (*George Santayana's America*, 74).

44. Stanley Cavell, *Contesting Tears: The Hollywood Melodrama of the Unknown Woman* (Chicago: University of Chicago Press, 1996), 65.

45. Stanley Cavell, *The Senses of Walden* (Chicago: University of Chicago Press, 1992), 137.

46. John Dewey, *Experience and Nature*, in *The Later Works of John Dewey*, vol. 1, ed. Jo Ann Boydston (Carbondale: Southern Illinois University Press, 1981), 57.

47. Steve Odin, *The Social Self in Zen and American Pragmatism* (Albany: State University of New York Press, 1996), 399, 344–45.

48. *Ju-Yon-Sai: Kokoro no Fukei (Fourteen-Year-Olds: The Scenery in their Minds)*, ed. Nihon-Hoso-Kyokai, "Ju-Yon-Sai: Kokoro no Fukei" Project (The Project for "Fourteen-Year-Olds: The Scenery in their Minds" in Japan Broadcasting Corporation) (Tokyo: Nihon-Hoso Shuppan-Kyokai, 1998), 45–46. Original in Japanese with my translation.

49. John Dewey, *Human Nature and Choice*, in *The Middle Works of John Dewey*, vol. 14, ed. Jo Ann Boydston (Carbondale: Southern Illinois University Press, 1983), 200.

50. Ralph Waldo Emerson, "Circles," in *Ralph Waldo Emerson*, 167.

51. Friedrich Nietzsche, "Schopenhauer as Educator," in *Untimely Meditations*, trans. R. J. Hollingdale, ed., Daniel Breazeale (Cambridge, UK: Cambridge University Press, 1983), 128, 183. This essay of Nietzsche starts with the Emersonian question, "How can we find outselfes again?", a question addressed by Emerson in "Experience" and concludes with the citation from his "Circles."

52. Earlier versions of parts of this chapter were published in the *Journal of Philosophy of Education* ("Pragmatism and the Tragic Sense: Deweyan

Growth in an Age of Nihilism," 36.2 [2002]: 247–63) in *Transactions of the Charles S. Peirce Society* ("Transcending the Tragic with Dewey and Emerson: Beyond the Morse-Boisvert Debate," 39.2 [2003]: 275–92), and in *Philosophy of Education 2003* ("Education's Hope: Transcending the Tragic with Emerson, Dewey, and Cavell [2004]: 182–90).

CHAPTER NINE

THE REKINDLING OF THE GLEAM OF LIGHT

Toward Perfectionist Education

1. John Dewey, *Construction and Criticism*, in *The Later Works of John Dewey*, vol. 5, ed. Jo Ann Boydston (Carbondale: Southern Illinois University Press, 1984), 135 (hereafter cited as *CC*).

2. Ralph Waldo Emerson, "The Over-Soul," in *Ralph Waldo Emerson*, ed. Richard Poirier (Oxford: Oxford University Press, 1990), 155–56 (hereafter cited as "OS").

3. John Dewey, *Experience and Education* (New York: Macmillan, 1938), 17 (hereafter cited as *EE*).

4. John Dewey, *Democracy and Education*, in *The Middle Works of John Dewey*, vol. 9, ed. Jo Ann Boydston (Carbondale: Southern Illinois University Press, 1980), 338 (hereafter cited as *DE*).

5. John Dewey, "Creative Democracy—The Task Before Us," in *The Later Works of John Dewey*, vol. 14, ed. Jo Ann Boydston (Carbondale: Southern Illinois University Press, 1988), 92 (hereafter cited as "CD").

6. John Dewey, *The Public and Its Problems*, in *The Later Works of John Dewey*, vol. 2, Jo Ann Boydston (Carbondale: Southern Illinois University Press, 1984), 368 (hereafter cited as *PP*).

7. John Dewey, "I Believe," in *The Later Works of John Dewey*, vol. 14, ed. Jo Ann Boydston (Carbondale: Southern Illinois University Press, 1988), 92 (hereafter cited as "IB").

8. Ralph Waldo Emerson, "The American Scholar," in *Ralph Waldo Emerson*, 45 (hereafter cited as "AMS").

9. Ralph Waldo Emerson, "Self-Reliance," in *Ralph Waldo Emerson*, 131 (hereafter cited as "SR").

10. Stanley Cavell, *Conditions Handsome and Unhandsome: The Constitution of Emersonian Perfectionism* (La Salle, IL: Open Court, 1990), 11 (hereafter cited as *Conditions*).

11. John Dewey, *Art as Experience* in *The Later Works of John Dewey*, vol. 10, ed. Jo Ann Boydston (Carbondale: Southern Illinois University Press, 1987), 28, 328 (hereafter cited as *AE*).

12. John J. McDermott, "From Cynicism to Amelioration: Strategies for a Cultural Pedagogy," in Robert. J. Mulvaney and Philip M. Zeltner, eds. *Pragmatism: Its Sources and Prospects* (Columbia: University of South Carolina Press, 1981), 91.

13. John Dewey, *Human Nature and Conduct*, in *The Middle Works of John Dewey*, vol. 14, ed. Jo Ann Boydston (Carbondale: Southern Illinois University Press, 1983), 181.

14. Stanley Cavell, *The Senses of Walden* (Chicago: University of Chicago Press, 1992), 136 (hereafter cited as *Senses*).

15. John Dewey, *Experience and Nature*, in *The Later Works of John Dewey*, vol. 1, ed. Jo Ann Boydston (Carbondale: Southern Illinois University Press, 1981), 286, 290–91.

16. Ralph Waldo Emerson, "Considerations by the Way," in *Ralph Waldo Emerson*, 396.

17. Ralph Waldo Emerson, "Fate," in *Ralph Waldo Emerson*, 345.

18. Stanley Cavell, *Contesting Tears: The Hollywood Melodrama of the Unknown Woman* (Chicago: University of Chicago Press, 1996), 212, 221 (hereafter cited as *Tears*).

19. Steve Odin discusses Dewey's critique of "artistic detachment" and emphasis on "participation" (Steve Odin, *Artistic Detachment in Japan and the West: Psychic Distance in Comparative Aesthetics* [Honolulu: University of Hawaii Press, 2001], 78–88.)

20. Friedrich Nietzsche, "Schopenhauer as Educator," in *Untimely Meditations*, trans. R. J. Hollingdlale, ed. Daniel Breazeale (Cambridge, UK: Cambridge University Press, 1983), 161. George J. Stack points out that this essay of Nietzsche was written under the influence of Emerson (George J. Stack, *Nietzsche and Emerson: An Elective Affinity* [Athens, OH: Ohio University Press, 1992], 16–17, 105).

21. Stanley Cavell, *A Pitch of Philosophy: Autobiographical Exercises* (Cambridge, MA: Harvard University Press, 1994) (hereafter cited as *Pitch*).

22. In connection with the theme of conversation for democracy, Garrison discusses the importance of *listening* as a mode of democratic listening (Jim Garrison, "A Deweyan Theory of Democratic Listening," *Educational Theory*, 46.4 [1996]: 429–51).

23. Dewey, *Democracy and Education*, 93, in Garrison, "A Deweyan Theory of Democratic Listening," 430.

24. John Dewey, "Emerson—The Philosopher of Democracy," in *The Middle Works of John Dewey*, vol. 3, ed. Jo Ann Boydston (Carbondale: Southern Illinois University Press, 1977).

25. John Dewey, *A Common Faith* in *The Later Works of John Dewey*, vol. 9, ed. Jo Ann Boydston (Carbondale: Southern Illinois University Press, 1986).

26. Emerson, "The Poet," in *Ralph Waldo Emerson*, 200 (hereafter cited as "Poet").

27. Emerson, *Representative Men*, ed. Pamela Schirmeister (New York: Marsilio Publishers, Co., 1995), 38.

28. Richard Poirier, *Poetry and Pragmatism*, (Cambridge, MA: Harvard University Press, 1992), 31.

29. Harold Bloom, *Agon: Towards a Theory of Revisionism* (New York: Oxford University Press, 1982), 172, 177.

30. Bloom, *Agon*, 171–72.

31. See Paul Standish, "Ethics before Equality: Moral Education after Levinas," *Journal of Moral Education*, 30.4 (2001): 339–48.

32. Steve Odin points out that William James's idea of the self in stream of consciousness and pure experience is characterized by "a focus / fringe pattern grounded by the datum of felt wholeness." The Jamesian idea of the "focal self with the center" in the whole field that Odin discusses matches Dewey's idea of the self as the center in the field (Steve Odin, *The Social Self in Zen and American Pragmatism* [Albany: State University of New York Press, 1996], 157).

33. Ralph Waldo Emerson, "Experience," in *Ralph Waldo Emerson*, 228.

34. Parts of this chapter were published in different versions in the *Journal of Philosophy of Education* ("Pragmatism and the Tragic Sense: Deweyan Growth in an Age of Nihilism," 36.2 [2002]: 247–63) and in *Teachers College Record* ("Education for Global Understanding: Learning from Dewey's Visit to Japan," 105.9 [2003]: 1758–1773).

Bibliography

Works by John Dewey

The collected works of John Dewey, edited by Jo Ann Boydston and published by Southern Illinois University Press, are listed chronologically with the following abbreviations: "EW" (The Early Works [1882–1898]; "MW" (The Middle Works [1899–1924]; and "LW" [The Later Works [1925–1953]). The dates in parentheses are those of the original publication.

Dewey, John. *Psychology* (1887). EW2, 1967.
———. *Outlines of a Critical Theory of Ethics* (1891). EW3, 1969.
———. *The Child and the Curriculum* (1902). MW2, 1976.
———. "Emerson—The Philosopher of Democracy" (1903). MW3, 1977.
———. *Ethics* (1908). MW5, 1978.
———. "Maeterlink's Philosophy of Life" (1911). MW6, 1978.
———. *Democracy and Education* (1916). MW9, 1980.
———. *Essays in Experimental Logic*. New York: Dover, 1916.
———. *Reconstruction in Philosophy*. Boston: Beacon Press, 1920.
———. *Human Nature and Conduct* (1922). MW14, 1983.
———. *Experience and Nature* (1925). LW1, 1981.
———. *The Public and Its Problems* (1927). LW2, 1984.
———. *The Quest for Certainty* (1929). LW4, 1984.
———. *Individualism Old and New* (1930). LW5, 1984.
———. *Construction and Criticism* (1930). LW5, 1984.
———. "From Absolutism to Experimentalism" (1930). LW 5, 1984.
———. "Qualitative Thought" (1930). LW5, 1984.
———. *Ethics* (1932). LW7, 1985.
———. *How We Think* (1933). LW8, 1986.
———. Contributions to *The Educational Frontier* (1933), LW8, 1986.
———. *A Common Faith* (1934). LW9, 1986.
———. *Art as Experience* (1934). LW10, 1987.

———. *Logic: The Theory of Inquiry* (1938). LW12, 1986.
———. *Experience and Education.* New York: Macmillan, 1938.
———. "Creative Democracy—The Task Before Us" (1939). LW14, 1988.
———. "I Believe" (1939). LW14, 1988.
———. "Time and Individuality" (1940). LW14, 1988.
———. "James Marsh and American Philosophy" (1941). LW5, 1984.
———. "Anti-Naturalism in Extremis" (1943). LW15, 1989.

Other Works

Alexander, Thomas M. *John Dewey's Theory of Art, Experience, and Nature: The Horizons of Feeling.* Albany: State University of New York Press, 1987.
———. "The Human Eros." In *Philosophy and the Reconstruction of Culture: Pragmatic Essays after Dewey.* Edited by John J. Stuhr. Albany: State University of New York Press, 1993.
Anderson, Douglas R. "American Loss in Cavell's Emerson." *Transactions of the Charles S. Peirce Society,* 29.1 (1993): 69–89.
Arcilla, René V. "Tragic Absolutism in Education." *Educational Theory,* 42.2 (1992): 473–81.
Aristotle. *Nicomachean Ethics.* In *Classic and Contemporary Readings in the Philosophy of Education.* Edited by Steven M. Cahn. New York: McGraw-Hill, 1997. (Originally translated by David Ross, revised by J. L. Ackrill and J. D. Urmson [Oxford: Oxford University Press, 1980]).
Arnold, Matthew. *Culture and Anarchy.* Edited by Samuel Lipman. New Haven: Yale University Press, 1994.
Bernstein, Richard J. *John Dewey.* New York: Washington Square Press, 1966.
———. "The Resurgence of Pragmatism." *Social Research,* 59 (Winter 1992): 813–40.
Blake, Nigel, Paul Smeyers, Richard Smith, and Paul Standish. *Education in an Age of Nihilism.* London: Routledge-Falmer, 2000.
Bloom, Allan. *The Closing of the American Mind.* New York: A Touch Stone Book, 1987.
Bloom, Harold. *Agon: Towards a Theory of Revisionism.* New York: Oxford University Press, 1982.
Bode, Boyd H. *Progressive Education at the Crossroads.* New York: Newson and Company, 1938.
Boisvert, Raymond D. *Dewey's Metaphysics.* New York: Fordham University Press, 1988.

———. "The Nemesis of Necessity: Tragedy's Challenge to Deweyan Pragmatism." In *Dewey Reconfigured*. Edited by Casey Haskins and David I. Seiple. Albany: State University of New York Press, 1999.

———. "Updating Dewey: A Reply to Morse." *Transactions of the Charles S. Peirce Society*, 37. 4(2001): 578–83.

———. "Forget Emerson, Forget Growth, Embrace Anaximander: Pragmatism and the Tragic Sense." Paper presented at Society for the Advancement of American Philosophy, 8 March 2002, Portland, ME.

———. "Toward a Programmatic Pragmatism: A Response to Naoko Saito." *Journal of Philosophy of Education*, 36. 4 (2002): 621–28.

Boler, Megan. "An Epoch of Difference: Hearing Voices in the Nineties." *Educational Theory*, 50.3 (2000): 357–81.

Boller, Paul F. *American Transcendentalism, 1830–1860: An Intellectual Inquiry*. New York: G. P. Putnam's Sons, 1974.

Bourne, Randolph. *The Radical Will: Selected Writings 1911–1918*. Edited by Olaf Hansen. Berkeley: University of California, 1977.

Buell, Lawrence. *Emerson*. Cambridge, MA: Belknap Press of Harvard University Press, 2003.

Cavell, Stanley. *The Claim of Reason: Wittgenstein, Skepticism, Morality, and Tragedy*. Oxford: Oxford University Press, 1979.

———. *This New Yet Unapproachable America: Lectures after Emerson after Wittgenstein*. Albuquerque, NM: Living Batch Press, 1989.

———. *Conditions Handsome and Unhandsome: The Constitution of Emersonian Perfectionism*. La Salle, IL: Open Court, 1990.

———. *The Senses of Walden*. Chicago: University of Chicago Press, 1992.

———. *A Pitch of Philosophy: Autobiographical Exercises*. Cambridge, MA: Harvard University Press, 1994.

———. *Philosophical Passages: Wittgenstein, Emerson, Austin, Derrida*. Oxford: Blackwell, 1995.

———. *Contesting Tears: The Hollywood Melodrama of the Unknown Woman*. Chicago: University of Chicago Press, 1996.

———. "What's the Use of Calling Emerson a Pragmatist?" In *The Revival of Pragmatism: New Essays on Social Thought, Law, and Culture*. Edited by Morris Dickstein. Durham, NC: Duke University Press, 1998.

———. "Nichijosei he no Kaiki: Watashi no Koe, Amerika no Koe" ("Return to the Ordinary: The Voice of Myself and the Voice of America." Interviewed and translated by Naoko Saito [11 November 1997]. *Gendai-Shiso (Contemporary Thoughts)* 26.1 (1998): 50–59.

———. *Emerson's Transcendental Etudes*. Stanford: Stanford University Press, 2003.

Chambliss, J. J. "Common Ground in Aristotle's and Dewey's Theories of Conduct."*Educational Theory*, 43.3 (1993): 249–60.
Colapietro, Vincent M. "The Question of Voice and the Limits of Pragmatism: Emerson, Dewey, and Cavell." *Metaphilosophy*, 35.1–2 (2004):178–201.
Conant, James. Introduction to *Realism with a Human Face* by Hilary Putnam. Cambridge, MA: Harvard University Press, 1990.
Coughlan, Neil. *Young John Dewey: An Essay in American Intellectual History*. Chicago: University of Chicago Press, 1973.
Diggins, John Patrick. *The Promise of Pragmatism: Modernism and the Crisis of Knowledge and Authority*. Chicago: University of Chicago Press, 1994.
Dykhuizen, George. *The Life and Mind of John Dewey*. Carbondale: Southern Illinois University Press, 1973.
Eames, Morris S. "The Cognitive and the Non-Cognitive in Dewey's Theory of Valuation." *The Journal of Philosophy*, 58 (March 1961): 179–95.
Emerson, Ralph Waldo. "The American Scholar." *Ralph Waldo Emerson*. Edited by Richard Poirier. Oxford: Oxford University Press, 1990.
———. "Circles." *Ralph Waldo Emerson*.
———. "Compensation." *The Portable Emerson*. Edited by Carl Bode in collaboration with Malcolm Cowley. New York: Viking Penguin, 1946; Penguin Books, 1977.
———. "Considerations by the Way." *Ralph Waldo Emerson*.
———. "Experience." *Ralph Waldo Emerson*.
———. "Fate." *Ralph Waldo Emerson*.
———. "Friendship." *Ralph Waldo Emerson*.
———. "History." *Ralph Waldo Emerson*.
———. "Intellect." *Ralph Waldo Emerson*.
———. "The Over-Soul." *Ralph Waldo Emerson*.
———. "The Poet." *Ralph Waldo Emerson*.
———. *Representative Men*. Edited by Pamela Schirmeister. New York: Marsilio Publishers Co., 1995.
———. "Self-Reliance." *Ralph Waldo Emerson*.
———. "The Transcendentalists." *Ralph Waldo Emerson*.
———. *The Heart of Emerson's Journals*. Edited by Bliss Perry. New York: Dover, 1958.
———. *The Selected Letters of Ralph Waldo Emerson*. Edited by Joel Myerson. New York: Columbia University Press, 1997.
Feenberg, Andrew. "Pragmatism and Critical Theory of Technology: Reply to Hickman." Paper presented at a meeting for the Society for Philosophy and Technology, Aberdeen, Scotland, 10 July 2001.

———. "Pragmatism and Critical Theory of Technology." *The Proceedings for the UTCP International Symposium on Pragmatism and the Philosophy of Technology in the 21st Century*, 2. Tokyo: The University of Tokyo Center for Philosophy, 2003: 115–25.

———. *Heidegger and Marcuse: The Catastrophe and Redemption of History*. New York: Routledge, 2005.

Feinberg, Walter. "Dewey and Democracy: At the Dawn of the Twenty-First Century." *Educational Theory* 43.2 (1993): 195–216.

Frankena, W. K. "The Naturalistic Fallacy." *Mind*, 48 (October 1939): 464–77.

Fujita, Hidenori. "Shin-Jidai no Kyoiku o Do Koso Suruka: Kyoiku-Kaikaku Kokumin Kaigi no Nokoshita Kadai" ("How to Envision Education in New Era: Tasks Left by the National Commission on Educational Reform"). *Iwanami Booklet*, 533 Tokyo: Iwanam: Shoten, 2000.

Garrison, Jim. "Realism, Deweyan Pragmatism, and Educational Research. *Educational Researcher*, 23.1 (1994): 5–14.

———. *Dewey and Eros: Wisdom and Desire in the Art of Teaching*. New York: Teachers College Press, 1997.

———. "Dewey and the Education of Eros." Paper presented at the International Conference on the Philosophy of John Dewey, Cosenza, Calabria, Italy, 10–13 April 2000. Photocopied.

———. "A Deweyan Theory of Democratic Listening." *Educational Theory*, 46.4: 429–51.

Goodman, Russell B. *American Philosophy and the Romantic Tradition*. Cambridge, UK: Cambridge University Press, 1990.

———. "Moral Perfectionism and Democracy: Emerson, Nietzsche, Cavell." *ESQ: A Journal of the American Renaissance*, 43, 1–4(1997): 159–80.

Gouinlock, James. "What Is the Legacy of Instrumentalism? Rorty's Interpretation of Dewey." In *Rorty and Pragmatism: The Philosopher Responds to His Critics*. Edited by Herman J. Saatkamp, Jr. Nashville: Vanderbilt University Press, 1995.

Hickman, Larry. "Pragmatism, Technology, and Scientism." In *Pragmatism: From Progressivism to Postmodernism*. Edited by Robert Hollinger and David Depew. Westport, CT: Praeger, 1995.

Hiei, Toshio. "'Kokoro no Kyoiku' tte Nani?" ("What Is the 'Education of the Heart'?" *The Yomiuri Newspaper*, 5 October 1997.

Hofstadter, Richard. *Anti-intellectualism in American Life*. New York: Alfred A. Knopf, 1963.

Hook, Sidney. "Naturalism and Democracy." In *Naturalism and the Human Spirit*, Edited by Yervant H. Krikorian. New York: Columbia University Press, 1944.

———. "John Dewey: Philosopher of Growth." *The Journal of Philosophy*, 56 (December 1959): 1010–18.

———. *Pragmatism and the Tragic Sense of Life*. New York: Basic Books, 1974.

Hurka, Thomas. "The Well-Rounded Life." *The Journal of Philosophy*, 84 (December 1987): 727–46.

———. "Perfectionism." In *Routledge Encyclopedia of Philosophy*, 7. Edited by Edward Craig. London: Routledge, 1998: 299–302.

James, William. *The Will to Believe: And Other Essays in Popular Philosophy*. New York: Dover, 1956.

Joas, Hans. *The Creativity of Action*. Chicago: University of Chicago Press, 1996.

Ju-Yon-Sai: Kokoro no Fukei (Fourteen-Year-Olds: The Scenery in their Minds). Edited by Nihon-Hoso-Kyokai, "Ju-Yon-Sai: Kokoro no Fukei Project (The Project for Fourteen-Year-Olds: The Scenery in their Minds" in Japan Broadcasting Corporation). Tokyo: Nihon-Hoso Shuppan-Kyokai, 1998.

Kandel, I. L. *The Cult of Uncertainty*. New York: Macmillan, 1943.

Kateb, George. *Emerson and Self-Reliance*. Walnut Creek, CA: Altamira Press, 2000.

Kosugi, Takashi. *Ushinawareta "Kokoro no Kyoiku" o Motomete: Niju-Isseiki ni Okuru Kyoiku-Kaikaku (In Search of the Lost "Education of the Heart": Educational Reform for the 21st Century)*. Tokyo: Diamond-Sha, 1997.

Levinas, Emmanuel. *Totality and Infinity: An Essay on Exteriority*. Translated by A. Lingis. Pittsburgh: Duquesne University Press, 1969.

———. *Collected Philosophical Papers*. Translated by A. Lingis. Pittsburgh: Duquesne University Press, 1998.

McDermott, John. "From Cynicism to Amelioration: Strategies for a Cultural Pedagogy." In *Pragmatism: Its Sources and Prospects*. Edited by Robert J. Mulvaney and Philip M. Zeltner. Columbia, SC: University of South Carolina Press, 1981.

Moore, G. E. *Principia Ethica*. In *Ethics*. Edited by Peter Singer. Oxford: Oxford University Press, 1994.

Mulhall, Stephen. *Stanley Cavell: Philosophy's Recounting of the Ordinary*. Oxford: Clarendon Press, 1994.

Nicholson, Marjorie H. "James Marsh and the Vermont Transcendentalism." *Philosophical Review*, 34 (January 1925): 28–50.

Nietzsche, Friedrich. *Untimely Meditations*. Translated by R. J. Hollingdale and edited by Daniel Breazeale. Cambridge, UK: Cambridge University Press, 1983.

Nishihira Tadashi, and René V. Arcilla, "Nihilism and Education." Lecture given at the University of Tokyo, Tokyo, 21 July 1999.
Noddings, Nel. "Thoughts on John Dewey's 'Ethical Principles Underlying Education.'" *The Elementary School Journal*, 98 (May 1998): 479–88.
Odin, Steve. *The Social Self in Zen and American Pragmatism*. Albany: State University of New York Press, 1996.
———. *Artistic Detachment in Japan and the West: Psychic Distance in Comparative Aesthetics*. Honolulu: University of Hawaii Press, 2001.
O'Hear, Anthony. *Father of Child-Centredness: John Dewey and the Ideology of Modern Education*. London: Centre for Policy Studies, 1991.
Okihara, Yutaka. *Shin-Kokoro no Kyoiku* (*New Education of the Heart*). Tokyo: Gakuyo-Shobo, 1997.
Peters, R. S. *John Dewey Reconsidered*. London: Routledge and Kegan Paul, 1977.
Plato. *The Republic*. Translated by G. M. A. Grube. Indianapolis: Hackett Publishing, 1992.
Poirier, Richard. *Poetry and Pragmatism*. Cambridge, MA: Harvard University Press, 1992.
Putnam, Hilary. *Realism with a Human Face*. Cambridge, MA: Harvard University Press, 1990.
———. *Renewing Philosophy*. Cambridge, MA: Harvard University Press, 1992.
———. *Words and Life*. Edited by James Conant. Cambridge, MA: Harvard University Press, 1994.
———. *Pragmatism: An Open Question*. Oxford: Blackwell, 1995.
———. "Are Moral and Legal Values Made or Discovered?" *Legal Theory*, 1 (1995): 5–19.
———. *The Threefold Cord: Mind, Body, and World*. New York: Columbia University Press, 1999.
———. "Dewey's Central Insight." Paper presented at the International Conference on the Philosophy of John Dewey, Cosenza, Calabria, Italy, 10–13 April 2000. Photocopied.
———. "Pragmatism and Neo-Pragmatism." Lecture given at Harvard University, Cambridge, MA, 17 April 2000. Tape recording.
———. *The Collapse of the Fact / Value Dichotomy and Other Essays*. Cambridge, MA. Harvard University Press, 2002.
———. *Ethics without Ontology*. Cambridge, MA: Harvard University Press, 2004.
Rockefeller, Steven C. *John Dewey: Religious Faith and Democratic Humanism*. New York: Columbia University Press, 1991.

Rorty, Richard. *Philosophy and the Mirror of Nature.* Princeton: Princeton University Press, 1979.
———. *Consequences of Pragmatism.* Minneapolis: University of Minnesota Press, 1982.
———. *Contingency, Irony and Solidarity.* Cambridge, UK: Cambridge University Press, 1989.
———. "Response to Thelma Lavine." In *Rorty and Pragmatism: The Philosopher Responds to His Critics.* Edited by Herman J. Saatkamp, Jr. Nashville: Vanderbilt University Press, 1995.
———. *Truth and Progress: Philosophical Papers,* 3. Cambridge: Cambridge University Press, 1998.
———. "Pragmatism as Romantic Polytheism." In *the Revival of Pragmatism: New Essays on Social Thought, Law, and Culture.* Edited by Morris Dickstein. Durham, NC: Duke University Press, 1998.
———. *Philosophy and Social Hope.* London: Penguin Books, 1999.
Ryan, Alan. *John Dewey and the High Tide of American Liberalism.* New York: W. W. Norton, 1995.
Saito, Naoko. "Owari Naki Seicho he no Cosen: Hegel to Darwin no Aida no Dewey." ("A Challenge to Growth without Ends: Dewey between Hegel and Darwin"). *Gendai-Shiso (Contemporary Thoughts),* 28.5 (2000): 167–89.
———. "Perfecting Democracy through Holistic Education: Dewey's Naturalistic Philosophy of Growth Reconsidered." *Philosophy of Education 2000* (2001): 155–63.
———. "Reconstructing Deweyan Pragmatism in Dialogue with Emerson and Cavell." *Transactions of the Charles S. Peirce Society,* 37.3 (2001): 389–406.
———. "Education for the Gleam of Light: Emerson's Transcendentalism and Its Implications for Contemporary Moral Education." *Philosophy of Education 2001* (2002): 144–52.
———. "Pragmatism and the Tragic Sense: Deweyan Growth in an Age of Nihilism." *Journal of Philosophy of Education,* 36.2 (2002): 247–63.
———. "Transcending the Tragic with Dewey and Emerson: Beyond the Morse-Boisvert Debate." *Transactions of the Charles S. Peirce Society,* 39.2 (2003): 275–92.
———. "Education for Global Understanding: Learning from Dewey's Visit to Japan." *Teachers College Record,* 105.9 (2003): 1758–73.
———. "Education's Hope: Transcending the Tragic with Emerson, Dewey, and Cavell." *Philosophy of Education 2003* (2004): 182–90.

Santayana, George. *George Santayana's America: Essays on Literature and Culture.* Collected and with an Introduction by James Ballowe. Urbana: University of Illinois Press, 1967.
———. *The Genteel Tradition: Nine Essays by George Santayana.* Edited by Douglas L. Wilson. Lincoln: University of Nebraska Press, 1967.
Sato, Manabu. "Kodomotachi wa Naze 'Manabi' kara Toso Suru ka?: 'Gakuryoku-Teika' ni Miru Nihon-Shakai no Bunka-teki Kiki" ("Why Are Children Escaping from 'Learning?': Cultural Crisis of Japanese Society Indicated by a 'Decline of Knowledge Level'"). *Sekai (The World),* 674 (2000): 77–85.
———. "Gakuryoku o Toi-naosu: Manabi-no Curriculum he" ("Re-questioning Academic Achievement: Toward a Curriculum for Learning"). *Iwanami Booklet,* 548. Tokyo: Iwanami: Shoten, 2001.
Scheffler, Israel. *Four Pragmatists: A Critical Introduction to Peirce, James, Mead and Dewey.* London: Routledge and Kegan Paul, 1974.
Sleeper, Ralph W. *The Necessity of Pragmatism: John Dewey's Conception of Philosophy.* New Haven: Yale University Press, 1986.
Stack, George J. *Nietzsche and Emerson: An Elective Affinity.* Athens, OH: Ohio University Press, 1992.
Standish, Paul. "Ethics before Equality: Moral Education after Levinas." *Journal of Moral Education.* 30.4 (2001): 339–48.
———. "From Moral Education to Citizenship: Principles and Problems in UK Policy." *International Christian University, Publications* 1-A, *Educational Studies,* 44 (March 2002), 243–62. Tokyo: The International Christian University, 2002.
———. "Democratic Participation and the Body Politic. Paper to be published in *Educational Theory.*
———. "Shimin-sei to Kyoiku no Mokuteki: Eikoku ni Okeru Seisaku to Jissen no Igi" ("Citizenship and the Aims of Education"). Translated by Naoko Saito. In *Shimin-sei no Kyoiku (Education for Citizenship)* (temporary title). Edited by Manabu Sato, Ryoko Tsuneyoshi, and Hidenori Fujita. Tokyo: Tokyo Daigaku Shuppan-kai (to be published in 2005).
Stuhr, John J. *Genealogical Pragmatism: Philosophy, Experience, and Community.* Albany: State University of New York Press, 1997.
Takahashi, Tetsuya, and Akiko Miyake. "Kore wa 'Kokumin Seishin Kaizo Undo' da." ("This Is the 'Movement for Reconstructing the National Spirit'"). *Sekai (The World),* 712 (2003): 33–47.
Taylor, Charles. *Sources of the Self: The Making of the Modern Identity.* Cambridge, MA: Harvard University Press, 1989.

Varela, Francisco, Evan Thompson, and Eleanor Rosch. *The Embodied Mind: Cognitive Science and Human Experience*. Cambridge, MA: MIT Press, 1993.

Versluis, Arthur. *American Transcendentalism and Asian Religions*. Oxford: Oxford University Press, 1993.

West, Cornel. *The American Evasion of Philosophy: A Genealogy of Pragmatism*. Madison: University of Wisconsin Press, 1989.

———. *The Cornel West Reader*. New York: Basic Civitas Books, 1999.

Westbrook, Robert B. *John Dewey and American Democracy*. Ithaca: Cornell University Press, 1991.

White, Morton. *Social Thought in America: The Revolt against Formalism*. New York: Viking Press, 1952.

Williams, Bernard. *Ethics and the Limits of Philosophy*. Cambridge, MA: Harvard University Press, 1985.

Index

Abandonment, 147. *See also* Detachment; Nonattachment
Absolutism, 9, 12, 29, 41, 121, 136, 139; moral, 131, 160; tragic, 124; metaphysical, 170*n*69
Acknowledgment, 56
Alexander, Frederick M., 72, 179*n*8
Anaximander, 123
Antifoundationalism, 7, 9, 10, 15, 25, 35, 96; Antifoundationalist, 17; Emersonian, 121, 132, 134–36; Rorty's, 8–9, 124, 135–36
Aristotle, 32, 51, 53, 74–75, 78–79, 180*n*14; Aristotelian, 54; perfectionism, 175*n*7
Arnold, Matthew, 51–52, 153
Asian religion, 102
Augustine, 103
Austin, J. L., 173*n*31

Bergson, Henri, 186*n*30
Bhagavad Gita, 102
Behaviorism: Dewey and, 179*n*8; reductionist, 72; Rorty's linguistic, 26–27
British empiricism. *See* Empiricism
Buddhism, 180*n*13. *See also* Zen Buddhist

Cartesian: dualism, 179*n*13; materialism, 179*n*13; rationalism, 71
Chance, 113–14, 122
Child/children: and escape from learning, 131; Cavell on, 10, 90–92, 97; -centeredness, 141; -centered education, 6, 19, 140; death of, 47; Dewey on, 5, 63, 94–95; disciplining of, 130; Emersonian, 90, 93, 97, 138 ; exceptional, 88; immaturity of, 5, 99; George Eliot on childhood, 145; recalcitrant, 14, 85–89, 93, 95, 99, 119, 136; romanticization of childhood, 126, 149; speech of, 44, 81; teacher's seeing of, 182*n*9
Circle(s), 4, 10, 14, 70, 76–79, 94, 108, 110, 112, 119, 132, 145, 147–48, 161, 177*n*22, 181*n*22, 186*n*33
Coleridge, Samuel Taylor, 37, 171*nn*11, 12, 184*n*15; *Aids to Reflection*, 37; "art of reflection," 39
Common good, 1, 22
Communitarian, 28; Communitarianism, 160
Compensation, 133
Conformity, 1, 3, 54, 57, 61, 64, 125–26, 154; anticonformist, 66; anticonformity, 100; non-, 55, 61, 73, 87, 89, 103; non-conformist, 88
Consummation: of experience, 115, 189*n*19; Consummatory moment, 111, 159
Courage, 132, 148, 155, 157–58; Cavell on, 138; Dewey and, 59, 70, 87, 109, 123, 139, 143, 146; Emerson and, 60, 87, 113–14, 158; pragmatism as philosophy of, 121
Crick Report, 129
Criteria/criterion, 5, 13, 23–24, 117–18, 149–50; directive, 14, 115, 117–19, 135,

{ 205 }

137, 149; missing, 167*n*33; revisable, 83; revised, 94; social reconstruction of, 81–83, 85–89, 94, 119; socially revised, 14; universal set of, 32; Wittgenstein's concept of. *See* Wittgenstein

Darwin: Darwinian evolutionary theory, 18, 113, 187*n*37; Darwinian experimentalism, 21; Darwinian naturalism, 5, 17, 23, 25, 40, 61, 96, 169*n*62: *See also* naturalism; Darwinian naturalistic philosophy of growth, 6, 8, 25, 33, 79; Hegel and, 8–9, 11–13, 17–18, 14–16, 29–30, 35–37, 40–41, 49, 51, 67–68, 79, 159
Derrida, Jacques, 124, 134
Despair, 113, 119, 138, 172*n*29
Detachment, 16, 148; art of, 147; artistic, 193n19. *See also* Abandonment; Nonattachment
Deviancy, 87–88; assimilation of, 94.
Discontinuity: discontinuous continuity, 114, 118; discontinuous moment, 115; prophesy in, 4; prophetic impulse and, 14
Disobedience, 103
Dissident, 157

Eccentricity, 88
Edwards, Jonathan, 101, 104
Eliot, George, 145
Empiricism, 7, 46; British, 18, 71; Lockean, 37–38, 107; Empiricist, 42, 101, 173*n*46
End: Dewey's Emersonian view of, 69, 73–76, 78, 80; in Deweyan growth, 62, 81, 83; -in-view, 76, 80, 180*n*18; means-ends relationship, 13, 75–76, 96, 180*n*16; pragmatism's lack of, 6
Enlightenment, 43, 47, 101; anti-, 44; pragmatist, 173*n*46
Equality, 57, 137, 157
Experiment: Dewey and 47, 109, 121; Emerson and, 97, 103; Emerson as experimenter, 101, 113

Experimental: Dewey and experimental method, 20, 30; Dewey and experimental inquiry, 29
Experimentalism: Dewey's experimentalism, 41; Darwinian: *See* Darwin; from absolutism to, 60
Experimentalist: Emerson as experimentalist, 42
Experimentation: Dewey on experimentation, 180*n*18; in Dewey's scientific method, 83, 105

Facts and values, 22, 96; Putnam on, 32, 34, 169*n*65, 169*n*67
Fate, 113, 147–48
Finding as founding, 134–37
Free will, 39
Freedom, 2, 66–67, 125, 128–32, 136–37, 148, 186*n*33; democratic, 6, 29; individual, 3; unbridled, 6
Freudian, 54; psychoanalysis, 71
Functional psychology, 18
Friends, 182*n*17
Friendship, 16, 53, 56–57, 66, 146, 151–51, 177*n*22
Fuller, Margaret, 133

Genius, 55, 65, 103, 103, 142, 146
German idealism. *See* Idealism
Gleam of Light. *See* Light

Habit reconstruction, 13, 61, 69–73, 76–77, 79, 83, 86, 95, 99, 105, 109, 127
Happiness, 53, 56, 62, 75, 111, 147, 175*n*7
Harris, William T., 38; *The Journal of Speculative Philosophy*, 38
Hawthorne, Nathaniel, 123
Hegel, G. W. F., 79; Hegel's Absolute, 5; Hegel's view of perfection, 60–61, 79; Hegelian absolutism, 5, 21; Hegelian historicism, 25; Hegelian idealism, 23, 41; Hegelian self–realization, 19; American neo-Hegelians, 38; and Darwin: *See* Darwin; Dewey and Hegelianism, 21, 39, 42, 77
Heidegger, Martin, 51, 108, 136

Hinduism, 101–102. *See also* Indian philosophy
Holmes, Justice, 59
Hudson, W. H., 143–44

Ibsen, Henrik, 51
Idealism, 33, 96; Dewey's social, 59; Emersonian, 41; German, 38; Hegelian: *See* Hegel; Kant's transcendental: *See* Kant; Royce's, 122; transcendental, 26
Idealist: Dewey as, 21; Emersonian, 42, 60, 67, 101–102; teleology, 25: tradition in America, 38
Imagination, 14, 110, 116–18, 143, 145, 152, 187n42.
Impulse, 16, 73, 84, 86, 91, 94, 99–100, 110, 112, 143, 145, 160; and directive criteria, 118: *See also* Directive criteria; and the gleam of light; 10, 105–106, 108, 115: *See also* Gleam of Light; and emotion, 116; and intelligence, 4, 70–71, 127 : *See also* Intelligence: prophetic, 14–15, 132, 140, 159; James on, 187n37; stifled, 125; and whim, 103, 107, 114: *See also* Whim
Independence, 88, 103, 125
Indian philosophy, 102. *See also* Hinduism
Individual(s), 63–67, 115, 119, 125–26, 129, 142, 146, 151, 159, 186n33, 187n37; and community, 22; lost, 11, 64; existential choice, 34; isolated, 159; potential of, 25; recalcitrant, 88; right of, 58; self-reliant, 100; what is distinctively, 87
Individualism, 1; American, 56, 125; Emerson's, 176n19; ethical, 88; isolated, 4, 65; new, 159; rugged, 1; robust, 7; selfish, 2, 142, 146, 149; talented, 153
Individuality, 22, 66, 108, 115, 129; genuine, 114; integrated, 65; novel, 115
Individuation, 56, 114, 146–47, 157
individualization, 148
Inquiry, 47, 109, 156, 179m13, 187n42; cooperative, 83, 169n68; democratization of, 32, 83; free, 66

Instinct, 101, 103–104, 107, 113; instinctive preference, 115; theory, 179n8
Instrumentalism, 29; instrumentalist attitude, 7
Integrity, 2, 101–102, 125
Intellect, 62; Dewey on, 37, 118; Emerson on, 45–46, 108, 118: *See also* Thinking
Intelligence, 10, 20, 29, 31, 46, 62, 79, 110, 151, 167n33, 172n29, 173n46; Cavell on, 44–45; Coleridge and Marsh on, 39; creative, 15, 146, 159; critical, 42; Emerson's idea of, 64, 108–109; experimental, 83; and impulse, 4, 70–71, 105: *See also* Impulse; scientific, 10, 29, 123; scientific method and, 30, 35, 43, 47, 49, 107; social, 34, 83, 94, 99, 118–19, 127
Intensity, 2, 111, 144–45, 159, 161
Interaction: Cavell's idea of, 93–94; Dewey's idea of, 5, 18, 69–70, 73, 83–86, 89, 96, 105–106, 115–16, 119, 144
Intersubjectivity, 34
Intuition: Dewey on, 120, 142, 186n30: *See also* Bergson; Emerson and, 101, 107–108, 176n19; in Scottish realism, 37; Marsh and Coleridge on, 39, 171n12, 184n15: *See also* Intuitionism
Intuitionism, 37, 171n12; New England, 185n15; Scottish, 104

James, William, 41, 104–105, 109, 114, 187n37, 194n32
Japanese education, 128–31, 136–37, 190nn30, 32
Justice, 56–57; social, 151

Kant, Immanuel, 51, 56, 77, 108, 117, 147, 180m18; Kant's transcendental, 101, 184nn7, 15; Kantian; Putnam's, 170n69; Kantianism, 51
Keats, John, 153
Kierkegaard, Søren, 24
Kleist, Heinrich von, 51
Kokoro no Kyoiku (Education of the Heart), 130
Kokoro no Note (Notebook for the Heart), 130

Levinas, Emmanuel, 164*n*24
Leaving, 147–48
Liberal: -communitarian democracy, 3; neo-, 128, 131, 136; progressive education, 89, 164*n*16; utopia, 28
Liberalism, 160; neo-, 130, 139
Liberalization, 130
Liberty, 56–57, 139
Light, 1–3; Gleam of, 4, 8–12, 14, 16, 99–120 passim, 126–27, 132, 137–49 passim, 157–61, 184*n*15, 185*n*17: *See also* Impulse; Whim; inner, 119, 150; lost, 11, 142, 146; prophetic, 115–17, 140, 150, 153, 157

Man Thinking. *See* Thinking
Marsh, James, 37, 171*nn*11, 12; "Preliminary Essay," 38
Mead, G. H., 72, 106, 114–15, 135–36
Miall, Bernard, 185*n*24
Moods, 77; epistemology of, 77, 184*n*7
Morris, George Sylvester, 39
Mourning, 124, 126, 132–33, 137; as morning, 147; morning comes after, 4
Mutual recognition, 157

Naturalism, 20, 32, 41, 95; anti-, 20; antireductionist, 20, 33; Darwinian naturalism: *See* Darwin; Dewey's, 166*n*16; experimental, 180*n*14; naturalistic ethics, 19–25, 28, 34; naturalistic fallacy, 22; naturalistic spiritualist, 42; reductive, 108
Nietzsche, Friedrich, 24, 51, 54, 136, 138, 148, 158, 174*n*1, 191*n*51, 193*n*20; Nietzschean Emerson, 176*n*19
Nihilism, 1–3, 6, 9, 11, 15, 31, 124, 127, 131–32, 138, 160, 190*n*36; nihilistic tendencies, 7
Nishida, Kitaro, 114, 136, 184*n*13; Zen philosophy, 135
Nonattachment, 102. *See also* Abandonment; Detachment

Over-Soul, 147
Otherness, 4, 132, 147–48, 157–58, 160. *See also* Self-transcendence

Patience, 44, 142
Perception: aesthetic, 157; Dewey and, 106, 109, 143, 145; Emerson and, 40, 113, 135; George Eliot on, 145
Peirce, Charles S., 72, 179*n*13; *tychism*, 113
Plato, 24, 51–53, 74, 101, 103, 129; Emerson's Platonic origin, 102; neo-Platonism, 101
Plotinus, 101
Poiesis, 15, 153
Positivism: logical, 170–71*n*68
Positivist: bifurcation of goods, 170*n*74; objectivism, 33; positivistic scientism, 29, 96
Potential, 5, 132, 140, 161; Dewey on, 20–21, 25, 95, 145, 148, 158; in Emersonian moral perfectionism, 54, 176*n*17; Potentiality/-ies: Dewey on, 71, 74, 115–16
Possibility/-ies, 122; in Dewey's idea, 18, 64, 79, 116, 123, 125, 139, 141, 153, 179*n*9, 180*n*15, 187*n*42; in Emerson's idea, 78, 134, 148, 157
Private and public, 2–3, 11, 15, 128–32, 140–42, 176*n*19
Progress: in Dewey's idea, 7–8, 11, 18, 21, 26, 29–30, 35, 63, 69, 79, 87, 98, 120, 123, 125, 135, 160; in Emerson's idea, 107, 191
Progressive: Dewey's view, 72, 113–14, 117–18; Dewey on progressive growth, 3, 6–7, 9, 11, 14, 29, 69, 120–21, 124–25, 127; education, 9, 15, 19, 89, 126, 140, 160, 164n16; Emerson's view, 181n22
Progressivism, 16, 164*n*17; Dewey's, 161
Pure experience, 194n32. *See also* James, William
Puritanism, 71; puritan moral thinking, 177*n*26

Rationalist, 173*n*46
Rawls, John, 54, 174*n*1; *Theory of Justice*, 54
Realism, 32, 77, 96; essentialist, 33; metaphysical, 32. Putnam's, 32; Scottish, 37–38

Realist, empirical, 42
Reason, 41; Dewey on, 40, 62, 70, 96, 109, 171*n*12, 186*n*30; Cavell on, 90–91, 93–94, 172*n*29; Emerson on, 184*n*15; in Marsh and Coleridge, 38–39, 184*n*15; in Scottish realism, 37
Relativism, 121, 140; moral, 6, 160; Putnam on, 32–33, 170*n*69; Rorty and, 8, 12, 18, 25–26, 31–32, 136
Representation theory, 31; of language, 26
Representativeness: Emerson and, 56, 176*n*15, 176*n*20, 177*n*22
Romanticism: Emersonian, 42
Rousseau, Jean-Jacques, 129
Royce, Josiah, 122

Santayana, George, 116, 133, 145, 164n17, 191*n*43
Sartre, Jean-Paul, 34
Schopenhauer, Arthur, 122
Science, 22, 24, 30, 172*n*29; Cavell on, 43–44, 97, 172n29; Dewey's view on, 7, 29, 45–48, 66, 97, 146, 173*n*47; Dewey's scientific concept of intelligence, 29, 108, 123, 173*n*46; Dewey's scientific discourse, 10, 61; Dewey's scientific method, 12, 16–20, 23–24, 29–32, 34–35, 43–44, 46–47, 49, 83, 96–97, 105, 107, 146, 169*n*68; Dewey's scientific knowing, 62; Dewey's scientific tendency, 97; scientific horizon in Dewey's philosophy, 82, 98
Scottish: intuitionism, 104; philosophy, 184*n*15.
Self: -aggrandizement, 157; aristocracy of, 54; -assertion, 143; authentic selfhood, 136; autonomous, 57, 157; better state of, 52; the attained and the unattained, 14, 53, 60, 68, 112, 119; care for, 148; -centeredness, 147; -conformity, 45; -creation, 42–43, 149; -criticism, 55, 66, 142, 160; -discovery, 44; -effacing, 59; individual, 62, 157; -indulgence, 16; in Emersonian moral perfectionism, 52–54, 76, 78, 111; in stream of consciousness,

194*n*32; -interest, 52; introspective, 126; isolated, 157; -knowledge, 39, 157; -lessness, 147; loss of, 131; noumenal, 147; -overcoming, 53, 78, 161; -realization, 5, 18, 19, 28, 38–39, 48, 51, 53, 74; -reliance, 4, 45, 52, 54, 142–43, 146, 157, 176*n*15, 177*n*22, 185*n*17; -respect, 125; -righteousness, 156; social being, 96; social theory of, 88, 157; -sufficient, 88; -transcendence, 4, 15, 101, 146–47, 154, 157–58, 160; -transformation, 44, 48, 153; true, 175*n*7; William James on, 194*n*32
Shame, 53–54, 57, 62, 64, 75, 119, 130, 134
Shaw, Bernard, 51
Situation: Dewey's idea of, 18–19, 33, 43, 62, 71–73, 82–86, 94–95, 115, 118, 179*nn*5, 13, 185*n*20
Skepticism, 173*n*46; Cavell's view of, 183*n*21
Skinner, B. F., 72
Social inclusion, 137, 140, 156
Solipsism, 77

Teleology: Dewey's, 25; Greek, 73–75
Teleological perfectionism, 53, 61, 74, 175*n*7
Telos, 3, 13, 74, 149, 158; perfectionist, 175*n*9
Tennyson, Alfred, Lord, 110
Thinking: Cavell on, 43, 55–56; Dewey's, 30, 46, 95, 109, 186*n*30; Emerson's, 40, 44–47, 101, 107–109, 117, 146–47, 175n13: *See also* Intellect; Man, 64, 66; scientific method of: *See* Scientific method
Thoreau, Henry David, 148
Torrey, H. A. P., 37
Tragedy, 11, 121–22, 124–25, 134; absolutism of, 126, 136; of the lost individual, 1–4, 8, 15, 120, 125–26; sense of, 7
Tragic, 2–3, 7– 9, 11, 14–15, 120–24, 126–27, 131–36, 138, 145–46, 151, 156, 181*n*23, 189*n*19
Transaction, 71–72, 120

Transactional holism, 13–14, 70, 72–73, 75–78, 94
Transcendence, 103, 112, 134, 154, 161; art of, 156; immanent, 184*n*13
Transcendental: Emersonian, 111; idealism: *See* Idealism; idealist, 42, 101
Transcendentalism, 102; American, 102; Emerson's, 41, 45, 101, 104, 147–48; New England, 184*n*15; Vermont, 37, 40
Transcendentalist, 184*n*15; American, 38; New England, 38
Translation, art of, 152–57
Tuition, 107, 101

Understanding: Coleridge on, 38, 184*n*15; Emerson on, 77

Utilitarianism, 51

Warranted assertibility, 32–33, 83
Watson, J. B., 72
Whim, 107, 112–13; and the gleam of light, 103–104, 106; prophetic, 114, 137–38. *See also* Gleam of Light; Impulse
Whitehead, Alfred North, 114–15, 135–36
Whitman, Walt, 24
Wilde, Oscar, 51
Wittgenstein, Ludwig, 44, 51, 172*n*29, 173*n*31; concept of criteria, 90–93, 182*n*19
Wordsworth, William, 144

Zen Buddhist, 186*n*32. *See also* Buddhism

AMERICAN PHILOSOPHY SERIES
Douglas R. Anderson and Jude Jones, series editors

1. Kenneth Laine Ketner, ed., *Peirce and Contemporary Thought: Philosophical Inquiries.*
2. Max H. Fisch, ed., *Classic American Philosophers: Peirce, James, Royce, Santayana, Dewey, Whitehead,* second edition. Introduction by Nathan Houser.
3. John E. Smith, *Experience and God,* second edition.
4. Vincent G. Potter, *Peirce's Philosophical Perspectives.* Edited by Vincent Colapietro.
5. Richard E. Hart and Douglas R. Anderson, eds., *Philosophy in Experience: American Philosophy in Transition.*
6. Vincent G. Potter, *Charles S. Pierce: On Norms and Ideals,* second edition. Introduction by Stanley Harrison.
7. Vincent M. Colapietro, ed., *Reason, Experience, and God: John E. Smith in Dialogue.* Introduction by Merold Westphal.
8. Robert J. O'Connell, S.J., *William James on the Courage to Believe,* second edition.
9. Elizabeth M. Kraus, *The Metaphysics of Experience: A Companion to Whitehead's "Process and Reality,"* second edition. Introduction by Robert C. Neville.
10. Kenneth Westphal, ed. *Pragmatism, Reason, and Norms: A Realistic Assessment—Essays in Critical Appreciation of Frederick L. Will.*
11. Beth J. Singer, *Pragmatism, Rights, and Democracy.*
12. Eugene Fontinell, *Self, God, and Immorality: A Jamesian Investigation.*

13. Roger Ward, *Conversion in American Philosophy: Exploring the Practice of Transformation.*
14. Michael Epperson, *Quantum Mechanics and the Philosophy of Alfred North Whitehead.*
15. Kory Sorrell, *Representative Practices: Peirce, Pragmatism, and Feminist Epistemology.*